Praise for *The Meat Lover's Meatless Cookbook*

"The landscape of childhood has changed—no longer are our children guaranteed a safe and healthy future—not in the face of climate change, obesity, and heart disease. In *The Meat Lover's Meatless Cookbook*, Kim O'Donnel inspires us, using wit and wisdom, to recreate our families' carnivorous plates. With poignant reason, practical 'how to' advice, and a sensitivity to our culinary challenges and restrictions, *The Meat Lover's Meatless Cookbook* is an invaluable resource to anyone who eats."

—Robyn O'Brien, mother of four, Founder, AllergyKids Foundation

The

MEAT LOVER'S
MEATLESS
COOKBOOK

The
MEAT LOVER'S
MEATLESS
COOKBOOK

VEGETARIAN RECIPES
CARNIVORES WILL DEVOUR

KIM O'DONNEL

PHOTOGRAPHY BY MYRA KOHN

Da Capo

LIFE
LONG

A Member of the Perseus Books Group

Copyright © 2010 by Kim O'Donnel
Photographs by Myra Kohn
Foreword by Robert S. Lawrence

Design and production by Trish Wilkinson
Set in 11.5 point Goudy

Library of Congress Cataloging-in-Publication Data

O'Donnel, Kim.
    The meat lover's meatless cookbook : vegetarian recipes carnivores will devour / Kim O'Donnel ; photography by Myra Kohn.
        p.   cm.
    Includes bibliographical references and index.
    ISBN 978-0-7382-1401-6 (alk. paper)
    1. Vegetarian cookery. I. Title.
TX837.O28 2010
641.5'636—dc22   2010013471

First Da Capo Press edition 2010
ISBN: 978-0-7382-1401-6

Published by Da Capo Press
A Member of the Perseus Books Group
www.dacapopress.com

Note: The information in this book is true and complete to the best of our knowledge. This book is intended only as an informative guide for those wishing to know more about health issues. In no way is this book intended to replace, countermand, or conflict with the advice given to you by your own physician. The ultimate decision concerning care should be made between you and your doctor. We strongly recommend you follow his or her advice. Information in this book is general and is offered with no guarantees on the part of the authors or Da Capo Press. The authors and publisher disclaim all liability in connection with the use of this book.

Da Capo Press books are available at special discounts for bulk purchases in the U.S. by corporations, institutions, and other organizations. For more information, please contact the Special Markets Department at the Perseus Books Group, 2300 Chestnut Street, Suite 200, Philadelphia, PA, 19103, or call (800) 810-4145, ext. 5000, or e-mail special.markets@perseusbooks.com.

10 9 8 7 6 5 4 3 2 1

CONTENTS

Foreword by Robert S. Lawrence | *xi*

Introduction | 3
How to Use This Book | 9
MLMC FAQ | 10
MLMC Pantry Lexicon | 13

═══ 52 MENUS ═══

Spring

Tara's Mushroom Ragout ★ Broccoli Pick-Up Sticks | 24
Rocket Lasagna | 26
Risotto, Two Ways | 30
Spinach & Feta Crostata ★ Arugula & Seasonal Fruit | 34
Chickpea-Turnip Chili ★ Barley Pilaf | 38
Egg-in-the-Hole ★ Family-Style Latke | 41
Spring Cassoulet ★ Seared Romaine Wedges | 44
Jig-Inducing Falafel Burgers ★ Oven Sweet Potato Fries or Tabbouleh | 48
West Indian–Style Channa Wrap ★ Top-Shelf Potato Salad | 52
Tempeh Hoagie-letta ★ Kale Chips | 55
Huevo y Frijoles ★ Romaine with Toasted Pepitas & Lemon Vinaigrette | 58
Jerk Tempeh ★ Zesty Pineapple Salad ★ Jamaican-Style Peas & Rice | 60

Summer . . .

Garlic Scape Pesto Pasta ★ Romaine & Balsamic-Gingery Strawberries — 66

Chickpea "Crab Cakes" ★ Yogurt Rémoulade ★ Cocktail Sauce ★ Corn Kernel Salad — 69

Hummus-Stuffed Tomatoes ★ Fattoush Salad ★ Seared Halloumi — 73

Zucchini Boats ★ Quickie Couscous-Chickpea Salad — 76

Frittata, Three Ways ★ Gazpacho — 80

Southern Red Rice ★ Roasted Green Bean, Mushroom, & Shallot Medley — 84

RW's Snack Plate: Hummus, Tabbouleh, Roasted Cauliflower with Tahini Sauce, Kopanisti, Eggplant Rounds, Roasted or Grilled — 87

Tofu Barbecue ★ True-Blue Baked Beans ★ Vinegar Slaw — 92

Sesame Rice Noodles & Melon-Herb Salad — 96

Stuffed Bell Peppers ★ Romesco Toasts — 98

Susan's Eggplant Stack ★ Minty Chickpeas — 101

Zucchini & Corn-Studded Orzo ★ Goat Cheesy Roasted Peppers — 105

Fall . . .

Ratatouille — 110

Twice-Baked Sweet Potatoes ★ Pear-Arugula Salad — 112

Roasted Beans, Greens, & Squash Rings — 115

Blue Corn Cakes ★ Roasted Red Pepper Sauce ★ Whipped Feta — 117

Mushroom-Spinach Scramble ★ Rosemary-Garlic Roasted Potatoes — 120

Braised Winter Squash with Black Bean Sauce & Bok Choy ★ Coconut Rice — 122

Roasted Eggplant–Lentil Caviar on Oversized Crostini ★ Pistachio-Raisin Rice Pilaf — 125

Pepita-Crusted Tofu ★ Dino-Mash — 128

Thai-Style Red Curry Tempeh — 131

Red Lentil Dal with Cumin-Fried Onions & Wilted Spinach ★ Individual Flatbreads — 133

Stuffed Shells with Lentil Ragout & Spinach — 137

Beets & Greens Quesadilla ★ Roasted Red Pepper Soup — 139

Winter . . .

Black Bean–Sweet Potato Chili ★ Skillet Corn Bread   144

Smokin' Hoppin' John ★ Skillet Corn Bread ★ KOD's Quickie Collards   146

Brocco Mac & Cheese ★ Stewed Tomatoes ★ KOD's Quickie Collards   150

Winter Veg & Cilantro "Curry" with Dumplings   153

Penne with Tempeh, Caramelized Shallots, & Goat Cheese   155

Gumbo z'Herbes (Green Gumbo)   156

Nonna Caterina's Pasta e Fagioli ★ Wilted Greens in a Skillet Vinaigrette   159

Polenta Squares with Puttanesca Sauce & Broccoli Raab   162

Go-with-the-Flow Potpie with Cheddar-Biscuity Crust   165

Sicilian-Style Roasted Cauliflower with Pasta ★ Stir-Fried Cabbage & Cumin
(or Caraway)   169

Shepherd's Pie with Chard-Lentil Filling ★ Onion Gravy   171

Slurpy Pan-Asian Noodles   175

Wild Cards

Pizza Night with DIY Dough and Seasonal Toppings   180

Veggie Fried Rice Bowl   185

Grilled Cheese & Soup for All Seasons   186

Canned Beans & Rice: A Template Meant to Be Tweaked   190

Kitchen Tricks for Your Sleeve   *193*

Metric Conversions   *213*

Resources   *215*

Acknowledgments   *217*

Index   *221*

About the author   *237*

FOREWORD

"It may be difficult to convince the meat lover that he can radically reduce the proportion of meat in his diet without detriment to health. Many persons adhere to the notion that you are not nourished unless you eat meat; that meat foods are absolutely necessary to maintain the body strength. This idea is entirely without foundation, for the foods mentioned as meat substitutes earlier in this chapter can be made to feed the world, and feed it well—in fact, no nation uses so large a proportion of meat as America."

The above words did not come from a New Age vegetarian cookbook but first appeared almost a century ago, although they remain as timely today as when first written. The cookbook—*Foods That Will Win the War*—was published in 1918 in an effort to conserve food resources as the nation battled the "war to end all wars."

Americans have long had an affinity for red meat. The authors of *Foods That Will Win the War* cited statistics from the U.S. Food Administration: "As a nation we eat and waste 80 percent more meat than we require to maintain health." Fast-forward to the year 2010, and government data reveal that Americans still can't seem to get enough meat. The U.S. Department of Agriculture says men in the United States consume 170 percent of the recommended daily allowance (RDA) of meat, while women eat 135 percent.

Overconsumption and production of meat poses risks not only to our health but also to alleviating hunger and to the health of the planet. Global demand for food animal products is at an unsustainable level and continues to increase. Many health experts attribute the overconsumption of meat with its saturated fat to increased risk of obesity, diabetes, and cardio-vascular disease. Reducing the amount of meat we eat just one day a week, particularly meat from industrially produced food animals, can help reduce greenhouse gas emissions and many other negative environmental and public health effects attributed to industrial food animal production.

The U.S.-based Meatless Monday Campaign was first launched as a simple way for people to reduce their consumption of saturated fat, found mainly in meat and high-fat dairy products, by the 15 percent the Surgeon General's *Healthy People 2010* recommended in 2000 as a goal for the nation over the next decade. For the past seven years, the Johns Hopkins Bloomberg School of Public Health and the Johns Hopkins Center for a Livable Future (CLF) have supported the nonprofit initiative with technical assistance and scientific advice. Meatless Monday's mission has recently expanded to not only highlight health issues associated with high meat diets, but also to help communicate how less meat consumption can protect the health of our planet by reducing greenhouse gas emissions, minimizing water and fossil fuel usage, decreasing air and water pollution, and alleviating food shortages by using grains and legumes to feed people directly rather than to sustain pigs, poultry, and cattle.

The CLF promotes research about the interrelationships among diet, food production, environment, and human health. Much of our work focuses on understanding food environments and their influence on eating behaviors; identifying what helps people adopt healthier eating behaviors; and creating food environments so that people have access to nutritious, affordable, culturally appropriate, and healthy food on a regular basis.

As the director of the CLF and one of the first supporters of the Meatless Monday Campaign, I am delighted that Kim O'Donnel has written a practical cookbook that will help people who are used to eating meat almost every day of their lives discover the pleasure of cooking meatless meals without feeling as though a radical change in their diet or, more important, a sacrifice in taste is required. I look forward to trying out Kim's recipes every Monday, and I hope you do, too.

Robert S. Lawrence, M.D.
Founding Director, Johns Hopkins Center for a Livable Future
Center for a Livable Future Professor and Professor of Environmental
Health Sciences, Health Policy and International Health, Johns Hopkins
Bloomberg School of Public Health

The
MEAT LOVER'S
MEATLESS
COOKBOOK

INTRODUCTION

LIFE BEGINS WITH STEAK. . . .

At least mine did. See Exhibit A on the right. That's me, documented in gloriously greasy detail in this Polaroid, circa 1967. Yes, instead of a teething ring, my mother gave me a T-bone to gum on. I was hooked.

Back in the day, meat was what we had for dinner (and lunch *and* breakfast), with applesauce as a vegetable. My love for the bone was unbounded and soon expanded to poultry, fried chicken in particular. It's what I insisted on for my seventh birthday party. (I later used it to seduce the man who would become my husband, lest you think this story ends on the vegetarian side of the tracks.)

But in the 1980s my father's (and paternal grandmother's) fatal heart attacks brought an end to our family's meat marathon. Alarmed by our dangerously high cholesterol levels, the doctors insisted on it.

My mother did a clean sweep of the pantry. We went cold turkey on cold cuts. We switched from butter to margarine (as if we knew better then?). Full fat became skim milk, and to my great horror: no more bacon and eggs. It was hell. Our family's all-or-nothing approach showed no understanding of eating in moderation.

The pent-up cravings exploded a few years later when I was in college. I tossed aside the doctor's advice and renewed my relationship with an old friend, the pepperoni pizza. As a college grad, my budding interest in the kitchen literally fanned the flames, and I maintained a meat-heavy diet, adding a few new recipes from such books as *The New Basics Cookbook* by Julee Rosso and Sheila Lukins. When I needed a good rationalization for my meat-eating ways, I looked at my roommate, Kat, who called herself a vegetarian and lived on potatoes, grilled cheese sandwiches, and ice cream. How healthy could *that* be?

The next twenty years only led to more of the same. I have formal culinary training and a career as an established online food personality. I've traveled and studied cuisines, techniques, ingredients, and tastemakers. I've equipped my *batterie de cuisine* and built an impressive library of cookbooks. And to this day, meat still figures into my life in a big, big way.

As this bone-gnawing baby can attest, I truly understand what it means to have a one-track appetite, to believe in your heart and soul that there is nothing else for dinner but meat—that a meatless meal may happen now and then but can never really satisfy. I'm not alone; Americans eat more than 200 pounds of meat per capita a year. But my experiences have taught me to understand that if I succumb to every craving for crispy-coated, buttermilk-infused chicken thighs, well, I'll eventually look like a Macy's Thanksgiving Day parade balloon.

Exactly what inspired this meat lover to write a meatless cookbook came from an unexpected source, my mother's sausage-loving longtime companion.

He had just suffered a massive heart attack, and it wasn't his first. Although he survived, he stubbornly refused to make any dietary adjustments, regardless of the consequences. Exasperated, my mother called me for some low-fat dinner ideas for "Mister Sausage." On that particular day, she mentioned that she had an eggplant and some vine tomatoes from a local farm stand.

"Make eggplant stacks," I said. "Grill the eggplant, slather it with olive oil, then stack it with tomato, a small amount of feta. Repeat. Basil would be good, too."

"Sounds really good," Mom replied. "I'll give this a try." Off she went in pursuit of feta and basil. And whaddya know? Mister Sausage liked it. Meat was never mentioned. Although a pork chop was probably in his near future, this was a chink in his meaty armor.

For me, it was a revelatory moment. I wondered if I could just get Mom and Mister Sausage (and me and my husband) to be consistent with the meatless theme, even just once a week.

I knew about "Meatless Monday," a public health campaign that Johns Hopkins University had launched back in 2003 to help Americans reduce saturated fats by 15 percent by 2010. Intellectually, the idea made good sense, but gastronomically, I wondered, could it be truly tasty and satisfying?

Most of us meat lovers, this one included, know we could stand to lower our cholesterol and drop a few pounds. Our problem isn't *believing* the data, it's the fear of change and the threat to our very personal relationship with food.

To wit: While filming in Huntington, West Virginia, for his reality show, *Jamie Oliver's Food Revolution*, British celebrity chef Jamie Oliver met fierce resistance from residents of the "unhealthiest city in America." In the first episode, which premiered in March 2010, the camera meets a local radio announcer, who says: "We don't want to sit around and eat lettuce all day. I don't think Jamie has anything that can change this town. He can try all he wants."

And yet, there's never been a better opportunity for the change this book proposes. We've never been more concerned about where our food comes from, how it's processed, and what this means for our health.

In the months leading up to its 2010 goal, the Meatless Monday message hit the mainstream, both here and abroad. In the past year, Baltimore City public schools became the first school district in the country to offer a meatless day in its cafeterias. San Francisco became the first U.S. city to pass a resolution for a weekly "Veg Day." And celeb chef (and nose-to-tail lovin' guy) Mario Batali began observing Meatless Monday in all fourteen of his restaurants. Across the Atlantic, Sir Paul McCartney launched Meat Free Monday in the UK, and the mayor of Ghent, Belgium, declared Thursdays as "Veggiedag."

Such books as *Fast Food Nation* by Eric Schlosser and *The Omnivore's Dilemma* by Michael Pollan became runaway best sellers, changing the collective consciousness about where and how we buy our food and what we put in our mouth. Schlosser was a coproducer of (and both he and Pollan appeared in) the documentary *Food, Inc.*, an exposé of industrial agriculture that earned a 2010 Academy Award nomination. Today, according to USDA statistics, there are more than five thousand farmers' markets across the country—including one just outside the White House—almost double what there were just ten years ago.

Healthy eating is now a priority at the White House; for the first time since World War II, there is an edible garden on the South Lawn. First lady Michelle

Obama is now leading a nationwide effort to combat childhood obesity that includes public, private, and nonprofit partnerships at the local, state, and national level. (According to the Centers for Disease Control and Prevention, 17 percent of American school-age children and teens are obese.)

Without a doubt, the eat-less-meat-for-health buzz had fueled my curiosity, but what truly got me off my reticent duff to put these ideas into practice is the environmental piece of this equation.

Specifically, the wake-up call was a 2008 speech by Rajendra Pachauri, an Indian economist and the chair of the UN Intergovernmental Panel on Climate Change (which shared the 2007 Nobel Peace Prize with Al Gore). Here's the gist of what Pachauri said: If there's one thing that average citizens of the world can do to help the planet, it's not recycling or trading in our gas-guzzlers for hybrid cars. It's eating less meat.

A year later, in December 2009, Pachauri and McCartney addressed the European Parliament, urging leaders to implement a meatless day as a way to fight climate change. At the hearing, McCartney read a statement from Al Gore, who agrees that a meatless day "is a responsible and welcome component to a strategy for reducing global pollution."

In a nutshell, here's why: According to a 2006 report from the UN Food and Agriculture Organization, livestock production is responsible for 18 percent of worldwide greenhouse gas emissions, major contributors to climate change. For daily meat eaters, one meatless day equals 15 percent less total consumption per week, not an insignificant number.

I needed no more convincing. The light bulb was officially shining brightly. Now I just needed to press the "start" button and commit, once and for all.

While writing a cooking blog for the *Washington Post*, I invited my readers to join me on a weekly meatless quest. When I asked them what they'd need to stick to the plan, the unanimous response was "recipes. We need tools, no talk."

And so, in September 2008, I did just that, offering a weekly recipe with nary a bone, feather, or fin. In pursuit of recipe ideas, I scoured my library of cookbooks, quickly learning, as Tony Geraci, of Baltimore City schools, has so aptly pointed out, that "there's not a culture on the planet that doesn't have vegetarian offerings." The food: filling, varied, and, as my mother would say, totally scrumptious. This wasn't the scary sacrifice I had anticipated; in fact, it was an exciting, eye-opening experience, both as an eater and as a cook.

After a few months of helping my readers, I noticed a pattern in my own kitchen: We loved eating this way so much that we increased our meatless days to two or more per week, and our craving for meat began to wane.

For the next year, I developed my own take on classic comfort favorites—potpie, a Philadelphia hoagie, and stuffed shells—without meat or meat analogues. I've shaped falafel into burgers, braised winter squash with black bean sauce, and smoked tofu into barbecue-worthy chow. The result: a personal cooking journey and a collection of fifty-two tried-and-true menus—one for every week of the year—with the meat lover in mind every step of the way.

Come as you are, with your appetite, and get ready to lick your chops.

HOW TO USE THIS BOOK

The menus on the following pages are grouped by season. Within each season, you'll find twelve meals, one to try each week, plus four additional "wild card" seasonless menus that I turn to year-round in my own kitchen. I also dish up some of my favorite go-to basics, a mix of DIY sauces, sides, and condiments that I like to think of as flavor zipper-uppers. Some menus are comprised of one-pot meals, which may seem like a dream come true for some cooks and not enough chow for others. For those with a bigger appetite, you'll see a "Make It a Meal" sidebar in various places throughout the book. This includes a list of my favorite sides with mix-and-match versatility.

There is no official beginning or end or right way to work your way through the year. Choose the dishes that speak to you, regardless of what the calendar says. Use the chapters as a guide to what's in season in your neck of the woods and as inspiration for the many special occasions sprinkled throughout the year, from birthdays to Memorial Day cookouts.

You'll notice icons designating recipes that address specific dietary issues, such as gluten-free, dairy- and egg-free (a.k.a. vegan), as well as dairy-optional. I've also given a special shout-out to menus that resonate with kids, and for those that make excellent leftovers. Here's the key:

GF = gluten-free

KIDDO = kid friendly

DO = dairy optional

V = vegan, also known as dairy- and egg-free

XTRA = leftover bonus

For the lowdown on ingredients, techniques, and where to find stuff, check out the pantry lexicon, and if you're in need of brushing up on some basics, the Kitchen Tricks section should set you straight.

In the back of the book, I've put together a list of both online and print resources for keeping on your mindful toes, regardless of your meat-eating tendencies.

And if that doesn't cover the bases, I've anticipated a few questions that might swirl around you and your family's brains with an FAQ. Curtain, please . . .

I KNOW WHAT YOU'RE THINKING. . . MEAT LOVER'S MEATLESS COOKBOOK FAQ

I have a Mister Sausage, too. How do I tell him we're not having meat for dinner?

Maybe he'll try it and like it and not say a thing. If he does, tell him you're about to go on a new eating adventure that you'd like to give a try just once a week for one month. Tell him what kind of meat will be on the table tomorrow and the rest of the week, so he knows it's not gone forever. And ask that he taste everything before issuing a veto.

What do I do when he asks, "Did we run out of money?" and "Is this some kind of punishment?" Because he will, you know.

You tell him, "No silly, we're not broke, but eating this way is definitely going to save us money!" By and large, a meatless meal will cost a fraction of what you're used to. As for punishment, that's just crazy talk. This book is designed to expand your culinary horizons, not deprive you of your most favorite things.

Does this mean I can't have eggs, milk, and cheese?

But of course you can! This is not about depriving you of the things you love. Eggs and dairy are featured throughout the collection, though in some cases, you'll find neither.

So does that mean you include fish and seafood? They're not meat, either.

Right you are. But they're not fruits, vegetables, or whole grains, either. I wanted to offer a collection of truly delicious recipes that keeps meat (no wings, fins, or feet) out of the equation.

Is there anything to else to eat but pasta?

My friend Peter asked me that, too. A lot of folks find comfort in the familiarity of pasta, which is why I kick off the January chapter with a variety of noodle items. But the answer is yes, there are all kinds of tasty pasta-free dishes to try, including West Indian–style curried chickpeas and baked polenta with puttanesca sauce.

But I *like* pasta!

Great! Then when you find one you like here, make it as much as you want. I hope the nonpasta dishes expand your horizons but don't be afraid to make your favorite pasta dishes from these pages whenever you want.

Will I have to learn how to cook all over again? Is this going to be hard?

I hope the hardest part will be in deciding what to cook, as there are lots of choices! Still, I know that the most challenging part will be to keep it going all year long. That's why I give you lots of choices. But have no fear: The recipes are designed for beginner and advanced beginner cooks with an adventurous spirit.

Will it take more time? Because I'm short on time as it is.

A roast chicken takes about two hours. So does my veggie potpie with cheddar biscuit crust. The only exception is the tofu barbecue, which calls for some smoking time on the grill. In most cases, you'll have dinner on the table in about an hour.

Will I have to drive all over town to buy weird ingredients?

I have no interest in having you drive all over town, which keeps you away from the kitchen and adds to the environmental impact of a meal. All of the ingredients used in the book are readily available at the supermarket, online stores, or at your local farmers' market. And while I'm confident you know what kale is, maybe you've never cooked with it, which is why I've put together a pantry lexicon

Okay, fine, I see your point. But honestly, will it taste good without the meat?

Allow me to quote my mother, a fan of London broil on the grill and the lady who gave me a T-bone as a teething ring: "It's not like you're giving someone a piece of lettuce and a noodle. With these recipes, your taste buds are aroused."

THE MEAT LOVER'S MEATLESS PANTRY LEXICON

WHAT I MEAN WHEN I SAY . . .

KOD: That's me referring to myself in the third person. You can call me KOD, too.

Aromatics: This refers to any combination of onions, celery, carrots, bell pepper, and garlic, often the foundation of soups, stews, and sauces.

Beans: Canned or dried? That is a darn good question, and a decision that will ultimately be up to the cook. Personally, I prefer the texture and flavor of dried beans, particularly when they're young and they come from a local source. Generally speaking, I also find they hold up better after cooking. The downside (and the reality): Most dried beans and legumes need several hours of soaking, which means planning ahead in a hectic week.

No one can argue against the convenience of opening a can of beans and having dinner ready in minutes. As you'll see in these pages, I'm a big fan of canned chickpeas, which maintain their textural integrity in chili and other braises. The downside: Many brands of canned beans are high in sodium, so keep that in mind when shopping and look for low or no-sodium varieties when possible. Then there's the BPA piece. BPA is bisphenol-A, a chemical that is used in canned goods manufacturing, and it has been the center of a recent controversy over potential associated health risks. As of this writing, Eden Foods is the only company I know of that packs beans in cans that are free of BPA.

Butter: Unsalted, please. Salted butter is great at the table, but it's a wild card at the stove. Salt content varies from brand to brand, so it's hard to know just how much salt you're adding to a dish. You have more control adding salt on its own.

Chard: Short for Swiss chard, a quick-cooking leafy green from the beet family. Available during cool months, with a variety of gorgeous, almost neon-colored stalks and can be used interchangeably with spinach.

Eggs: Large eggs were used in developing all of the relevant recipes. Brown or white? Your pick. My preference: farmstead eggs laid by hens that are outside during the day and cared for by a real person who lives within 250 miles of your neighborhood. The difference in taste from a commercial battery-cage egg is mind blowing.

Fresh parsley: I prefer flat-leafed over curly purely for aesthetic reasons, but I wouldn't let curly hold up the works if that's what was available. Chopped, you can hardly tell which is which; whole, it has a different look and feel.

Mise en place: Pronounced MEEZ ON PLAHZ, this is an old-school French term that refers to the process of locating and prepping all ingredients for a dish. A culinary "getting your ducks in a row."

Oil: I like all-purpose, high heat–friendly, and mostly neutral-flavored oils and choose organic varieties whenever possible.

> *Safflower:* One of my two workhorse oils. Consistently reliable and relatively inexpensive.

> *Olive:* My second workhorse oil. Unrivaled source of heart-healthy monosaturated fatty acids and antioxidants. But at the stove, it shouldn't be used for everything. Its distinctive fruitiness clashes with Asian and Indian spice-intensive dishes in the book, and its lower smoking point creates a challenge for longer sautés. On the other hand, this oil is tailor-made for vinaigrettes and for drizzling over pasta just before serving.

> *Grapeseed:* Love its high-heat capability, but can be pricey.

> *Sesame:* The Asian variety, made from toasted sesame seeds, which is darker and richer in flavor. Use as a flavor enhancer rather than as a cooking medium, as too much can be overwhelming and unlike its lighter counterpart, can burn quickly. Good idea to combine in a fifty-fifty ratio with a neutral oil (such as safflower or grapeseed) with a higher smoking point.

Onion: Unless specified, I'm referring to the yellow onion (also known as yellow storage onion), an all-purpose, year-round allium with a good balance of sweetness and pungency. Come spring, I make room for the mild, sweet onion (Walla Walla, Vidalia, to name a few) for salads and sandwiches.

Salt: Kosher salt was used in developing all of the recipes and what I recommend you give a try in your own kitchen. It is as all-purpose as it gets, with larger crystals than table salt. Sold in 5-pound boxes in the same vicinity as the Morton's free-running canister. Don't worry; you'll find it.

A sprig of thyme: Given a choice, I always prefer fresh herbs to dried, which oxidize and lose their flavor spunk quickly. In the case of thyme, use it like a bay leaf, allowing flavor to steep, then remove from dish before serving.

Consider buying herbs from the bulk sections in supermarkets such as Whole Foods. This allows you to buy in amounts only as you need. Store herbs (and spices) in a cool, dark place, and do label them with a date of purchase; you'd be amazed at how fast spice time flies.

Tomato puree: Use commercially processed tomatoes with minimal salt and seasonings (or none, if possible). Preferred brands: Pomi (box), Bionaturae (jar), Rao's (can). Choose whole plum tomatoes over "spaghetti sauce" and puree yourself.

Veg stock: For the purposes of this book, the strained liquid of simmered aromatics, herbs, and spices. DIY details are available on page 211 of the Kitchen Tricks section. Although a snap to make, veg stock is often not the first thing that comes to mind for the home cook. I keep Rapunzel brand bouillon cubes on hand for instant-presto veg stock. It's the only brand of veg bouillon that I've found without salt and with true veg flavor.

WHAT IN THE WORLD IS . . .

Arborio rice: A short-grained, high-starch rice from Italy that is used to make risotto (page 30).

Black bean–garlic sauce: Made from fermented beans, this Chinese condiment is a mix of pungent, sweet, and spicy. Available in Asian groceries and some conventional supermarkets.

Blue cornmeal: Made from blue corn, this has a slightly sweeter flavor and somewhat heartier texture. Commercially available brand: Arrowhead Mills.

Bok choy: A member of the very large and extensive Brassica vegetable family, *bok choy* refers to several varieties of leafy greens with white or green stalks or stems and a mild cabbage-y flavor. Also sold as Chinese white cabbage. Available in many conventional supermarkets, Asian groceries, and farmers' markets, when in season (spring or fall).

Broccoli raab: Also known as broccoli rabe and rapini, raab looks like skinny broccoli but is more closely related to the turnip. Its flowering stem and leaves are both good eating, with a slightly bitter flavor.

Bulgur wheat: First order of business is defining the **wheat berry**, which isn't a berry at all; rather, a whole, hulled wheat kernel. When the berry is parboiled or steamed, then dried and ground, it becomes **bulgur**—a ready-to-eat grain after a short soak. It's a staple in Middle East cookery and featured in tabbouleh (page 88).

Chipotle chiles in adobo sauce: When jalapeño chile peppers are smoked, they become chipotle chiles. Sold in little cans in a rich tomato-based sauce, chipotles pack a lot of flavor and heat. Great pantry item to have on hand; keep leftovers in an airtight container in fridge or freezer. Available in Latino groceries and in most conventional supermarkets.

Coriander: Lemon is what you smell and taste in ground coriander, but there's something else. Mustard, maybe? Sage? Both bright and subtle, coriander adds an extra layer of flavor to curries and marinades, and it's frequently paired with the more robust cumin (see below). Available in both berrylike seed and ground form, and don't forget its love-it-or-hate-it leafy plant, also known as cilantro.

Cumin: Available in both seed and ground form. The small pointy seeds (which resemble caraway) impart terrific flavor when toasted. Used in Middle Eastern, Mexican, and Caribbean cooking, cumin has a musky smell and warm feel on the tongue. Featured regularly throughout the book.

Garlic scape: The curlicue green shoot of a developing garlic bulb. Tender like a scallion, with a mild garlic flavor. Makes amazing pesto (page 66). Because it represents a specific stage in the life of the garlic plant, available for a limited time in early summer.

Gomasio: A Japanese condiment of salted sesame seeds. Try it on a plain pot of rice, steamed rice, or popcorn. Changes everything! Available through spice resources or in Asian groceries.

Halloumi: A sheep's milk cheese from Cyprus. Out of the package, its consistency is reminiscent of Armenian string cheese. It is the one cheese I know of that doesn't melt when heated and sears instead. Available in some conventional supermarkets and in Middle Eastern groceries.

Hoisin sauce: A Chinese condiment made from soybeans, sugar, chile peppers, garlic, and some kind of starch (check labels if you are gluten intolerant). It can be used as a dipping sauce, as part of a marinade, or in stir-fries. Available in conventional supermarkets as well as Asian groceries.

Jerk sauce: A highly aromatic and flavorful marinade and barbecue sauce from Jamaica. There are several reliable commercial brands: Busha Browne's Spicy Jerk Sauce, Walkerswood Jerk Barbecue, Dave's Gourmet Jammin' Jerk Sauce & Marinade—look in the condiments section of your supermarket; also available on Amazon. Try to avoid brands using high-fructose corn syrup, such as A.1.

Kale: A member of the cabbage family, kale is an all-purpose, leafy cool-weather green loaded with nutrients. It has become one of my favorite, go-to vegetables. Lacinato (a.k.a. Dinosaur) kale is at the top of my list, but the Red Russian and curly varieties do an equally delightful job.

Lentils: One of the first known domesticated crops, with links to the fertile crescent of the Stone Age, the lentil is as ancient as food gets. Revered in nearly every corner of the world, the lentil is finally catching on in the United States, where its quick-cooking (no soaking required), versatile personality is attracting attention. A Meat Lover's Meatless pantry staple of the highest order. In these pages, the following varieties are used:

Brown or green: Also sold as Egyptian lentils. What you'll likely find on any supermarket shelf. I'm also a big fan of the smaller, darker French *lentilles du Puy*, which have a more refined texture.

Red: Coral-colored when raw; marigold yellow when cooked. Cook very quickly and practically self-puree.

Madras curry powder: A premixed Indian spice blend catered for the Western home cook. (In India, such spice blends are mixed at home.) Usually some combination of the following: coriander, cumin, chile pepper, cinnamon, turmeric, black pepper, ginger, mustard, cardamom, fennel, and fenugreek. In the supermarket, a jar labeled "curry powder" is typically milder than

"Madras." For the West Indian–style channa on page 52, Madras is preferred but not mandatory. For details on making your own Madras curry, check out page 210 in the Kitchen Tricks section.

Parmigiano-Reggiano: Many of us grew up with the tall green can of shelf-stable "Parmesan" that we dutifully sprinkled atop spaghetti and meatballs. Now we've got a taste of the real thing—hard, aged cow's milk cheese from the Parmigiano-Reggiano area of Italy. Parm-Regg virgins may balk at the price tag, but I promise you: A little goes a long way, and when stored in an air-tight container, the cheese keeps for a few months. With a rich, nutty flavor and encompassing mouthfeel, Parm-Regg takes many of the dishes in this book to satisfying, meat-worthy territory.

Pearl barley: A form of this ancient grain that has been "pearled" (polished and steamed) to remove both the bran and the outer husk. As a result, it is considered a refined rather than whole grain and cooks more quickly than its less processed counterparts. Even with the processing, pearl barley is a respectable source of fiber; ½ cup of cooked pearl barley contains 3 grams of dietary fiber.

Pepitas: Also known as hulled pumpkin seeds, olive-shaded pepitas add richness and texture, and when toasted, become nutty. Available in bulk in some supermarkets and in Latino groceries.

Quinoa: This supernutritious, delicious, and versatile seed of an ancient plant acts like a grain, and is native to the Andean regions of South America. It is a complete protein, cooks as easily as rice, and is a terrific gluten-free alternative. Available in shades of white/khaki, red, and black, depending on your fancy.

Rice noodles: Rice flour noodles from Vietnam and Thailand do not require boiling, just a soak in a hot bath to soften. Readily available in conventional supermarkets and Asian groceries.

Shallot: A member of the allium family, the shallot looks like garlic (bulbs, thin skin) but cuts like a red onion, and is more delicate and sweeter in flavor than a storage onion. A personal pantry favorite.

Shaoxing rice wine: A type of rice wine from China, Shaoxing is amber in color and similar in flavor to dry sherry (but not cooking sherry). Although becoming increasingly available in conventional supermarkets, your best bet is an Asian grocery or online source. White rice wines are fine substitutes, but not as flavorful.

Smoked paprika: Also known as *pimentón de la vera* in Spain, smoked paprika is made from peppers that have been slowly smoked, resulting in a sublime mixture of heat, sweet, and smoke. This is probably my most beloved spice. Increasingly available in conventional supermarkets or through spice resources that follow.

Tahini: Made from ground sesame seeds, tahini has the look and feel of creamy peanut butter. It is a staple of Middle East cuisine, including hummus (page 87). Keep in the fridge, as the oils will eventually oxidize and go rancid. Available in some supermarkets and in Middle East groceries.

Tempeh: Native to Indonesia, tempeh is a "cake" of fermented soybeans. Its texture is toothy and appealing to meat eaters. Brand recommendations: Lightlife, SoyBoy, Wildwood, and WestSoy, all organic; choose from plain, rice, or flax varieties. Available in many conventional supermarkets, health food stores, and Asian groceries.

Thai red curry paste: A pounded mixture of herbs, spices, and chile peppers, this paste is ready made and available in conventional supermarkets and Asian groceries. I like Mae Sri brand curry paste, sold in a can; Thai Kitchen brand is sold in a small jar. Leftover paste can be stored in an airtight container in the fridge.

Tofu: Made from soybean curd, tofu comes in a variety of textures, from silken to extra firm. For the recipes in this book, firm or extra firm is preferred, organic whenever possible. Available in most conventional supermarkets, Asian groceries, and health food stores.

Udon noodles: Japanese wheat flour noodles, udon are about the same thickness as linguine. Available in conventional supermarkets and Asian groceries.

Winter squash: "Winter" refers to larger, thicker-skinned varieties that must be cooked (unlike the tender zucchini). Flesh comes in various shades of yellow or orange, rich in disease-fighting beta carotene. For the recipes in this book, I recommend exploring a world beyond the same ole acorn squash with the following: butternut (beige and shaped like an elongated pear, somewhat sweet); delicata (yellow with green stripes with a thin, edible skin, shaped like a cucumber, flesh a cross between sweet potato and corn); Hubbard (thick, green/blue skin, ball shaped, "meaty" orange flesh); and kabocha (orange or green, sometimes striped, pumpkin shaped, yellow, creamy/custardy flesh).

RESOURCES

It's not always easy to get your hands on pantry staples that are so readily available in big cities. For details on where and how to find them, check out my list of go-to favorites on page 215.

Spring . . .

. . . can really hang you up the most.

One minute, you're admiring the popped-up crocuses, the next minute, a lionlike gust bites your collar, a reminder that it ain't quite sandal time. There's still a need for belly warmers, such as a tray of lasagna and a potful of beans, but in anticipation of breaking ground and brighter days, you can fluff up the pasta pillows with emerald leaves of arugula and lighten up those beans with early-season leeks and the zest of sunny lemons.

While Mother Nature moves the furniture and whistles in the birds (and the bees) from down south, we mere mortals clean house, take stock, and wait for her cue that spring is here in earnest.

Meanwhile, we are brooding, simultaneously giddy and melancholy. We anticipate (farmers' markets) and procrastinate (Tax Day). At the Easter or Passover table, we might get our first taste of green garlic with the ham or asparagus spears alongside the charoset, and maybe if we're lucky, we'll fete Mom with the first batch of strawberries.

And what is it about spring that makes us hopelessly yearn for summer and all the requisite outdoor feasting? Ants in the pants be damned; instead, let's turn up the radio and whip up a Jamaican-style spread—jerk tempeh, peas and rice, and a kicky salad of sunny-side-up pineapple—that melts away the remaining chill and reroutes us to the land of sultry eves and swaying fruit trees. If it's a cookout you crave, re-create the magic indoors and fire up a skillet of falafel burgers that have earned major grill marks from high-ranking members of the two-all-beef-patty club. Get ready to jig!

TARA'S MUSHROOM RAGOUT

No mushrooms for me. Unfortunately, that's the rule, unless I want to throw caution the wind and always carry an EpiPen. Allergies aside, I couldn't have a meatless cookbook without mushrooms, among the "meatiest" plants for vegetarians. I sought counsel from fungi-loving friends and writers willing to both develop and test 'shroom-centric recipes for the collection. The first out of the gate comes from West Coast writer Tara Austen Weaver, a lifelong vegetarian who dabbled in meat for a while; she chronicles her pendulum-swinging adventures in *The Butcher and the Vegetarian: One Woman's Romp Through a World of Men, Meat, and Moral Crisis.*

INGREDIENTS

2 pounds mixed mushrooms (button, cremini, and/or shiitake)

3 tablespoons butter

1 tablespoon olive oil

3 medium-size leeks, washed thoroughly, root and dark green tops removed, cut lengthwise in quarters, and sliced thinly (about 3 cups)

½ cup carrots, minced finely

3 cloves garlic, peeled

1¼ teaspoons salt

½ cup dry white wine

¼ cup vegetable stock or water

¼ cup heavy cream

Ground black pepper

Cooked rice or pasta, to serve (1 to 1½ cups per person)

HERE'S WHAT YOU DO:

Clean the mushrooms: Mushrooms easily get waterlogged, so if you use water, rinse quickly and lightly. Otherwise, use a soft-bristle brush or dish towel to remove any dirt.

Cut the mushrooms in half and then slice into ¼-inch pieces (Tara uses an egg slicer for this). Set the mushrooms aside.

In a medium-size saucepan over medium-high heat, heat the butter and oil. Once the butter has melted and the mixture has warmed, add the leeks, carrots, and whole garlic cloves. Add the salt and sauté until the leeks and carrots are soft, 8 to 10 minutes.

Add the mushrooms and wine. Cook, stirring regularly, for 5 minutes, as the wine reduces. Add the stock, lower the heat to medium, and continue to cook until the mushrooms soften, 10 to 15 minutes. Add the cream and cook for another 5 minutes. By this time, the garlic cloves should be soft enough to mash coarsely into the wine cream sauce. The flavor will have mellowed, so don't worry about a strong garlic taste (you can actually leave them whole if you like).

Taste; add pepper and additional salt to taste.

Serve over rice or pasta. This is especially wonderful over fresh, homemade pasta cut into 1-inch-wide ribbons.

Makes 4 servings

BROCCOLI PICK-UP STICKS

Did you grow up on frozen veg in easy-breezy boil pouches, too? I had my first taste of fresh broccoli when I was eighteen—and had no idea what I had been missing! Here's an irresistible broccoli trick to change your life forever. Broccoli florets get slathered with a zesty seasoning mix of fresh ginger, garlic, and a smidge of cayenne for heat. Into a hot oven they go and roast for about 10 minutes, plenty of time to check e-mail or contemplate the meaning of life. Like this idea but prefer cauliflower to brocc? Head over to page 204 in the Kitchen Tricks section for those details.

INGREDIENTS

1 pound broccoli, separated into florets

1 (2 x 1-inch) piece fresh ginger, peeled and minced

1 to 2 cloves garlic, minced

½ teaspoon salt, plus more to taste

¼ teaspoon cayenne or smoked paprika

3 tablespoons olive oil

HERE'S WHAT YOU DO:

Preheat the oven to 400°F.

In a large mixing bowl, combine the broccoli, ginger, garlic, salt, cayenne, and olive oil. With your hands, mix until the broccoli is well coated. The broccoli should glisten with oil; if it seems dry, feel free to add more oil. Taste a floret for salt and add more if needed. Transfer the broccoli to a baking tray and place in the oven.

Roast until fork tender, 15 to 16 minutes. Serve warm or at room temperature.

Makes 4 side-dish servings

ROCKET LASAGNA

Rocket is the Brit word for arugula, the sassy, peppery green that stars in this irresistible lasagna, which really should be called Goldilocks Lasagna—not too heavy, not too light, but jusssst right. I've also developed this recipe with Passover in mind, swapping in matzoh, which does a superb job. Details follow.

KITCHEN NOTES: I like to work through this dish by component: arugula-ricotta filling, marinara sauce, and the overall assembly. To make your own marinara sauce or to pour it out of a jar is the cook's choice; I've included details for a simple yet flavorful "gravy" that is worth the extra half hour or so. Added benefit for the DIY route: Double amounts and freeze half for later!

🙢 Make It a Meal 🙠

Is your appetite bigger tonight than anticipated? Consider one of these versatile sides to round out your plate. Mix-and-matching encouraged!

Wilted Greens in a Skillet Vinaigrette (page 161)

Roasted Broccoli or Cauli Pick-up Sticks (page 204)

Seared Romaine Wedges (page 47)

Arugula & Seasonal Fruit (page 37)

Stir-fried Cabbage & Cumin (or Caraway) (page 169)

Mixed greens with seasonal crunch—thinly sliced apples, fennel, cucumber, radishes, jicama, or julienned carrots, with Lemon-Garlic Vinaigrette (page 199)

Sliced avocado, watercress, a squeeze of lime or grapefruit, and a sprinkling of gomasio

---

ROCKET LASAGNA

Greens-Ricotta Filling

INGREDIENTS

2 bunches arugula, washed
thoroughly, stemmed, and
spun dry (about 8 cups), or
equal amounts of spinach

2 tablespoons olive oil

3 cloves garlic, sliced thinly

½ teaspoon red pepper flakes
(add up to 1 teaspoon if you
like heat)

¼ cup walnuts (optional)

½ teaspoon salt

Ground black pepper

½ cup ricotta cheese, beaten
lightly with a fork

⅛ teaspoon grated nutmeg

HERE'S WHAT YOU DO:

Divide the arugula between two bowls. At first, it will seem like an excessive amount of greens, but it will all be put to use.

Heat 1 tablespoon of the olive oil in a 10-inch skillet over medium heat and add the garlic and half of the arugula. With tongs, turn the arugula to coat it with the oil; it will wilt (and shrink) rather quickly. Cook for about 2 minutes.

Transfer the wilted arugula and garlic to the bowl of a food processor. Add the remaining uncooked arugula, red pepper flakes, and nuts (if using) to the food processor, in batches if necessary. Whiz until the mixture becomes an emerald green puree. Add the remaining oil and whiz for another minute or so. Add the ½ teaspoon of salt and whiz for a few seconds. Taste, adjust the salt as needed, and add black pepper as you see fit.

Remove the blade from the food processor and measure out 1 cup of the puree. Transfer to a medium-size mixing bowl. (You will have a scant ½ cup of leftover puree; store in the fridge in an airtight container and use within 2 days as a sandwich spread, over rice, or devoured with an egg. It's a wonderful cook's treat.)

Add the ricotta and nutmeg, and with a rubber spatula, fold in until well integrated. Taste again for salt, and add more if you wish.

ROCKET LASAGNA

Marinara Sauce

You'll need approximately 2½ to 3 cups of sauce for the lasagna assembly. If you're merely warming up a jar of meatless spaghetti sauce from the supermarket, choose labels with as little sugar and salt as possible, two elements that can mask the flavor of the tomatoes.

INGREDIENTS

2 tablespoons olive oil

1 small onion, chopped

3 cloves garlic, minced

1 medium-size carrot, peeled and minced

1 to 2 sprigs fresh oregano or thyme (optional but nice)

¼ cup red wine of choice (optional)

1 (23- to 28-ounce) container tomato puree (see page 15 for recommendations)

Salt and ground black pepper

HERE'S WHAT YOU DO:

In a medium-size saucepan, heat the oil over medium heat, then add the onions, garlic, and carrot, cooking until slightly softened, about 5 minutes. Add the herbs and wine, if using; cook until the wine is reduced by half. Stir occasionally to minimize sticking.

Add the tomato puree and stir to combine. Bring to a lively simmer, then lower the heat, so the sauce can simmer over low heat. Cover the pot and cook for about 30 minutes; remove the herb sprigs and add salt and pepper to taste. Keep warm until ready to assemble the lasagna.

ROCKET LASAGNA

Assembling the Lasagna

INGREDIENTS

1 box no-boil lasagna noodles
(Passover option: 8 to 10
matzoh boards—less than
1 box)

About 1½ cups arugula-ricotta
filling

About 2½ cups marinara sauce

12 to 16 ounces mozzarella
cheese, sliced or shredded

1 cup grated Parmigiano-
Reggiano cheese

HERE'S WHAT YOU DO:

Preheat the oven to 350°F.

Grease a 9 x 13-inch rectangular baking dish. Before assembly, it's a good idea to check how the noodles fit inside the dish; ideally, you want a maximum of four per layer (overlapping is totally fine).

Passover option: Wet each matzoh under warm running water to moisten. Stack the damp matzohs on a plate and cover with a damp paper towel.

Spoon enough marinara sauce onto the bottom of the baking dish to cover its surface. Place a layer of lasagna noodles side by side, so that they're snug, on top of the sauce. With a rubber spatula, spread *half* of the arugula-ricotta filling on top of the noodles, covering the surface, and add one-fourth of the mozzarella and Parmigiano-Reggiano.

Create a new layer of noodles, and this time, spoon in enough marinara sauce to cover the surface, followed by another ¼-cup addition of each cheese.

For the third layer of noodles, add the remaining arugula-ricotta filling, then top with both cheeses.

For the top layer, place the remaining noodles, marinara sauce, and cheese in the baking dish, in that order.

Cover with foil and bake the lasagna until fork tender and bubby, 50 to 60 minutes. At 50 minutes, remove the foil and allow the cheese to brown for a few minutes before removing the baking pan from the oven.

Cut and serve while still hot.

Makes 6 to 8 servings

RISOTTO, TWO WAYS

GF

When it comes to risotto, I owe it all to a guy named Sergio. Ten years ago, I studied at a cooking school in Piedmont, Italy, and Sergio was one of my chef instructors. It was a chilly Saturday morning in March, and Chef decided that it was time for me to learn the fine art of coaxing short-grain rice into creamy submission. What he didn't tell me was that my maiden voyage on the risotto train would also be lunch for forty.

You might say that Chef poured on the tough love that day. For a few hours, I hated the guy, but I remember everything he taught me.

KITCHEN NOTES: Unless you've got a risotto partner at your side, I highly recommend prepping all ingredients before you begin cooking the rice, which requires your full attention. If you end up short on veg stock, you can use hot water in a pinch.

Basic Risotto

INGREDIENTS

5 to 6 cups risotto stock (Rapunzel unsalted bouillon cubes are terrific in a pinch; DIY details follow)

2 tablespoons olive oil

1 tablespoon butter (Don't do butter? Use all olive oil instead.)

½ medium-size onion, diced very finely (think baby food)

2 cups uncooked Arborio rice, or short-grained Carnaroli or Vialone Nano

¼ cup white wine that you enjoy drinking (optional)

½ cup grated Parmigiano-Reggiano cheese, plus more to taste

½ teaspoon salt

HERE'S WHAT YOU DO:

Keep the veg stock warm over low heat while you prepare the rest of the recipe.

In a 10- or 12-inch heavy-bottomed skillet (think wide and shallow versus tall and deep), combine the oil and butter and heat over medium heat. Add the onion, stirring with a wooden spoon, being mindful not to let it brown, about 3 minutes. Add the rice, coating it with the onion mixture, toasting it for about 1 minute.

If using, stir in the wine and allow it to boil off, occasionally stirring the rice; otherwise, ladle in 1 cup of the stock and stir the rice with a wooden spoon until the liquid is almost completely absorbed.

Ladle in more stock, in ½-cup increments, stirring constantly to keep the rice from sticking and helping it to release its starch, for a creamy result. With each addition of liquid, you'll notice the rice transforming from hard pellets to creamy yet al dente morsels. Estimate 25 to 30 minutes after first addition of liquid to arrive at al dente stage. The rice should be creamy and firm, but not mushy.

Turn off the heat, then stir in the cheese. Taste and add the salt, plus more to taste.

Stir in the add-on veg (details follow), and serve immediately.

Makes 4 servings

RISOTTO, TWO WAYS

Mushroom Variation

INGREDIENTS

3 tablespoons olive oil, or a combination of butter and oil

1 shallot bulb, minced

1 pound mushrooms (any or all of the following: oyster, shiitake, cremini, rehydrated porcini or chanterelles, depending on availability and preference), washed and sliced thinly

1 sprig fresh thyme, or ½ teaspoon dried (optional)

¼ cup balsamic or sherry vinegar

½ teaspoon salt

Ground black pepper

HERE'S WHAT YOU DO:

In a 10- or 12-inch skillet, heat the oil over medium heat and add the shallot. Cook until slightly softened, about 2 minutes. Add the mushrooms and sauté, stirring occasionally to keep them from sticking, until browned, up to 10 minutes. Add the thyme, if using. If the pan gets too dry, add 2 tablespoons of water.

As the mushrooms brown, add the vinegar and stir continuously to coat the mushrooms evenly. Remove the thyme sprig, if using. Add the salt and season with the pepper as you see fit.

Turn off the heat, cover, and set aside while the risotto cooks. When the risotto is done, transfer the mushroom mixture to the risotto and stir in.

RISOTTO, TWO WAYS

Spring Meadow Variation

INGREDIENTS

3 tablespoons olive oil, or a
combination of butter and oil

1 shallot bulb, minced

A total of 2 cups veg, including
any or all of the following:
1 cup asparagus, woody
stems removed, cut into
1-inch pieces; 1 medium-size
leek, thoroughly cleaned,
white part only, quartered
lengthwise, and cut into
¼-inch slices; ½ cup fresh or
frozen green peas

¼ cup white wine, or
2 tablespoons lemon juice

Zest of 1 lemon

¼ cup chopped fresh parsley

½ teaspoon salt

Ground black pepper

HERE'S WHAT YOU DO:

In a 10- or 12-inch skillet, heat the oil over medium heat and add the shallot. Cook until slightly softened, about 2 minutes. Add the asparagus and leeks, if using (if using peas, wait to add them), and stir well.

Add the wine and cook the veg until tender, about 7 minutes. If using peas, add now, plus the lemon zest and parsley. Stir to combine, add the salt and pepper, taste, and reseason as you see fit.

Turn off the heat and set the veg mixture aside while the risotto cooks. When the risotto is ready, transfer the veg mixture to the risotto and stir in.

Makes 4 servings

RISOTTO, TWO WAYS

Risotto Stock

I like the mild flavor that leeks impart in a stock, but don't fret if they're unavailable where you live. Use an extra onion instead.

INGREDIENTS

2 medium-size leeks, thoroughly cleaned, trimmed of their roots and cut into fourths (dark green part can be used)

1 large onion, cut into quarters, with skin on (clean if necessary)

1 stalk celery, cleaned and cut into thirds

3 cloves garlic, peeled but left whole

10 black peppercorns

5 whole sprigs fresh parsley

6 cups cold water

HERE'S WHAT YOU DO:

Place all the ingredients in a large saucepan. Bring to a lively simmer, then cook over medium-low heat for 30 minutes. Strain and return to the saucepan, and keep at a low simmer, covered, until ready to use.

Makes 5 cups

SPINACH & FETA CROSTATA

XTRA

In Italy, her name is *crostata*; in France, *elle s'appelle galette*, but at the end of the day, she's an easygoing free-form tart that don't need no stinkin' tart pan.

Going pan free is a liberating experience; by eliminating the pa(i)n-staking step of fitting delicate, tearable dough into a precious flute-edged pan, the crostata/galette eliminates the anxiety, too, letting cooks be cooks and not pseudo–pastry chefs.

My filling of choice features cool-weather greens seasoned with feta, but feel free to experiment with your own mix of textures and flavors. Following the recipe are details for an autumnal filling with caramelized onions, pears, and goat cheese.

KITCHEN NOTE: *Cold* is the operative word for this butter-centric dough. Cold flour, fat, and water are all key to keeping dough taut yet flexible and friendly. While the dough is resting in the fridge, make the filling.

INGREDIENTS:

Dough

1¾ cups all-purpose flour
¾ teaspoon salt
1½ sticks cold butter, diced
3 to 5 tablespoons ice-cold water
1 tablespoon cider vinegar

HERE'S WHAT YOU DO: Dough

Combine the flour and salt in a medium-size mixing bowl and place in the freezer for about 15 minutes.

Transfer the flour mixture to the bowl of a food processor. Add the butter and "cut" it into the flour, using the "pulse" function, until the mixture looks like cornmeal. (Alternatively, "cut" by hand, working the butter through your fingertips until it is integrated.)

Spoon the ice-cold water over the dough, starting with 3 tablespoons. (The amount needed will depend on temperature and climate on the day). Mix into the dough using the "pulse" function, followed by the cider vinegar. (*By hand: Use a fork to gently distribute.*) The dough should now be moist enough to press together with the squeeze of your hand.

Dust your hands with flour. Turn out the dough onto a lightly floured work surface and press together with your hands to flatten and shape into a well-formed disk, about 1 inch thick. Wrap in plastic and refrigerate for 1 hour. (May be made several hours or up to 2 days in advance, if wrapped snugly.)

SPINACH & FETA CROSTATA

INGREDIENTS:

Filling

1 tablespoon salt

About 8 cups quick-cooking greens, such as spinach or chard, washed, stemmed, and dried (Have 2 bunches on hand.)

2 tablespoons olive oil

1 small onion, chopped

2 cloves garlic, minced

⅛ teaspoon grated nutmeg

¼ cup fresh parsley, chopped

½ cup feta cheese, crumbled

Ground black pepper

2 eggs

HERE'S WHAT YOU DO: *Filling*

Have ready a large bowl filled with ice water. Bring about 6 cups of water to a rolling boil in a large saucepan. Add the salt. In batches, cook the greens for 60 seconds, then immediately transfer to the bowl, to halt the cooking process.

Remove the greens from the ice bath, and with your hands, squeeze out any remaining water. Chop coarsely.

In a 10-inch skillet set over medium heat, heat the olive oil, then add the onion and garlic. Cook until slightly softened, about 3 minutes. Stir in the greens and coat with the aromatics. Season with the nutmeg.

Transfer the greens to a medium-size mixing bowl and stir in the parsley and feta. Taste for salt and pepper, and season accordingly.

Beat one of the eggs and add to the greens mixture, stirring until well blended, and set the mixture aside.

ASSEMBLING THE CROSTATA:

Preheat the oven to 350°F. Lightly grease a baking sheet and set aside.

Lightly dust a work surface with flour and unwrap the chilled dough disk.

With a lightly floured rolling pin, gently pound on the dough to help soften and bring it to room temperature. From the middle of the dough, roll outward, turning 45 degrees after each movement, using a bench scraper to help move the dough. Roll out into a circle about 15 inches across.

With the bench scraper or a straight-edged spatula, fold the dough into half (and if necessary, into fourths) and transfer to the prepared baking sheet.

Completely unfold the dough.

Spoon the filling into the center of the dough and smooth out until well distributed, leaving a 2-inch margin all around. Working from the outer edges, gently fold the dough inward, over the filling. The

continues

dough will not completely cover the filling (the center will peek through), and that's totally fine. Pleat the dough edges as you see fit—or not.

Lightly beat the remaining egg in a small bowl, and with a silicone or pastry brush, apply the beaten egg to the surface of the crostata.

Place the crostata in the oven and bake for about 40 minutes, or until the pastry is golden brown.

Cut into wedges and eat hot or at room temperature.

Makes about 4 servings. Store leftovers in the fridge.

Caramelized Onion, Pear, and Goat Cheese Filling

INGREDIENTS

½ stick butter

5 cups onion (about 3 medium-size onions), sliced into half-moons

A handful of fresh thyme sprigs

½ teaspoon salt

Ground black pepper

3 ounces plain goat cheese

2 moderately ripe Bartlett pears, trimmed, cored, and sliced thinly

HERE'S WHAT YOU DO:

In a 10- or 12-inch skillet, melt the butter over medium heat and add the onions. Add the thyme sprigs. Cook over medium-low heat, stirring every 5 minutes and adjusting the heat to ensure that the onions are cooking evenly and not burning. Gradually the onions will soften, shrink, and sweeten, becoming caramelized and jamlike in about 1 hour.

Add the salt and season with the pepper, remove the thyme sprigs, and allow to cool.

Transfer the onions to a mixing bowl and, with a rubber spatula, combine with the goat cheese until well integrated. Transfer the mixture into the center of the dough and smooth out, leaving a 2-inch margin. Place the pear slices on top, in a concentric fashion.

ARUGULA & SEASONAL FRUIT

Ⓥ

INGREDIENTS

4 to 5 cups arugula (about
   1 bunch), washed thoroughly,
   dried, and trimmed as needed

⅛ teaspoon salt

1 tablespoon juice from a lemon,
   lime, or grapefruit

About 1 cup of seasonal fruit of
   choice: pomegranate seeds;
   2 clementines, 1 to 2 blood
   oranges or 1 grapefruit,
   segmented; strawberries,
   sliced into quarters

½ cup toasted walnuts or pecans,
   chopped

¼ cup toasted sunflower seeds
   (optional but really nice)

Extra-virgin olive oil that you love

HERE'S WHAT YOU DO:

Place the arugula in a wide salad bowl. Sprinkle with the salt, and with tongs or salad hands, turn to ensure even coverage. Taste a piece of arugula. Is it adequately salty? If not, add more. Add the citrus juice, and turn with your tools to distribute evenly and moisten.

Add the fruit, nuts, and seeds (if using), and gently toss all the ingredients until well integrated. Drizzle the oil over the salad (a trickle, not a rainfall), gently toss again, and taste for the salt-acid-fat balance.

Makes 4 servings

CHICKPEA-TURNIP CHILI

In the world of chili, ever notice how no one ever talks about chickpeas? It's too bad—and incomprehensible. These little balls of wonder deserve a shot at the next chili cook-off, y'all. Now about that turnip: Don't scoff. A slightly more bitter version of a potato, ye olde turnip is a refreshing change of pace that plays nicely with the mélange of spices and cocoa. Should you remain unconvinced, by all means, go with the spud.

KITCHEN NOTES: Adjust the chile pepper amounts as you see fit. Chili is a very personal creation, and you know your tolerance better than anyone else. This is killer served with a pot of pearl barley. Although preparing pearl barley is as simple as cooking a pot of rice, it does need a bit more time—about 45 minutes—so plan accordingly (in other words, get it on the stove before starting the chili).

INGREDIENTS

1 medium-size turnip, washed, peeled and cut into ½-inch cubes (about 2 cups)

3 tablespoons vegetable oil

1 medium-size onion, diced

3 stalks celery, cut into ½-inch slices

1 medium-size carrot, peeled and diced

1 (2 x 1-inch) hunk fresh ginger, peeled and minced

3 cloves garlic, minced

½ chile pepper of choice, seeded and minced

HERE'S WHAT YOU DO:

Prepare the turnip: Bring 4 cups of water to a boil over high heat. Add the chopped turnip and parboil for 5 minutes. The turnips will still be toothy, but are well on their way to tenderness. With a skimmer or sieve, transfer the turnips to a small bowl.

In a large saucepan or soup pot, heat the oil over medium heat, add the onion, celery, and carrot, and cook until slightly softened, 6 to 8 minutes. Add the ginger, minced garlic, and chile pepper, stirring to mix in, about 2 minutes, then add the cocoa, spices, and salt. The mixture will seem a little pasty; that's okay.

Add the turnips; stir to coat with the spice mixture and aromatics, and let everything talk to one another. Pour in the tomato puree and water and bring to a lively simmer. Cook, stirring occasionally, over medium-low heat, 10 to 15 minutes. The sauce will thicken and reduce a bit. Taste for salt, and add more if needed.

CHICKPEA-TURNIP CHILI

1 teaspoon unsweetened cocoa
   powder
2 teaspoons ground cumin
1 teaspoon ground coriander
½ teaspoon ground cinnamon
¼ teaspoon cayenne
⅛ teaspoon grated nutmeg
⅛ teaspoon ground cloves
1 teaspoon salt
2 cups tomato puree
1 cup water
2 (15-ounce) cans chickpeas,
   drained and rinsed thoroughly
2 tablespoons tomato paste,
   dissolved in 2 tablespoons
   water (optional)

HERE'S WHAT YOU DO:

continued

Stir in the chickpeas and cook as one big happy chili, until the chick-peas have arrived at your desired state of tenderness, 10 to 30 minutes. The wide time range is intentional, allowing for cook's choice. If you find that the chili needs thickening, add the optional tomato paste mixture at this time.

Will keep in an airtight container for at least 5 days.

Makes 6 servings

BARLEY PILAF

INGREDIENTS

2 tablespoons vegetable oil
½ medium-size onion, minced
1 cup uncooked pearl barley
3 cups warm water
½ teaspoon salt

HERE'S WHAT YOU DO:

Pour the oil into a medium-size saucepan and heat over medium heat. Add the onion and cook until slightly softened, about 5 minutes. Add the barley and stir until well coated with the oil, about 1 minute. The barley will glisten and maybe even make a popping noise.

Pour in the water and bring to a lively simmer. Add the salt. Lower the heat to low, cover, and cook for 30 to 35 minutes, or until tender and liquid is absorbed. If a small amount of liquid remains, turn off the heat, keep the pot covered, and leave the barley to continue absorbing the liquid, 10 to 15 minutes.

Serve with the chili.

Makes 4 cups

EGG-IN-THE-HOLE

Who knew that an egg cracked into a cut-out piece of bread would have so many names. Maybe you know it as the bull's-eye, one-eyed jack, eggs in basket, or bird's nest? Until recently, I ate my eggs scrambled or omelet-style, squeamish about runny yolks and squishy whites. What a dope I've been.

But really, I had a change of heart only when I swore off supermarket eggs and started buying locally raised eggs from small farms. The difference in flavor, texture, and color is remarkable; wait till you see that brilliant orange yolk!

Speaking of yolks, this menu is a kick in the pants to put together. Everyone gets an individual parcel, with a liner of greens. Instead of hash browns, you'll fry up a potato latke that's bigger than your head—with just one potato.

KITCHEN NOTES: Do all prep for the latke first, including boiling the potato. While the eggs are in the oven, fry the latke. Should the eggs finish first, turn off the heat and keep in the oven until ready to serve.

For the toad, it's ideal to use an ovenproof skillet that is no smaller than 12 inches across. That doesn't mean you should run out and buy a 12-inch ovenproof skillet. Plan B is to use the skillet you have on hand, then transfer the greens to a baking dish that can snugly accommodate all four slices of bread.

As for the latke, I boil the potato whole, then grate it, which creates a starchier result, eliminating the need for egg, matzo meal, or any binder whatsoever.

The latke should be fried in a skillet no wider than 10 inches across, and the shallower the skillet, the better.

continues

EGG-IN-THE-HOLE

INGREDIENTS

4 slices sandwich bread

3 tablespoons vegetable oil

½ cup minced shallot
(from 1 large bulb)

6 cups chard or spinach, washed
thoroughly and stemmed
(My preference is to completely
remove the stem from the
chard leaves, but it's cook's
choice.)

1 teaspoon salt, plus more for
sprinkling

¼ teaspoon cayenne

4 large eggs

½ cup grated Gruyère or sharp
cheddar cheese

Olive oil, for drizzling

HERE'S WHAT YOU DO:

Preheat the oven to 325°F.

With a 2½-inch biscuit cutter or an inverted drinking glass, cut a hole in the center of each slice of bread.

In an ovenproof 12-inch skillet, heat the vegetable oil over medium heat. Add the shallot and cook until slightly softened, about 3 minutes. Add the greens, turning with tongs regularly to coat with the shallot mixture. As the greens wilt, add 2 tablespoons of water to the skillet, cooking for a total of 10 minutes. Add the salt and the cayenne.

Turn off the heat. Spread the greens so that they're evenly distributed in the skillet. Place one bread slice at a time on top of the greens, making sure that all four slices fit comfortably.

Crack an egg directly into each bread hole. Sprinkle cheese around the perimeter of each egg, so that it both moistens the egg and melts on the bread.

Sprinkle additional salt over each egg, and drizzle olive oil over each bread slice, then place the pan in the oven. Bake for 15 minutes, or until the whites are opaque and the yolks are slightly set. (You can cook longer if you like your eggs harder.)

To serve, use a spatula to lift each egg-in-the-hole and surrounding greens.

FAMILY-STYLE LATKE

INGREDIENTS

2½ teaspoons salt

1 large potato, about 12 ounces
(or 2 smaller potatoes totaling
12 ounces), scrubbed
thoroughly

½ medium-size onion

Ground black pepper

3 tablespoons vegetable oil

HERE'S WHAT YOU DO:

Bring 4 cups of water and 2 teaspoons of the salt to a boil. Add the potato, cover, and boil for 22 minutes (the potato will only be slightly tender). Have ready a bowl of ice-cold water.

While the potato is cooking, coarsely grate the onion, using a box grater.

Remove the potato from the boiling water and transfer to the bowl of cold water. Allow to cool for about 10 minutes.

Peel away the skin and coarsely grate the potato. Before mixing with the onion, drain the onion of any residual water. Combine the potato and onion, then add the remaining salt and black pepper, gently stirring with a rubber spatula.

In a shallow skillet, heat 2 tablespoons of the oil over medium heat, tilting the skillet for even coverage. Move the skillet off the heat and transfer the potato mixture to the skillet, pressing it evenly until entire surface is covered with potatoes, looking like a pie.

Place the pan back over high heat, high enough that oil sizzles but doesn't burn the latke. Fry the first side for about 12 minutes, keeping a close eye on the latke cooking progress.

Have a clean heatproof cutting board at the ready. Turn off the heat and place the cutting board on top of the skillet. With one hand on top of the cutting board and the other hand on the skillet handle, invert the latke. Return the skillet to the burner, add the remaining oil, and carefully slide the latke into the skillet. Use the spatula to help reshape, if necessary, and cook the second side for 10 minutes.

Cut the latke into wedges and serve from the skillet.

Makes 4 to 6 servings

SPRING CASSOULET

Is a cassoulet still a cassoulet when the duck, goose, and pig have taken the day off? That's the question I sought to answer in my pursuit of a country French white bean stew sans *confit* or *saucisson*.

In this version, the beans are the star of the show, rather than an afterthought, with a supporting cast of leeks, lemon, and sage. But it's the head of roasted garlic, buttery and unctuous, that meats up this dish and helps to earn it cassoulet status.

Although my preference is to use dried beans for this dish, which get really creamy, I'm quite happy with the results using canned beans, which save considerable kitchen time.

INGREDIENTS

1 head garlic

Olive oil

3 tablespoons vegetable oil

1 dried cayenne pepper, cut in half

2 stalks celery, cleaned and sliced into ½-inch pieces

2 medium-size leeks, washed thoroughly, root and dark green tops removed, sliced lengthwise and cut into half-moons

1 medium-size carrot, cleaned, peeled, and diced

1 shallot bulb, diced

¼ teaspoon smoked paprika

½ teaspoon salt

Ground black pepper

HERE'S WHAT YOU DO:

Preheat the oven to 375°F.

Trim the top of the garlic and peel away most of the outermost layer of skin. Pour a small amount of olive oil into the palm of your hand and slather the garlic. Place in a small dish, cover with foil, and roast until the cloves are soft, 30 to 40 minutes.

Remove from the oven and allow to cool slightly. With one hand at root, use the other hand to squeeze out the garlic pulp, which should emerge easily. Set aside. Lower the oven temperature to 350°F.

In a deep skillet, heat the vegetable oil over medium heat, add the cayenne pepper halves, and allow to roast for about 15 seconds. Add the celery, leeks, carrot, and shallot and cook until slightly softened, about 6 minutes. Add the smoked paprika, salt, and black pepper to taste and stir to combine. Remove the cayenne. Taste for salt and black pepper and adjust as you see fit.

Transfer the drained beans to a large mixing bowl. Season with the lemon zest and juice, sage leaves, wine, and roasted garlic. Stir until the mixture is well combined. Taste for salt and adjust as you see fit.

Transfer the skillet veg to the bowl of seasoned beans, and stir in until well combined.

SPRING CASSOULET

3 (15-ounce) cans cannellini or great northern beans, rinsed and drained, or 2 cups dried white beans, soaked for 4 hours (Details for dried-bean version follow.)

Zest of 1 lemon

Juice of ½ lemon

12 sage leaves, stemmed and chopped roughly

½ cup white wine or water

¼ cup chopped fresh parsley

½ cup bread crumbs

½ cup grated Parmigiano-Reggiano cheese

½ teaspoon salt

1 tablespoon butter (optional)

HERE'S WHAT YOU DO:

continued

Grease a 9-inch casserole dish or something similar in proportion. Transfer the beans to the dish.

In a small mixing bowl, combine the parsley, bread crumbs, Parmigiano-Reggiano, and salt. Cover the beans with the bread crumb mixture and dot with butter, if using.

Cover the dish with foil and bake for about 25 minutes, or until slightly bubbly on the edges. Remove the foil and allow the cheese to brown for 3 to 4 minutes. Remove from the oven and serve hot.

Makes 6 servings

continues

SPRING CASSOULET

Plan B: Cassoulet with Dried White Beans

HERE'S WHAT YOU DO:

Begin by cooking the soaked beans with 4 cups of water and a sachet of aromatics (six black peppercorns, lemon zest from ½ lemon, and 3 sprigs fresh parsley) wrapped in cheesecloth.

Bring the beans to a rolling boil and cook at a hard boil for 5 minutes. Lower the heat and cook at a simmer until tender to the bite, at least 1 hour. Add more water as needed (you want the beans always to be covered). Remove the sachet. Add 1 teaspoon of salt and stir.

While the beans are cooking, roast the garlic.

When the beans are tender, stir in the roasted garlic. Lower the oven temperature to 350°F.

As with the canned version, cook the aromatics in skillet and add to the beans. Taste for salt and pepper and season accordingly.

Proceed to assemble in the casserole dish with the seasoned bread crumb topping and bake the same way, covered.

SEARED ROMAINE WEDGES

INGREDIENTS

3 tablespoons lemon juice
1 clove garlic, minced
¼ teaspoon salt
4 tablespoons olive oil
1 head romaine lettuce

HERE'S WHAT YOU DO:

In a small bowl, combine the lemon juice, garlic, and salt, whisking with a fork until the salt is dissolved. Whisk in the olive oil until well combined. Set aside the vinaigrette.

Cut the romaine in half, keeping the root in intact. Wash and dry carefully, keeping the halves in one piece, then cut into fourths.

Heat a griddle or skillet over medium-high heat. No oil is necessary. Place the romaine wedge onto the griddle, cut side down, in batches (don't crowd the pan). Lower the heat, then allow the lettuce to char slightly, about 90 seconds. Use tongs to check on doneness and transfer to a platter.

Drizzle the vinaigrette over the wedges and serve immediately.

Makes 4 servings

Jig-Inducing Falafel Burgers ★
Cooler-weather side: Oven Sweet Potato Fries ★
Warmer-weather side: Tabbouleh

JIG-INDUCING FALAFEL BURGERS   (XTRA) (KIDDO) (V)

I've taken the deep-fry out of this popular Middle Eastern snack and given it a new lease on life. Instead of little balls, which tend to get hard and dry in a deep pool of oil, I've shaped the spiced chickpea batter into burgers, which get pan-fried and finished in the oven. The result: Crispy and golden on the outside, tenderly moist on the inside, and soft enough to serve on a hamburger bun.

KITCHEN NOTES: Admittedly, falafel requires extra time, namely soaking dried chickpeas for at least 8 hours (canned chickpeas are simply too soft), so plan accordingly. I've had good results with shaping the patties a day in advance and frying to order; and the cooked patties make excellent leftovers.

Tabbouleh details can be found on page 88.

INGREDIENTS

1 cup dried chickpeas
1½ cups onion, chopped finely (not quite 1 large onion)
2 cloves garlic, crushed
½ cup fresh cilantro or parsley, or ¼ cup each, chopped
½ teaspoon baking powder
1 teaspoon ground coriander
1 teaspoon ground cumin
⅛ teaspoon cayenne
1½ teaspoons salt
¼ teaspoon ground black pepper
¼ to ½ cup olive oil
Optional fixins: 1 cucumber, peeled and cut into thin rounds; thinly sliced red onion, radishes, or tomatoes; your favorite hot sauce

HERE'S WHAT YOU DO:

Cover the chickpeas with water and soak for at least 8 hours at room temperature. (If your kitchen is very warm, you may want to place in the fridge to minimize chances of fermentation.) Drain and set aside. You will end up with 2 cups of soaked chickpeas.

Using a food processor or heavy-duty blender, pulverize the chickpeas, using the "pulse" function, until the beans just form a paste that sticks together when you squeeze it in your hand. Be careful not to overprocess the chickpeas; too smooth, and the batter will fall apart when cooking.

Add the rest of the ingredients, except the oil, and combine using the "pulse" function. After being pulsed approximately twelve times, the batter will be somewhat grainy and speckled with herbs.

Refrigerate the batter about 1 hour, until firm.

Meanwhile, make the tahini sauce (details follow).

Preheat the oven to 350°F.

Remove the batter from the fridge and shape into patties, using a scant ⅓-cup measure. Be careful not to overhandle the batter.

JIG-INDUCING FALAFEL BURGERS

Place the patties on a plate or baking tray and cover with plastic wrap or parchment paper. Return to the fridge and chill for an additional 10 to 15 minutes.

In a shallow 12-inch skillet set over medium-high heat, heat the oil. Gently place the patties in the hot oil in small batches (don't crowd the pan) and fry until golden brown, about 3 minutes. (If you're the impatient sort, set a timer and relax. These things don't like to be fussed with.)

Gently turn onto the second side and cook for an additional 3 minutes. Transfer to a baking tray and continue cooking in the oven for 8 minutes.

Meanwhile, prepare your fixins and the tahini sauce.

May be served in a pita, on a warmed-up soft hamburger bun, or atop romaine lettuce. Make sure you add plenty of that finger-licking tahini sauce.

Makes 8 patties. Leftover alert: Reheats well for next day's lunch.

---

continues

Tahini Sauce

Made from ground sesame seeds, tahini has the look and feel of creamy peanut butter. A staple of Middle East cuisine, it is the star player of this addictive sauce, which takes about 3 minutes to whiz in the food processor. Try it with roasted cauliflower, which is featured on page 204.

INGREDIENTS

1 cup tahini, stirred well before using
¼ to ½ cup lemon juice
1 to 2 cloves garlic, smashed
1½ teaspoons salt
½ cup water

HERE'S WHAT YOU DO:

In a medium-size bowl or a food processor, mix together all the ingredients and blend until smooth; add extra water if necessary to make a pourable sauce. Keeps in the fridge for a few days.

Makes about 2 cups

OVEN SWEET POTATO FRIES

First things first: These orange oven fries are fab. But I must warn you: If you're looking for the equivalent crispiness of potato fries, move on. Sweet potatoes will never win the crispy contest, and it's even more of a long shot when they're "fried" in the oven. They also like to stick to the pan. After several tries, I've come up with a few tricks that both eliminate the sticky syndrome and maximize the crispy quotient.

INGREDIENTS

2 medium-size sweet potatoes
(total weight: 24 to 32 ounces)
¼ to ½ cup cornstarch
4 tablespoons olive oil
1 teaspoon salt
1 teaspoon cayenne (optional)
1 teaspoon ground cumin
(optional)
Oil spray, for greasing the baking
pan

HERE'S WHAT YOU DO:

Preheat the oven to 425°F.

Peel the sweet potatoes and cut in half, then slice each half lengthwise. Cut each chunk into "fry" spears, about 4 inches long and 1 inch across. Fries that are too wide will fail to crisp. You should get about thirty pieces from each sweet potato.

Pour the cornstarch into a small, shallow bowl. Dredge the sweet potato spears, tapping off any excess.

Grease a baking pan with oil spray and preheat in the oven for 2 minutes.

Transfer the sweet potatoes to a medium-size bowl and add the oil. With your hands, toss the sweet potatoes to completely coat with the oil. The cornstarch will begin to disappear. Add the salt and cayenne and cumin, if using. Toss the sweet potatoes again to make sure it's evenly distributed.

Remove the baking pan from the oven and immediately place the sweet potatoes on the hot pan. You may hear a sizzle.

Bake for 20 minutes, removing from the oven at the halfway point to turn the sweet fries onto a second side to ensure even browning. At the 18-minute mark, check for doneness and browning and turn again, if necessary. The fries are done when both tender to the bite and crispy on the outside.

Remove from the oven and eat while hot, as they get soggy quickly.

Makes 4 servings

WEST INDIAN–STYLE CHANNA WRAP

The farther east you go in the West Indies, the more Indian (as in India) the food gets, the result of a massive import of indentured laborers in the nineteenth century. Curry is a way of life in Trinidad, where 40 percent of the population has South Asian roots. These culinary influences are also felt in neighboring islands such as Grenada and Barbados, where chickpeas are called channa.

In keeping with Indian cookery, the channa are curried and tongue popping, often rolled into a paper-thin roti or cushioned between two pieces of fried bread for a head-spinning sandwich called Doubles.

As a tribute to time spent in countless West Indian gas stations where channa-filled morsels are often sold, I've come up with my own take on channa that I reckon would do my island friends proud. Here, I tuck the peas into a whole wheat tortilla that's wrapped like a parcel. With a cooling cucumber or tomato garnish, and a quick glug of hot sauce, I'm back where the ocean really is blue.

Makes over-the-top lunch leftovers.

NOTE: On a spicy scale, this recipe is 4 stars out of 5. You may tone down the heat by eliminating the cayenne or reducing the curry powder, but I recommend using at least 1½ tablespoons of the curry powder.

WEST INDIAN–STYLE CHANNA WRAP

INGREDIENTS:

Curry

3 tablespoons vegetable oil

2 cups diced onions

5 cloves garlic, minced

½ chile pepper of choice, seeded and diced

1 (2 x 1-inch) hunk fresh ginger, peeled and minced

3 tablespoons curry powder (preferably Madras-style)

1 teaspoon ground cumin

¼ teaspoon cayenne

¼ teaspoon ground turmeric

1 teaspoon salt

2 (15-ounce) cans chickpeas, drained and rinsed thoroughly

1 (17.5-ounce) package 8-inch whole wheat tortillas (10-inch tortillas work well, too)

Optional add-ons: Your favorite hot sauce; ½ red onion, sliced thinly; ½ cucumber, diced

HERE'S WHAT YOU DO:

In a deep skillet, heat the oil over medium heat. Add the onions and cook until slightly softened, about 8 minutes. Add the garlic, chile pepper, and ginger, and cook for about 2 minutes. Add the spices and salt, and stir well. You'll end up with a paste.

Add chickpeas, plus enough water to barely cover (at least 3 cups). Bring to a lively simmer, then lower the heat and cook at a gentle simmer, stirring occasionally, until most of the liquid evaporates, 50 to 60 minutes. You're looking for very soft chickpeas with a thick gravy, not soup.

Taste for salt and season accordingly.

Place a few tablespoons of channa inside a warmed tortilla (one per person to start), with any or all of the optional add-ons, and you've got a sandwich of champions. The channa is also great over rice. To heat the tortillas, there are a few options: Wrap in plastic and heat for 20 seconds in the microwave; wrap in aluminum foil and heat for 10 minutes in the oven at 325°F; place on a dry skillet or griddle, one by one, for 30 seconds each side, over medium heat.

Keeps well in an airtight container in the fridge for at least five days.

Makes at least 8 servings

TOP-SHELF POTATO SALAD

Mayonnaise, the white goop in a jar that everyone but me seems to adore, is conspicuously absent from this potato salad. My condiment of choice is mustard, and here, it's part of a vinaigrette, with plenty of lemony notes chiming in. But really, the key to my potato salad's top-shelf-ness is neither the mustard nor the lemon, but the way I boil the potatoes. Less water and more salt in the pot makes for a starchier, well-seasoned cooking liquid and potato-y morsels that are, dare I say, palate perfect. What's more, you won't have to worry about your potato salad curdling at the next company picnic!

INGREDIENTS

2 pounds waxy potatoes (Yukon Gold, Yellow Finn, new, or red-skinned), washed, trimmed, and peeled as necessary

2 teaspoons salt

3 tablespoons lemon juice

2 teaspoons Dijon mustard

3 tablespoons olive oil

¼ cup scallions, white and light green parts only, diced

¼ cup fresh parsley, chopped finely

Ground black pepper

HERE'S WHAT YOU DO:

Cut the potatoes into 1-inch pieces and place in a medium-size pot with a lid. Add the salt and 4 cups of water (Note: This is important.) and cover. Set over medium-high heat and bring to a boil. Lower the heat to medium and cook for 18 to 20 minutes.

While the potatoes cook, combine the lemon juice, mustard, and olive oil in a small bowl, whisking with a fork until well blended.

When the potatoes are fork tender, remove with a skimmer or sieve, allowing the residual water to drain, and transfer to a medium-size serving bowl.

Pour the sauce directly on top of the potatoes, and with a rubber spatula, gently stir until the potatoes are well coated. Stir in the scallions and parsley, until evenly distributed, then add the black pepper. Taste. This should make you very happy.

Serve warm or at room temperature.

Makes 4 servings

TEMPEH HOAGIE-LETTA   **DO**

> Born and raised outside of Philadelphia by two Philly natives, I cut my teeth (not long after the T-bone from my high chair days) on footlong sandwiches that are my hometown's cultural icons.
>
> I'm talking about the cheese steak and the hoagie, possibly two of the greatest artery cloggers ever invented, a mound of meat and fixins tucked into a freshly baked Italian roll, always made to order with homegrown "atty-tude" in a neighborhood joint—a luncheonette, corner sandwich shop, or street cart.
>
> I wondered if it was possible to recreate the hoagied bliss of my youth, but without the cold cuts. Here, pan-fried tempeh (which you'll also meet on page 131) stands in for the Italian meats and cozies up with an olive salad that is reminiscent of the dressing on a muffaletta, the hoagie's distant and equally scrumptious cousin from New Orleans.
>
> Ladies and gents, meet the hoagie-letta.
>
> P.S. Do take the additional 15 minutes to try out the kale chips. They're life changing.

INGREDIENTS:

Tempeh

¼ cup soy sauce

2 teaspoons Dijon mustard

1 teaspoon sesame oil

Juice ½ lime

1 clove garlic, chopped, plus
    1 whole clove

1 teaspoon hot sauce of choice
    (optional)

1 (8-ounce) package soy tempeh
    (multigrain or flax is fine,
    too; see page 19 for
    recommendations), sliced
    into thumb-size pieces, about
    ½ inch thick

3 tablespoons vegetable oil

Salt

4 (6-inch) hoagie rolls (baguette
    is too hard; look for something
    soft)

HERE'S WHAT YOU DO:

In a shallow baking dish, combine the soy sauce, mustard, sesame oil, lime juice, garlic, and hot sauce (if using) and whisk with a fork to blend. Add the tempeh, making sure it's covered in marinade. Allow to marinate about 30 minutes, turning to coat the second side after 15 minutes.

In a medium-size mixing bowl, combine the onion, oregano, oil, celery, and lemon juice and stir. Allow to sit for about 15 minutes. The onion will mellow out a bit with the citrus.

Stir in the olives, pepperoncini, roasted peppers, and parsley. Taste for salt and pepper, and season accordingly (the olives and pickled peppers are salty, FYI).

Can be made several hours or day in advance. The salad gets better the next day.

Heat the oil in a wide skillet over medium heat. Remove the tempeh from the marinade and transfer to the skillet to pan-fry. Don't crowd the skillet; if necessary, cook the tempeh in batches.

Cook until golden brown on both sides, about 10 minutes. With tongs, transfer to a paper towel to drain. Sprinkle immediately with salt.

continues

TEMPEH HOAGIE-LETTA

INGREDIENTS:

Tempeh

continued

Olive oil, to moisten the rolls

A few slices of smoked Gouda or provolone cheese per sandwich (optional tasty treat)

INGREDIENTS:
Fixins Salad

½ medium-size onion, cut through the root in half, then sliced into half-moons

1 teaspoon dried oregano

2 tablespoons olive oil

1 large or 2 small celery stalks, washed thoroughly, halved lengthwise, and cut into ½-inch slices

Juice ½ lemon

½ cup good-quality olives (green and/or black), pitted and chopped roughly

¼ cup pepperoncini or your favorite pickled pepper, chopped roughly

¼ cup roasted peppers (½ to 1 medium-size pepper), chopped roughly (see page 194 for how-to details; jarred variety also fine)

¼ cup fresh parsley, chopped finely

Salt and ground black pepper

HERE'S WHAT YOU DO:

continued

Slice the rolls in half (but not all the way through; keep attached along one edge). In a dry skillet or under the low setting of your broiler, toast the rolls, cut side toward the heat source, until slightly crisp on the inside. Remove from the heat and rub the insides with the whole garlic clove.

Drizzle a small amount of olive oil on each roll half to moisten. Add the cheese, if using, followed by ½ cup of salad, topped off with four pieces of tempeh. Push the tempeh down to meet the salad, squish both sides of roll, and dig in.

Makes 4 sandwiches

KALE CHIPS

INGREDIENTS

1 bunch (4 to 5 cups) Lacinato kale (also sold as Dinosaur kale)

1 tablespoon olive oil

½ teaspoon salt

¼ teaspoon red pepper flakes (optional)

HERE'S WHAT YOU DO:

Preheat the oven to 350°F.

With a sharp knife, remove the stem and middle rib of each kale leaf so that all you have left are leaves. Wash the leaves, then dry thoroughly, preferably in a salad spinner. With a knife, cut the leaves into small pieces (ideally 3 inches long, 2 inches wide).

Transfer the leaves to a medium-size mixing bowl and add the olive oil, salt and red pepper flakes (if using). With your hand, coat leaves with the seasonings; the leaves will glisten a bit.

Place the kale in a single layer on a baking sheet, giving the leaves plenty of room to roast. Cook for 8 minutes, maybe a few seconds more. Remove from the oven and enjoy.

**Makes enough chips for 4 sandwiches or a bowl of TV snacks.
Best eaten within 24 hours, stored in a paper bag.**

Huevo y Frijoles ★ Romaine with Toasted Pepitas & Lemon Vinaigrette

HUEVO Y FRIJOLES

KIDDO **GF**

This is a variation on huevos rancheros, the classic Mexican breakfast plate of fried eggs, refried beans, chili sauce, and various accoutrements on a bed of corn tortillas. Day or night, huevos has long been a personal favorite, but they inevitably put me into a food coma.

To lighten the load, I've slimmed down to just one huevo, and instead amped up the ratio of black beans (simmered in a saucepan, not refried, with aromatics and spices). Rather than frying the egg, I place it atop the bean mountain and let it bake in the oven.

INGREDIENTS

2 tablespoons vegetable oil, plus more for lubricating the tortillas
½ medium-size onion, diced
2 cloves garlic, minced
½ teaspoon ground cumin
¼ teaspoon cayenne
1 teaspoon dried oregano
1 (25-ounce) can black beans
Salt
4 (6-inch) soft corn tortillas
4 large eggs
½ to ¾ cup black bean–compatible grated cheese (Monterey Jack, cotija, cheddar)
½ cup fresh cilantro, chopped finely
Optional fixins: 1 ripe avocado, cut into slices; your favorite jarred salsa or hot sauce, thinly sliced radishes, sour cream or plain yogurt

HERE'S WHAT YOU DO:

Preheat the oven to 350°F.

In a medium-size saucepan or deep skillet, heat the oil over medium heat. Add the onion and cook until slightly softened, about 5 minutes. Add the garlic, cumin, cayenne, and oregano, and stir; mixture will be somewhat pasty.

Pour in the black beans, stir to mix well, and bring to a lively simmer. Cover and cook over low heat for about 15 minutes. The beans will reduce and thicken a bit.

The sodium amount in canned beans varies greatly, so do make sure to taste the beans before seasoning with salt.

In a shallow skillet or on a griddle, heat about ¼ teaspoon of the oil over medium-high heat. (If you can fit more than one tortilla on a griddle, use more oil.)

One by one, warm the tortillas in the skillet, so that they soften and relax. Measure out ½ cup of beans and spoon onto each tortilla. Then crack an egg on top, followed by the grated cheese. Using a spatula, transfer the egg-topped tortillas to a baking sheet.

Bake until the egg whites are translucent and yolks are slightly set, about 15 minutes. If you like, finish cooking the eggs under the broiler setting to brown the cheese.

Serve with any or all of the fixins.

Makes 4 servings

ROMAINE WITH TOASTED PEPITAS & LEMON VINAIGRETTE

INGREDIENTS

1 head romaine lettuce, washed thoroughly and dried, and trimmed as necessary

½ small jicama, peeled and julienned (optional)

½ teaspoon salt

½ cup pepita seeds (a.k.a. hulled pumpkin seeds)

2 tablespoons lemon juice

2 tablespoons olive oil

HERE'S WHAT YOU DO:

Cut the romaine into smaller, salad-size pieces and place in a salad bowl. Add the jicama, if using. Season with ¼ teaspoon of the salt.

Place the pepitas in a skillet over medium heat and toast, about 2 minutes. Stay close, as the seeds will quickly turn golden brown, and if you're not careful, will burn.

Transfer the seeds to the salad, and toss to mix with the lettuce.

In a small bowl, whisk the lemon juice and the remaining salt, with a fork, until dissolved. Drizzle in the olive oil, and whisk until emulsified.

When ready to serve, pour the vinaigrette over the salad, tossing with tongs or salad hands for even coverage.

Makes 4 servings

JERK TEMPEH

The seasonal stretch between February and March can be agonizing, when spring teases but doesn't quite commit. When I'm hankering for warmer times and climes but am too broke to get airborne, I let food transport me instead. With this trio of island-inspired vittles, we can all go on spring break. According to my friend Barbara, who for years lived with a Jamaican musician, the peas and rice are the real deal.

KITCHEN NOTES: While the tempeh is marinating, make the pineapple salad.
While the marinated tempeh is baking, make the peas and rice.

INGREDIENTS

1 (8-ounce) package tempeh
½ cup prepared jerk sauce
   (Look for sauce, not marinade
   or rub, as either of the latter
   will be too dry.)
Cooking spray or vegetable oil

HERE'S WHAT YOU DO:

Slice the tempeh into thumb-size pieces, about 2 inches long and ½ inch wide. You'll end up with at least twenty-five pieces, maybe more.

Test the baking dishes for size before marinating: Line up the tempeh in a single layer, row by row. You want a snug fit, but the dish must be at least 10 inches wide.

Transfer the tempeh to a medium-size mixing bowl and add the jerk sauce. Turn the tempeh to coat with the sauce on all sides, being careful not to break the tempeh. Allow to marinate for 30 minutes (or longer, if you want).

Preheat the oven to 350°F. Lightly grease a baking dish with oil spray or apply vegetable oil with a brush.

Transfer the marinated tempeh to the prepared baking dish and line up in a single layer, row by row, just like the test run.

Bake for 25 minutes, then cook the tempeh under the broiler for about 3 minutes, for a crusty top.

Remove from the heat and serve with Zesty Pineapple Salad and Jamaican-Style Peas & Rice (details follow).

Makes 4 to 6 servings. Great leftover alert!

ZESTY PINEAPPLE SALAD

INGREDIENTS

1 ripe pineapple, peeled and cut
into 1-inch chunks (How-to
details are on page 195.)

¼ cup fresh cilantro, chopped

⅛ cup unsalted peanuts, toasted
and chopped finely

Zest of 1 lime

¼ fresh chile pepper of choice,
seeded and diced (optional)

Juice of ½ lime

1 teaspoon brown sugar

2 teaspoons soy sauce

HERE'S WHAT YOU DO:

Place the pineapple chunks in a large bowl and add the cilantro,
peanuts, lime zest, and chile pepper (if using).

In a small bowl, combine the lime juice, brown sugar, and soy sauce
and stir until the sugar is nearly dissolved. Pour over the pineapple;
with a large spoon, stir to combine and coat the fruit with the dressing.

Can be made a day in advance.

Makes at least 4 servings

JAMAICAN-STYLE PEAS & RICE

INGREDIENTS

1 tablespoon vegetable oil

¼ cup minced shallot

1 cup long- or medium-grain rice

½ (14-ounce) can unsweetened coconut milk (you can make a rum cocktail with the rest, or keep in the fridge for a few days in an airtight container)

1¼ cups water

1 (15-ounce) can small red beans or red kidney beans, rinsed and drained

1 sprig fresh thyme, or ½ teaspoon dried

½ teaspoon salt

½ Scotch bonnet chile pepper, seeded and deveined, but kept whole (optional)

HERE'S WHAT YOU DO:

In a medium-size saucepan with a lid, heat the oil over medium heat. Add the shallots and cook until slightly softened, about 2 minutes.

Add the rice and stir to coat with the shallots, allowing it to toast for 1 minute.

Add the coconut milk, water, beans, thyme, salt, and chile pepper (if using). Bring the mixture to a lively simmer, then cover, lower the heat to low, and cook for 20 minutes. Check the rice for doneness; cook for an additional 5 minutes if necessary. Turn off the heat and keep covered; the rice will continue to cook.

Taste for salt and add more if needed. Remove the chile pepper, if using.

Makes 4 ample servings

Summer . . .

. . . is when the rules do not apply.

The inside moves outside; we live on our porches, stoops, and decks, in our backyards and parks, under the boardwalk and up on the roof. Our lap becomes our table and our hands become our plates.

We're ready for a ride on an herb-stuffed zucchini boat and for a date with a sun-kissed bell pepper, roasted for romesco sauce or filled with luscious goat cheese. We break out the steak knives to cut into vine-warmed tomatoes (they don't call them Beef Steaks and Big Boys for nothing), filled with hummus or pureed into a spritzy pitcher of gazpacho.

As much as we play with fire (tofu barbecue, grilled eggplant stacks), we embrace the raw (sesame rice noodles and melon-herb salad), an orgy of color and a heady perfume of basil, peaches, and muskmelon that is gone before you know it. Can we blame the alternative universe on midsummer night fairy dust? Absolutely. Meet you under the cherry tree!

GARLIC SCAPE PESTO PASTA

I should probably have a bumper sticker made that says: I BRAKE FOR GARLIC SCAPES. As soon as June arrives, I'm champing at the bit, waiting like a concert groupie for the crazy-looking green curlicues to debut at my farmers' market.

Here's the botany lesson: Garlic, as well as its relatives in the Allium family (leeks, chives, onions), grows underground, where the bulb begins its journey, soft and onion-like. As the bulb gets harder (and more like the garlic we know), a chlorophyll-green shoot like a scallion pokes its way through the ground. The shoot, called a scape, is long and thin and pliable enough to curl into gorgeous tendrils. Farmers clip it to encourage the bulb to grow, and lucky for us, those scraps, once destined for the compost pile, are now market fare. Garlicky yet smoother than the full-grown bulb, scapes make the most killer pesto in the world.

Mark your calendar! Scapes stick around for a limited time.

INGREDIENTS:

Pesto

1 cup garlic scapes (8 or 9 scapes), top flowery part removed, cut into ¼-inch slices

⅓ cup walnuts

¾ cup olive oil

¼ to ½ cup grated Parmigiano-Reggiano cheese

½ teaspoon salt, or to taste

Ground black pepper

HERE'S WHAT YOU DO:

Place the scapes and walnuts in the bowl of a food processor and whiz until well combined and somewhat smooth. Slowly drizzle in the oil and process until integrated. With a rubber spatula, scoop the pesto out of the bowl and into a mixing bowl. Add Parmigiano-Reggiano and the salt and pepper to taste.

Keeps for up to one week in an airtight container in the fridge. Also freezes well; add the cheese after the pesto has thawed.

Makes about ¾ cup

GARLIC SCAPE PESTO PASTA

Pesto Pasta Supper

1 (1-pound) package short pasta (penne, fusilli, farfalle)

1 tablespoon salt, plus more to taste

¼ cup garlic scape pesto

Optional add-ons: ½ cup cherry or grape tomatoes, sliced in half; ¼ cup fresh parsley, chopped finely; ¼ cup Parmigiano-Reggiano cheese

Ground black pepper

HERE'S WHAT YOU DO:

Bring 3 quarts of water and the 1 tablespoon of salt to a boil in a large pot. Add the pasta and cook until al dente, about 10 minutes. Stir occasionally to keep from sticking. Drain the pasta and transfer to a wide, shallow bowl.

Stir in the pesto until the pasta is well coated. If using, add the tomatoes, parsley, and/or Parmigiano-Reggiano. Taste for salt and pepper and season as you see fit.

Serve immediately.

Makes 4 servings

ROMAINE & BALSAMIC-GINGERY STRAWBERRIES

INGREDIENTS

1 head romaine lettuce
(about 8 cups), washed
thoroughly, dried, and trimmed

2 cups (1 pint) strawberries,
hulled and sliced into halves
or fourths, depending on size

1 tablespoon balsamic vinegar

1 teaspoon sugar

1 teaspoon peeled and minced
fresh ginger

½ medium-size red onion, sliced
very thinly

¼ teaspoon salt

Olive oil, for drizzling

HERE'S WHAT YOU DO:

Tear the romaine into bite-size pieces and place in a large salad bowl.

Place the strawberries in a medium-size bowl. In a small mixing bowl, combine the vinegar, sugar, and ginger, whisking with a fork until the sugar is dissolved. Pour over the strawberries and add the onion, stirring until well combined. Allow the strawberries to bathe in the liquid for about 15 minutes.

Sprinkle the salt all over the lettuce and toss until well distributed. Drizzle with the olive oil and toss again. The lettuce should glisten slightly from the oil. Stir in the strawberry mixture.

Makes 4 servings

Chickpea "Crab Cakes" ★ Yogurt Rémoulade ★ Cocktail Sauce ★ Corn Kernel Salad

CHICKPEA "CRAB CAKES"

KIDDO

True story: Less than two weeks before this manuscript was due, with most recipes edited and determined fit for public consumption, I pan-fried a batch of my falafel patties (featured on page 48) for me and my husband, Russ. He took one bite into his falafel-on-a-bun and looked at me with all seriousness. "This falafel looks and eats likes a crab cake."

He was right. With thirty combined years of living in Washington, D.C.—crab cake central—we could both see that this chickpea patty had Chesapeake potential.

With the wild eyes of a mad scientist, I immediately went to work, replacing Middle Eastern falafel spices with Old Bay, the iconic Maryland seafood seasoning that's had a cult following for three generations. Out with the tahini, in with a yogurt rémoulade and horseradishy cocktail sauce that transport you from the Mid-East to the Mid-Atlantic.

The result: Downright crab-shacky.

KITCHEN NOTE: As with the falafel, dried chickpeas are a must for this recipe; the canned version are simply too soft and patties will fall apart.

INGREDIENTS

1 cup dried chickpeas

1½ cups finely chopped onion (not quite 1 large onion)

2 cloves garlic, crushed

½ cup fresh cilantro or parsley, or ¼ cup each, chopped

½ teaspoon baking powder

2 teaspoons Old Bay seasoning

⅛ teaspoon cayenne

½ teaspoon dry mustard

½ teaspoon salt

¼ teaspoon ground black pepper

½ cup vegetable oil

8 soft hamburger buns or English muffins

HERE'S WHAT YOU DO:

Cover the chickpeas with water and soak for at least 8 hours at room temperature. (If your kitchen is very warm, you may want to place in the fridge to minimize chances of fermentation.) Drain and set aside. You will end up with 2 cups of soaked chickpeas.

Using a food processor or heavy-duty blender, pulverize the chickpeas, using the "pulse" function. Pulverize until the beans just form a paste that sticks together when you squeeze it in your hand. Be careful not to overprocess the chickpeas; too smooth, the batter will fall apart when cooking.

Add the rest of the ingredients (except the oil) and combine using the "pulse" function. After being pulsed approximately twelve times, the batter will be somewhat grainy and speckled with herbs.

Refrigerate the batter for about 1 hour, until firm.

Meanwhile, make the yogurt rémoulade or cocktail sauce (details follow).

continues

CHICKPEA "CRAB CAKES"

Remove the batter from the fridge and shape into patties, using a scant ⅓-cup measure. Be careful not to overhandle the batter.

Preheat the oven to 350°F.

Place the patties on a plate or baking tray and cover with plastic wrap. Return to the fridge and chill for an additional 10 to 15 minutes.

In a shallow 12-inch skillet, heat ¼ cup of the oil over medium-high heat. Gently place the patties into the hot oil in small batches (don't crowd the pan) and fry the first side until golden brown, about 3 minutes. (If you're the impatient sort, set a timer and relax. These things don't like to be fussed with.)

Gently turn onto the second side and cook for an additional 3 minutes. Transfer to a baking tray to finish cooking in the oven for 8 minutes. (Before frying the next batch, heat the remaining oil.) The patties will have a somewhat drier appearance on the outside, which is a good thing.

Serve on a bun with the rémoulade, cocktail sauce, or a schmear of mustard-mayo.

Makes 8 patties

YOGURT RÉMOULADE

INGREDIENTS

½ cup plain yogurt (if you like thick sauce, look for Greek-style yogurt)
¼ cup chopped fresh parsley
2 teaspoons Dijon mustard
Squeeze of ½ lemon
2 to 3 cornichons or bread-and-butter pickles, diced
1 teaspoon of your favorite hot sauce
⅛ cup onion or shallot, diced
¼ teaspoon salt

HERE'S WHAT YOU DO:

In a small mixing bowl, stir the yogurt with a fork, to loosen. Add the rest of the ingredients and stir to combine. Taste for salt, acid, and heat and season accordingly. This is an ad hoc sauce open to all kinds of kitchen improv. Have your way with this one!

Makes ¾ cup

COCKTAIL SAUCE

INGREDIENTS

½ cup ketchup
3 tablespoons prepared horseradish
Juice of ½ lemon, plus more to taste
⅛ teaspoon cayenne (optional)
Salt (optional)

HERE'S WHAT YOU DO:

Combine all the ingredients in a small bowl and stir to combine. It is unlikely you will need salt, but taste and add if need be.

Makes ¾ cup

CORN KERNEL SALAD

The constant in this dish is the corn kernels (and salt). Everything else is subject to cook's preferences, mood, and availability of ingredients. Tomato hater? Try ½ cup of blueberries instead. No red onion in the house? Use up the scallions. This is a template meant to be played with.

INGREDIENTS

4 ears corn (estimate 1 ear per person)

2 teaspoons salt

½ cup fresh basil leaves, torn, or fresh flat-leaf parsley or cilantro, finely chopped

½ cup red onion, diced

Juice of 1 lime

2 to 3 tablespoons olive oil

12 to 15 small tomatoes (such as cherry, grape, or pear), sliced in half

1½ teaspoons Madras curry powder (Plan B: ½ teaspoon ground cumin, ½ teaspoon ground coriander, ¼ teaspoon ground cinnamon, and ⅛ teaspoon cayenne)

Ground black pepper

HERE'S WHAT YOU DO:

Husk the corn thoroughly, including the interior silk. Lay the corn on a work surface. Use one hand to anchor the corn, while you place the edge of a sharp, wide knife against the kernels. Move the blade away from your anchoring hand, in a horizontal direction, allowing the kernels to fall as they are cut.

In a small saucepan, bring 2 cups of water to a boil. Add the salt and kernels and cook for about 60 seconds. Drain the kernels, using a strainer, and rinse under cold water.

Transfer the kernels to a medium-size bowl. Add the rest of the ingredients, stirring with a wooden spoon as you proceed, tasting for the intensity of the spices and salt. Season until you've hit all the right notes. Keeps for one day, covered, in the fridge.

Makes 4 servings. Amounts can be halved and doubled.

HUMMUS-STUFFED TOMATOES

With my broom in the shop, I've rented a magic carpet and invite you to climb aboard for our adventure to the Mediterranean coast. When I'm too hot to think, I like to imagine I'm somewhere else, particularly where there's a sea breeze whispering in my ear. This trio of goodies does the trick, and much of it can be made in advance, so that when evening calls, supper is a snap.

Halloumi is a cheese from Cyprus, made from sheep's and/or goat's milk. Straight out of the package, it has a texture reminiscent of Armenian string cheese, with a salty flavor. Unlike any other cheese I've come across, Halloumi doesn't melt into a pile of goo when heated. It gets nice and brown on the outside but stays solidly intact, resembling a boneless chicken breast or an egg-white omelet.

KITCHEN NOTES: Make the fattoush salad first, so it can marinate in its own juices. Then make the hummus, in preparation for the stuffed tomatoes. The Halloumi should be cooked just before serving, because it hardens as it cools.

FATTOUSH SALAD

INGREDIENTS

3 (8-inch) pita rounds, or 2 cups
  unsalted pita crisps

1 clove garlic, minced

3 to 5 scallions (depending on
  size), white and light green
  parts only, cleaned and
  minced finely

½ cup fresh flat-leaf parsley,
  chopped finely

1 cup mint leaves, chopped finely

1 medium-size cucumber, peeled,
  seeded, and chopped finely

½ cup grape or cherry tomatoes,
  sliced in half lengthwise

½ cup lemon juice

¼ teaspoon red pepper flakes

½ teaspoon salt

⅓ cup olive oil

HERE'S WHAT YOU DO:

Preheat the oven to 350°F. Place the pita rounds on a baking sheet and toast in the oven until crisp and brittle (but not burned), about 30 minutes. You may also toast for a while, turn off the heat, and keep the bread in the oven to continue drying out. (This may also be done in a toaster oven.) If using pita crisps, do not toast.

In a medium-size salad bowl, combine the garlic, scallions, herbs, cucumber, and tomatoes. With a wooden spoon, stir to mix well. Add the lemon juice, red pepper flakes, and salt, stirring again.

With your hands, break the crisped pitas into bite-size pieces and mix with the rest of the salad. The pita will absorb some of the juices and soften; that's a good thing. Pour in the olive oil, toss, and allow the salad to macerate while you prepare the other dishes.

Makes 4 side-dish servings

HUMMUS-STUFFED TOMATOES

INGREDIENTS

1 (15-ounce) can chickpeas, drained and rinsed

3 tablespoons tahini

1 clove garlic

¼ to ½ cup lemon juice

¼ to ½ teaspoon salt

4 medium-size vine-ripe tomatoes

4 fresh parsley or basil leaves and/or olive oil, for garnish

HERE'S WHAT YOU DO:

In a food processor, combine the chickpeas, tahini, and garlic. Puree for about 2 minutes, then stop the motor. With a rubber spatula, scrape down the sides of the bowl. Add 4 to 6 tablespoons of water, gradually, to help smooth things out, and then add the lemon juice. Continue pureeing until the mixture achieves your desired flavor, texture, and consistency. Add ¼ teaspoon of the salt and taste. Enough? And what about the lemon? The hummus should have a balance of lemony tang, earthy sesame, and salt. Scoop out of the food processor and into a small bowl.

Core and excavate the tomatoes: Insert a paring knife into the top of each tomato and move it around the core and stem end. Remove the core top. Place a teaspoon inside and gently remove first layer of seeds and pulp, creating a home for the hummus filling. (You may add the tomato seeds and pulp to the fattoush salad, if you like.) If using the spoon becomes too awkward, extract the pulp with your fingers.

Fill each tomato with about 1 tablespoon of hummus, more or less, depending on its size. (Leftover hummus will keep for at least three days in the fridge—if you can resist eating it all in one sitting!)

Garnish with herbs and/or a drizzle of olive oil.

Makes 4 servings

SEARED HALLOUMI

Halloumi is sold in some conventional supermarkets and in Mediterranean or Middle Eastern grocery stores. You can sear it in a skillet or grill pan or on an outdoor grill.

INGREDIENTS

1 (8-ounce) package Halloumi cheese

Juice of ½ lemon

1 teaspoon dried oregano

1 tablespoon olive oil or oil spray, for greasing the cooking surface

HERE'S WHAT YOU DO:

Slice the Halloumi into ½-inch slices; you'll get about six pieces. Place in a shallow dish and season with the lemon and oregano.

Grease a skillet or grill grate over medium heat.

With tongs, lift the cheese from the seasoning mixture and transfer to the skillet, in small batches, if necessary. Sear for 2 minutes on each side.

Eat immediately.

Makes 4 servings

ZUCCHINI BOATS

In *Animal, Vegetable, Miracle*, Barbara Kingsolver's account of eating locally for a year, there's a chapter called "Zucchini Larceny." The summer squash in the family garden had lived up to its reputation as the vegetable that keeps on giving, and Kingsolver suggests to her husband that they get a pig to help them with the surplus. Sound familiar?

Here's one way to deal with an embarrassment of zuke riches—transforming them into boats that are stuffed with a summery filling of tomatoes, garlic, and fresh herbs. I like to serve these edible containers with couscous-chickpea salad, my favorite on-the-fly combo during the hottest months. Note on herbs: *Fresh* is the operative word here, particularly during summer when they're flourishing and abundant. The one dried allowance I'd make is oregano.

INGREDIENTS

6 medium-size zucchini (about 2 pounds), halved lengthwise

5 tablespoons extra-virgin olive oil

1 medium-size onion, chopped finely

3 cloves garlic, chopped finely

2 medium-size vine-ripe tomatoes, cored and chopped

½ teaspoon ground coriander

½ teaspoon salt

Ground black pepper

¼ teaspoon red pepper flakes (optional)

¾ cup grated pecorino or Parmigiano-Reggiano cheese

¾ to 1 cup plain bread crumbs with texture (See page 195 for DIY details.)

¼ cup fresh flat-leaf parsley, chopped finely

HERE'S WHAT YOU DO:

Using a small spoon, scoop the pulp from each zucchini half, leaving a rim around the edges to minimize tearing. Reserve the pulp.

Heat 3 tablespoons of the olive oil in a 10-inch skillet over medium heat. Add the onion; cook, stirring occasionally, until slightly softened, about 5 minutes. Add the garlic, tomatoes, and reserved zucchini pulp, and cook, stirring occasionally, until the mixture is softened and slightly thickened, about 4 minutes. Stir in the ground coriander, salt, black pepper, and red pepper flakes (if using). Remove from the heat.

In a medium-size bowl, stir together ¼ cup of the cheese, ¼ cup of the bread crumbs, and the parsley, mint, and oregano. Transfer the onion mixture to join the cheese mixture. With a wooden spoon, stir everything together until well mixed. Taste for salt and pepper, and season as you see fit. Squeeze the lemon a few times over the mixture if you feel the need for a little acidic pop.

Heat the oven to the broil setting.

With a silicone or pastry brush, apply the remaining oil on the inside of zucchini halves, and sprinkle with salt.

With oil spray, lightly grease a rimmed baking sheet. Place the zucchini on the baking sheet, making sure that the top rack is about 6 inches away from broiler element. Broil for 3 to 5 minutes. Keep a

ZUCCHINI BOATS

INGREDIENTS

continued

2 teaspoons fresh mint leaves,
  plucked from stems, torn
  roughly

2 teaspoons fresh oregano
  leaves, plucked from stems,
  or 1 teaspoon dried

Juice of ½ lemon (optional
  finishing touch)

HERE'S WHAT YOU DO:

continued

close eye on the zucchini to make sure it does not char. (Alternatively, you can grill the zucchini, cut side down, over direct heat for 3 to 5 minutes.)

Remove the baking sheet from the oven and fill each zucchini boat with enough filling that it mounds slightly but doesn't spill over the edges of the zucchini.

Lower the oven temperature to 350°F.

Sprinkle each stuffed zucchini with the remaining bread crumbs and cheese.

Roast the zucchini until fork tender and the tops are golden, about 15 minutes. Cover the baking sheet with foil if the tops brown prematurely.

Serve hot or at room temperature with Quickie Couscous-Chickpea Salad (or quinoa for a gluten-free option).

Makes 5 to 6 servings

QUICKIE COUSCOUS-CHICKPEA SALAD

INGREDIENTS

1 cup water

½ teaspoon salt

1 cup dried couscous

1 (15-ounce) can chickpeas,
   rinsed and drained

Zest of 1 lemon

Juice of ½ lemon

1 teaspoon olive oil

¼ cup fresh parsley, chopped

HERE'S WHAT YOU DO:

Bring the water to a boil in a medium-size saucepan and add the salt and couscous. Give a quick stir, then cover and turn off the heat. Allow the couscous to "cook" for about 5 minutes.

Remove the lid, fluff with a fork, and add the chickpeas, lemon zest, lemon juice, olive oil, and parsley. Stir to combine and taste for salt, adding more as you see fit.

Makes 4 side-dish servings

QUICKIE COUSCOUS-CHICKPEA SALAD

Quinoa Variation

V

If you are the 1 in 100 Americans suffering from celiac disease, a debilitating autoimmune disorder that makes eating gluten a living nightmare, this all-purpose quinoa side is for you. If you've never had the pleasure, quinoa is an ancient seed native to South America that acts like a grain. Loaded with protein and fiber, it is truly a super food yet cooks up as easily as rice. Note: As of this writing, most quinoa must be rinsed to remove the bitterness of saponins, a naturally occurring residue that is also mildly toxic, although some brands are developing no-rinse-required varieties. If you are cooking with untreated quinoa, do make sure you rinse before using.

INGREDIENTS

2 cups water

½ teaspoon salt

1 cup quinoa (available in red, black, and white), rinsed in a sieve

1 (15-ounce) can chickpeas, rinsed and drained

Zest of 1 lemon

Juice of ½ lemon

1 teaspoon olive oil

¼ cup fresh parsley, chopped

HERE'S WHAT YOU DO:

Bring the water to a boil in a medium-size saucepan and add the salt and quinoa. Give a quick stir, then cover, lower the heat, and cook for 15 minutes.

Remove the lid, fluff with a fork, and add the chickpeas, lemon zest, lemon juice, olive oil, and parsley. Stir to combine and taste for salt, adding more as you see fit.

Makes about 6 side-dish servings
(quinoa expands more than couscous)

FRITTATA, THREE WAYS

DO

Picnic is the first word that comes to mind with this menu. You can't get much more Mediterranean than this—a skillet pie of eggs and seasonal veg, sliced into wedges for an informal lunch or supper, in the back yard or at the park. It's hard to screw up such an easygoing impromptu dish, but I've offered my favorite fillings along with a template for a blank-slate bunch of eggs.

To help take this from snack to supper, I've paired the frittata with a pitcherful of gazpacho, another Mediterranean classic celebrating the best of summer produce. On a hot day, gazpacho can be a lifesaver, Mother Nature's version of Gatorade.

KITCHEN NOTES: You can make both dishes in advance, but whatever you decide, always make the gazpacho first. Its flavor improves over time, and you'll get it out of the way allowing you to focus on the frittata.

INGREDIENTS:
Basic Frittata Template

6 large eggs
¼ teaspoon cayenne
1 teaspoon salt
Ground black pepper
4 tablespoons vegetable oil
1 medium-size onion, sliced into
   thin half-moons
¼ cup grated Parmigiano-
   Reggiano cheese (optional)

HERE'S WHAT YOU DO:

In a large mixing bowl, beat the eggs and season with the cayenne, salt, and pepper to taste.

FRITTATA, THREE WAYS

INGREDIENTS

continued

HERE'S WHAT YOU DO:

continued

Chard

1 bunch chard, stemmed
(about 4 cups)
1¼ teaspoons salt
¼ teaspoon freshly grated
nutmeg

CHARD VARIATION

Have ready a bowl of ice water. Bring 4 cups of water to a boil with 1 teaspoon of salt. Add the chard and cook for 60 seconds, then immediately transfer to the bowl. Lift the chard from the ice bath and, with your hands, wring out any excess water. Coarsely chop the chard.

In a 12-inch ovenproof skillet, heat 2 tablespoons of the oil over medium heat. Add the onion and cook until slightly softened, about 5 minutes. Add the chard, toss to coat with the onions, and allow to wilt. Season with the nutmeg and the remaining ¼ teaspoon of salt.

Remove the chard mixture from the skillet and combine with the eggs. Stir to mix well.

Wipe out the skillet and heat the remaining oil over medium-high heat. Pour the chard mixture into the skillet and tilt to ensure even distribution. Cover, lower the heat to medium, and cook until the eggs are just set, about 15 minutes, occasionally running a spatula around the edges.

Zucchini

1 large zucchini, sliced into very
thin rounds (⅛ inch if
possible) (about 2 cups)
¼ cup fresh parsley, chopped
finely, and/or ¼ cup fresh mint
leaves (optional, a really nice
extra add-on)
¼ teaspoon salt
Ground black pepper

ZUCCHINI VARIATION

In a 12-inch ovenproof skillet, heat 2 tablespoons of the oil over medium heat. Add the onion and cook until slightly softened, about 5 minutes.

Add the zucchini rounds and sauté, in batches if necessary, until tender and just slightly softened but not yet browned, 5 to 8 minutes. Stir in the parsley (and/or mint, if using), plus the salt and pepper, and set aside to cool for 5 minutes.

Remove the zucchini mixture from the skillet and combine with the eggs. Stir to mix well.

Wipe out the skillet and heat the remaining oil over medium-high heat. Pour the zucchini mixture into the skillet and tilt to ensure even distribution. Cover, lower the heat to medium, and cook until the eggs are just set, about 15 minutes, occasionally running a spatula around the edges.

continues

FRITTATA, THREE WAYS

Potato

3 medium-size potatoes (Yukon Gold or Yellow Finn recommended), sliced very thinly (about 2 cups)

2½ teaspoons salt

1 to 2 cloves garlic, minced

Needles from 2 fresh rosemary sprigs, chopped finely

POTATO VARIATION

Bring 8 cups of water to a boil with 2 teaspoons of the salt. Add the potatoes and parboil for 4 minutes. With a skimmer or sieve with a handle, extract the potatoes and run under cold water.

Transfer the potatoes to a rack to dry out for a few minutes. Pat with a towel if necessary.

In a 12-inch ovenproof skillet, heat 2 tablespoons of the oil over medium heat. Add the onion and cook until slightly softened, about 5 minutes.

Add the potatoes, and sauté, in batches if necessary, until tender and even a little bit browned, about 8 minutes. Stir in the garlic, rosemary, and remaining salt and pepper and cook for an additional 1 to 2 minutes, stirring regularly. Turn off the heat and allow to cool for 5 minutes.

Remove the potato mixture from the skillet and combine with the eggs. Stir to mix well.

Wipe out the skillet and heat the remaining oil over medium-high heat. Pour the potato mixture into the skillet and tilt to ensure even distribution. Cover, lower the heat to medium, and cook until the eggs are just set, about 15 minutes, occasionally running a spatula around the edges.

FINISHING IN THE OVEN

If using cheese, add it now, sprinkling evenly over the top.

Set the oven to the broiler setting. Transfer the pan to the oven (if the skillet handle is rubber, cover with aluminum foil) and broil for 3 to 4 minutes, until the top of the frittata is evenly browned.

Remove from the heat and slice into wedges. Serve with gazpacho.

Makes 6 servings

GAZPACHO

Gazpacho had its start in the Arab world as a bread-based soup, flavored with garlic, olive oil, vinegar, and salt. Tomatoes and peppers weren't part of the recipe until explorers brought them back from the New World. Purists will tell you that a "genuine" gazpacho includes tomatoes, garlic, bread, olive oil, salt, and vinegar. But really, the beauty of gazpacho is that you can add or subtract whatever you want. If you want to use a lime instead of a lemon, go right ahead. Parsley instead of basil? Sure thing. Hold the cukes? All right by me. After deciding on the lineup, it's a matter of a quick whiz in the blender or food processor.

KITCHEN NOTE: The other question to ask yourself is: Will bread be part of the gazpacho? I've included details for a bread variation, as it requires an extra step.

INGREDIENTS

Bread variation: About 4 ounces (1 or 2 slices) stale bread, crusts removed (a country-style loaf is a good choice)

2 cloves garlic, chopped roughly

About 2 pounds ripe tomatoes, quartered (if you hate seeds, remove them)

½ to 1 cucumber, peeled and chopped roughly

1 medium-size bell pepper of any color, seeded, deveined, and chopped roughly

½ medium-size red or yellow onion, chopped roughly

½ jalapeño or chile pepper of choice, seeded, deveined and finely chopped

Juice of ½ lemon, plus more to taste

1 tablespoon sherry vinegar or red wine vinegar, plus more to taste

10 to 12 fresh basil leaves

2 teaspoons salt

HERE'S WHAT YOU DO:

For the bread variation: Place the bread in a medium-size shallow bowl and moisten with 4 tablespoons of water for about 10 minutes. Squeeze out any excess water and place the bread in the bowl of a food processor. Add the garlic. Pulse until the bread starts to look like pulp. *Note: If omitting the bread, the garlic will be the first ingredient to go into the food processor bowl.*

Add the tomatoes gradually and pulse. Follow with the cucumber, bell pepper, onion, and chile pepper. Puree for 1 minute. Add the lemon juice and vinegar. Pulse and taste. Add the basil. Pulse. Open the bowl, have a spoonful, and decide what else is needed before seasoning with the salt.

Serve at room temperature or chill for at least an hour for a more refreshing experience on a hot day. Gazpacho keeps for at least three days in the fridge in an airtight container and the flavors improve with time. Can be sipped from a glass or spooned from a bowl.

Makes six 6-ounce portions

SOUTHERN RED RICE

When I make a pot of Southern red rice, I feel as if I'm taking a bite out of history.

Rice was a major contributing factor for a booming slave trade in South Carolina for more than one hundred years and has played a pivotal role in African American history, cuisine, and culture. In the 1730s, Charleston, South Carolina, was rice central, where some twelve thousand slaves from West Africa were indentured for this purpose. And in the cuisine of the Gullah people, descendants of these slaves, rice figures prominently. Red rice is one such dish, and it is believed to be an adaptation of Jollof rice, a tomato-based pilaf from the Wolof people of West Africa.

Traditionally, red rice is seasoned with pork fat, but this version gets its smoke from smoked paprika, a.k.a. pimentón de la vera. Tangy, garlicky, and pillowy on the tongue, the rice feels more like a risotto than a pilaf. It plays nicely with the roasted green bean medley, but would graciously welcome okra if the cook wants to go all-out southern.

KITCHEN NOTES: You may grill the veg in lieu of roasting them. Make sure you have a grill basket big enough for even cooking. The balsamic vinegar would be applied just before serving. Whatever you decide, prep the veg medley while the rice is simmering.

When in season, vine-ripe tomatoes, are the obvious choice for the "red" part of the rice. Use 2 pounds of tomatoes, cored and quartered.

SOUTHERN RED RICE

INGREDIENTS

1 (28-ounce) can whole Italian
tomatoes, preferably without
salt

1 teaspoon crushed red pepper
flakes

1 teaspoon smoked paprika

1 teaspoon salt

½ teaspoon ground black pepper

Leaves from 1 to 2 sprigs fresh
thyme (optional)

A glug of your favorite hot sauce
(optional)

3 tablespoons vegetable oil

1 medium-size onion, diced

3 cloves garlic, minced

1½ cups uncooked long-grain
rice

2 to 2½ cups water

¼ cup chopped fresh parsley, for
garnish

HERE'S WHAT YOU DO:

In a food processor or heavy-duty blender, puree the tomatoes until
well blended and season with the red pepper flakes, smoked paprika,
salt, pepper, and thyme and hot sauce (if using).

In a medium-size saucepan with a lid, heat the oil over medium heat
and add the onion. Cook, stirring occasionally, until slightly softened,
about 5 minutes. Add the garlic, stirring to keep from burning, and
sauté for 1 minute. The kitchen will begin to smell good.

Add the rice, stir to coat with the aromatics, and allow to toast for 1
to 2 minutes. The rice will become fragrant and slightly translucent.

Add 2 cups of the water and bring to a lively simmer. Transfer the
puree to the rice mixture, stir to combine, and return to a lively simmer. It will look very soupy, but don't fret.

Lower the heat to low, cover, and simmer for 20 minutes. Do not stir.
If the rice is getting too dry, add the balance of the water, 1 tablespoon at a time.

Return the cover and continue to cook for an additional 20 minutes,
until the liquid has been absorbed. The rice will be somewhat wet
and sticky (like a risotto) versus dry and fluffy (like a pilaf).

Makes 4 servings

ROASTED GREEN BEAN, MUSHROOM, & SHALLOT MEDLEY Ⓥ ⒼⒻ

INGREDIENTS

1 pound green beans, trimmed, or
   1 pound okra, trimmed and
   sliced in half, lengthwise

1 large shallot, sliced thinly

1 portobello mushroom, stemmed
   and cut into ½-inch slices

1 clove garlic, minced

½ cup lemon juice

¼ cup olive oil

½ teaspoon salt

Ground black pepper

Balsamic vinegar that you enjoy,
   for drizzling

¼ cup walnuts or almonds,
   toasted and chopped roughly
   (optional)

HERE'S WHAT YOU DO:

Preheat the oven to 400°F. With cooking spray or a smear of vegetable oil, lightly grease a 9 x 13-inch baking dish.

In a medium-size bowl, combine the green beans and shallot. If the mushroom slices are longer than the green beans, slice in half to shorten. Add to the bowl.

In a small bowl, combine the garlic, lemon juice, olive oil, and salt, whisking with a fork. Taste for salt; the mixture should be somewhat salty. Add more as need be.

Pour the vinaigrette over the veg, and with your hands, toss to coat. Lift the veg out of bowl, leaving behind the remaining vinaigrette, and transfer to the prepared baking dish. Distribute the veg evenly so that they have room to roast. Season with black pepper.

Drizzle the balsamic vinegar over the veg medley and place the dish in the oven. Roast for 15 minutes, remove the dish from the oven, and toss the veg to ensure even cooking.

Return the dish to the oven and cook for an additional 10 minutes. This will give the beans an al dente consistency. If you prefer a softer texture, cook for an additional 15 minutes. Remove from the heat and add the toasted nuts, if using. Serve hot.

Makes 4 servings

RW'S SNACK PLATE: HUMMUS, TABBOULEH, ROASTED CAULIFLOWER WITH TAHINI SAUCE, KOPANISTI, EGGPLANT ROUNDS, GRILLED OR ROASTED

XTRA
KIDDO

This menu is dedicated to my husband, RW (a.k.a. Russ), who loves nothing more for supper than a snack plate. He's come a long way from his favorite cheese and salami rotation (with the requisite cornichons), which, although delicious, is as dangerously tempting as a bag of chips.

The snack plate lives on at our house, but we've made some changes, incorporating more plant-based protein and more choices to keep things interesting and satisfying. For inspiration, we turned to meze, the smaller, tapas-style dishes of Middle Eastern cookery. I've served up a handful of options that allows you to mix and match (and make in advance), depending on your mood and time commitment. With three of these little dishes and a basket of pita or naan, you've got a snack plate that truly eats like a meal.

Hummus

INGREDIENTS

1 (15-ounce) can chickpeas, drained and rinsed
3 tablespoons tahini
1 clove garlic
¼ to ½ cup lemon juice
¼ to ½ teaspoon salt
Suggested serving partners: pita, cucumber spears, carrot sticks, celery stalks, and bell pepper strips

HERE'S WHAT YOU DO:

In a food processor, combine the chickpeas, tahini, and garlic. Puree for about 2 minutes, then stop the motor. With a rubber spatula, scrape down the sides of the bowl. Add 2 to 4 tablespoons of water, gradually, to help smooth things out, and then add the lemon juice. Continue pureeing until the mixture achieves your desired flavor, texture, and consistency. This takes a total of 5 minutes.

Add ¼ teaspoon of the salt and taste. Enough? And what about the lemon? Season accordingly. Scoop out of the food processor and into a shallow serving bowl. Serve at room temperature, with pita, or any of the suggested serving partners. Can be made a few days in advance.

Makes about 2 cups

Tabbouleh

I learned how to make tabbouleh from Nada Kattar, a Lebanese-American home cook in Chicago. She taught me to understand that tabbouleh is a parsley salad, not a bulgur salad, and that everything revolves around the "parsley drinking the juice" of the other ingredients.

INGREDIENTS

¾ cup fine- or medium-grain bulgur wheat

3 plum tomatoes

1 cup mint leaves

2 large bunches (about 3½ cups) flat-leaf parsley

6 scallions

½ cup lemon juice, from about 2 lemons

½ cup olive oil

½ teaspoon salt

1 head romaine lettuce, for garnish

HERE'S WHAT YOU DO:

Note: Everything going into the salad has to be as dry as possible. After you've washed all of the herbs, make sure to dry them well. It makes a huge difference to the end result.

In a medium-size bowl with some depth, cover the bulgur with water. Soak for about 20 minutes. You'll notice that the bulgur has absorbed the water and expanded. Add more water, just to cover, and allow to soak while you prep the rest of the ingredients.

Slice the tomatoes in half lengthwise, remove the seeds with your fingers or a teaspoon, and dice. Place in a large bowl.

Keep the mint and parsley separate at all times. Wash thoroughly, shake out the water, and dry in a towel or salad spinner.

Pull the mint leaves from their stems. Chop finely and place on top of the tomatoes.

Separate the parsley leaves and discard the stems. Chop the leaves until they are very fine, so small they almost look like a puree. Layer on top of the mint.

Thoroughly drain the water from the bulgur, then spread on top of the herb layer like a blanket. Spread around with a spoon if necessary. Cover the bowl and put in the fridge for at least 30 minutes to chill and set up.

Meanwhile, prepare the scallions: Wash, dry, and slice off roots. Using only the white and light green parts, chop very finely. Place in a small bowl and add the lemon juice.

**HERE'S WHAT
YOU DO:**

continued

When ready to serve the tabbouleh, incorporate the scallion mixture into the bulgur mixture. With your hands, mix thoroughly. ("The parsley is not drinking the juice if you use a spoon," tabbouleh-guru Nada proclaims.)

Add the oil and salt. Taste for seasoning. Traditionally, tabbouleh is served with romaine lettuce leaves that can also be used as garnish. The heart of the romaine can be placed in the center of the bowl or platter as decoration.

Makes about 3½ cups

Roasted Cauliflower with Tahini Sauce

INGREDIENTS

1 large head cauliflower, broken into florets

¼ cup olive oil

¼ teaspoon ground black pepper

¾ teaspoon salt

¼ cup tahini

¼ cup water

¼ cup fresh lemon juice (from about 1 lemon)

1 clove garlic, minced

¼ cup finely chopped fresh flat-leaf parsley

HERE'S WHAT YOU DO:

Preheat the oven to 400°F.

In a mixing bowl, toss the cauliflower with the oil, pepper, and ½ teaspoon of the salt until well coated. Spread in a single layer on a baking sheet and roast, stirring and turning once or twice, until the cauliflower is tender and crispy brown in spots, about 30 minutes.

While the cauliflower is roasting, puree the tahini, water, lemon juice, garlic, and remaining ¼ teaspoon of salt in a blender or food processor until well combined. Taste for salt and add more as needed. Add the parsley and blend in for a speckled result.

Remove the cauliflower from the oven and immediately transfer to a serving bowl or platter.

Pour the tahini in a smaller bowl for dipping the cauliflower.

Serve warm or let stand at room temperature.

Makes 3 to 4 servings

Kopanisti

GF

Kopanisti is a type of cheese only made in the Cyclades islands of Greece. Like Champagne and Parmigiano-Reggiano, kopanisti is kopanisti only if it's made in its country and region of origin. As such, the recipe below is an approximation of the real deal. One can dream, though.

INGREDIENTS

1 cup feta cheese
1 medium-size red bell pepper, roasted (For how to roast a pepper, see page 194.)
1 teaspoon dried oregano
¼ teaspoon red pepper flakes
Juice of ½ lemon
2 tablespoons olive oil
Pinch of salt
Ground black pepper

HERE'S WHAT YOU DO:

In the bowl of a blender or food processor, process the feta for 1 minute, until somewhat whipped. Using a rubber spatula, scrape down the sides of the bowl and process for another minute. Add the roasted pepper, oregano, red pepper flakes, and lemon and process until well blended. The color will be burnt orange. Scrape down the sides of the bowl and add the olive oil. Whiz for another minute. Taste for salt and pepper and add accordingly.

Serve at room temperature.

Makes 1 cup

EGGPLANT ROUNDS, ROASTED OR GRILLED

INGREDIENTS

1 medium-size globe eggplant
    (about 1 pound)
Salt, for leaching
Cooking spray or vegetable oil

HERE'S WHAT YOU DO:

Preheat the oven to 400°F or prepare your grill.

Slice the eggplant into ½-inch rounds. Place the eggplant on a rack in a single layer and sprinkle salt on top to help release the water content. Allow to leach for about 15 minutes.

With a towel, pat the eggplant dry.

Thoroughly grease two baking trays with cooking spray. Place the eggplant rounds in a single layer on both trays. Roast for 15 minutes, then remove from the oven, turn onto their second side, and roast for an additional 10 minutes, for a total of 25 minutes.

(On the grill: Using a brush, grease the grate. Grill using the direct method, making sure the eggplant does not burn. After 7 to 10 minutes, turn to grill on their second side. Yes, you can do this on a grill pan.)

Makes 4 servings

TOFU BARBECUE

The idea: Tofu barbecue. Not baked tofu with some tangy sauce slapped on top, but marinated and slow-cooked over wood, so that you can really taste the spice and smoke, like a brisket. A few rounds of testing revealed good flavor on the outside, but nada on the interior. We even tried one of those flavor-injector gizmos. I was about to hang up my cockamamie experiment, when my friend Jeanne suggested putting it in the freezer. As it turns out, freezing tofu changes both its texture (from cheesecakey to striated and chewy) and porousness (from No way, Jose, to Bring it on!). The result: Knee-slapping tanginess. It delivers both spice and smoke, just like that brisket. In fact, I'd like to make a declaration: Freezing takes the oxymoron out of tofu barbecue. Served up with baked beans and vinegar slaw, this is one helluva plate.

KITCHEN NOTES: Just as with ribs or brisket, tofu barbecue is a weekend/leisure time project. A block of tofu needs 24 hours in the freezer, then about 3 hours of thawing time. (You may also try thawing in the microwave, in 2-minute increments). And that's before you start the coals. Because of its newly acquired absorbability, the tofu needs relatively little marinating time—30 minutes is sufficient.

One last note: Given the time commitment involved, it's worth smoking two full-size blocks of tofu, which will keep in the fridge for five days for leftovers of the best kind. One batch of spice rub is plenty for two blocks.

INGREDIENTS

1 (14-ounce) package
  extra-firm tofu
2 teaspoons salt
1 teaspoon brown sugar
1 teaspoon smoked paprika
1 teaspoon ground New Mexico
  chile pepper (between paprika
  and cayenne in heat)
1 teaspoon granulated garlic
1 teaspoon granulated onion
¼ teaspoon ground black pepper
¼ teaspoon ground fennel seed
Vegetable oil, for brushing

HERE'S WHAT YOU DO:

Remove the tofu from its packaging and discard the water. Set on a plate and top it with a smaller plate, weighed down with a filled can. Allow to drain, about 20 minutes.

Place the tofu in a zippered plastic freezer bag and freeze for 24 hours. The tofu will turn a shade of pale yellow; do not be alarmed, as the color will return to its original shade of off-white when it thaws.

Meanwhile, prepare the spice rub: Mix the salt and spices together in a small bowl and place in an airtight container or jar. Stored in a dark, cool place, the rub will keep for a few months.

Remove the tofu from the freezer; allow to thaw in the refrigerator (6 hours) or in the microwave in 2-minute increments (20 minutes—just remember to remove the tofu from the plastic

TOFU BARBECUE

About 2 cups of wood chips of choice (hickory, alder, cedar), for smoking

About ½ cup of your favorite barbecue sauce, mixed with 1 tablespoon honey

Optional sauce: ½ cup soy or teriyaki sauce; 1 tablespoon hot water; 2 tablespoons honey; 1 tablespoon fresh ginger, peeled and minced; squeeze of ½ lime

bag before you start!). You may also start the thawing process on the counter for the first 30 minutes, then continue the process in the re-frigerator. Keep in mind that tofu is perishable, and food safety pre-cautions apply. Squeeze out any remaining water and pat the tofu dry.

With a sharp knife, slice the tofu block in half, so that you have two smaller blocks. Measure out ⅛ cup of the spice rub and apply the rub all over each block. With a silicone or pastry brush, apply the oil all over the surface of each block. Marinate for 30 minutes.

Meanwhile, prepare the coals and soak the wood chips for 30 min-utes, so they are ready for the grill. Prepare the grill for indirect cook-ing: Remove the wood chips from the water and place in a smoker tray or disposable aluminum pan or foil pouch, on the floor of the grill, off to one side. Fire up the grill according to the manufacturer's instructions and bring the temperature to 350°F.

Place both tofu blocks on the grate, on the opposite side of the wood chips (and charcoal, depending on what kind of grill you're using). Cover and allow to cook for 20 minutes on each side, while trying to maintain the 350°F heat.

Meanwhile, prepare for the final step of lacquering tofu with the fol-lowing sauce or use your favorite barbecue sauce.

In a small bowl, combine the remaining ingredients and stir well. Ap-ply your sauce of choice all over each tofu block and cook 10 min-utes on each side, closer to the coals, if you like, for some charring.

Remove from the grill and slice thinly. Serve with True-Blue Baked Beans and Vinegar Slaw.

Makes 4 to 5 servings

TRUE-BLUE BAKED BEANS

KITCHEN NOTES: Pickapeppa is a brand of sauce that is reminiscent of Worcestershire but sweeter and hotter. Use what you can get your hands on.

INGREDIENTS

1 cup tomato puree

¼ cup molasses

¾ cup brown sugar

1 tablespoon Pickapeppa sauce

1 tablespoon dry mustard

1 teaspoon New Mexico ground chile pepper (or another medium-heat pepper)

½ teaspoon ground cumin

½ chipotle chile in adobo sauce, minced

3 (15-ounce) cans pinto and/or kidney beans, rinsed and drained

2 tablespoons vegetable oil

1 medium-size onion, chopped

1 clove garlic, minced

HERE'S WHAT YOU DO:

Preheat the oven to 350°F.

In a large mixing bowl, combine the tomato puree, molasses, brown sugar, Pickapeppa sauce, mustard, ground chile, cumin, and chipotle, and stir until well blended.

Stir the beans into the sauce.

In a medium-size skillet, heat the oil over medium heat and add the onion and garlic. Cook for about 2 minutes, stirring regularly; the onion should still be a little crunchy.

Transfer the onion mixture to the saucy beans and stir until well combined.

Pour the beans into a lightly greased 9 x 13-inch baking dish and bake for 1 hour, or until bubbly. The beans should keep moist while they cook; cover with foil if necessary.

Will keep refrigerated for up to one week.

Makes 6 to 8 side-dish servings

VINEGAR SLAW

V

INGREDIENTS

1 head small green cabbage,
   shredded

1 medium-size carrot, peeled and
   diced

½ red bell pepper, seeded and
   diced

½ cup rice vinegar

1 teaspoon sugar, or to taste

1 teaspoon soy sauce, or to taste

1 teaspoon sesame oil

Squeeze of ½ lime

1 glug of your favorite hot sauce

Salt

HERE'S WHAT YOU DO:

Place the vegetables in a bowl and stir to combine. Into another bowl, pour the vinegar, sugar, soy sauce, sesame oil, lime juice, and hot sauce and stir to combine. Taste for seasoning; you're looking for a balance of pungent, salty, sweet, and spicy. Adjust as needed, tinkering gradually.

Pour over the vegetables and mix until well combined. Allow to marinate for at least 45 minutes before serving. The flavor improves with time.

Makes 4 servings

SESAME RICE NOODLES & MELON-HERB SALAD

This is my take on pasta salad, using no-cook Asian rice noodles, lots of fruit, and herbs. It's about as close to raw food as you'll get in this collection, the gist being cool food for the doggiest days of summer. While the noodles soak and soften, the melon, red onion, and cukes marinate in their respective baths. When everything comes together, it reminds me of a deconstructed Vietnamese salad roll, with cooling herbs and chopped peanuts.

KITCHEN NOTES: This is a multibowl affair: In addition to a large serving bowl for the entire salad, you'll need smaller bowls for preparing the cucumbers, melon, onions, and sauce. The salad should be eaten shortly after it's assembled; the herbs and melon are highly perishable and look mangy the next day.

Asian rice noodles come in a variety of sizes but even among the same type of noodle, packaging may greatly vary by weight. Soaked noodles will expand to four times their weight in volume.

There are many kinds of Chinese rice wine, but the amber-colored Shaoxing is my favorite. White rice wine will do the job; use pale dry sherry if you can't find rice wine of any kind. Do not use rice wine vinegar.

❧ Make It a Meal ❧

Is your appetite bigger tonight than anticipated? Consider a versatile side to round out your plate. Mix-and-matching encouraged! See Make It a Meal sidebar on page 26.

SESAME RICE NOODLES & MELON-HERB SALAD

INGREDIENTS

8 ounces flat rice noodles (available in many conventional supermarkets and at Asian groceries; also sold as rice sticks)

1 tablespoon soy sauce

1 teaspoon granulated or light brown sugar, plus more for sprinkling

5 tablespoons lime juice (from about 1½ limes)

1 tablespoon sesame oil

1 tablespoon vegetable oil

¾ teaspoon salt

1 medium-size cucumber, peeled, seeded and sliced into half-moons (about 1½ cups)

¼ cup Chinese rice wine, preferably Shaoxing

1 teaspoon red pepper flakes

½ red onion, sliced into very thin half-moons

4 cups cantaloupe and/or watermelon, peeled and cut into 1- to 2-inch chunks (similar in size to the cukes)

¼ cup fresh cilantro, chopped finely

1 cup fresh mint leaves, stemmed and chopped finely

10 to 12 fresh basil leaves, sliced into a chiffonade

½ cup unsalted peanuts, chopped roughly (optional garnish)

HERE'S WHAT YOU DO:

Soak the rice noodles in very hot, but not boiling, water for 30 minutes, until pliable, followed by a rinse under cold water. Drain thoroughly. If possible, dry the noodles in a salad spinner; the drier the noodles, the better. Transfer to a bowl large enough for the entire salad.

In a small bowl, combine the soy sauce, sugar, 2 tablespoons of the lime juice, 2 teaspoons of the sesame oil, the vegetable oil, and ¼ teaspoon of the salt. Whisk with a fork until the sugar and salt are dissolved.

Pour the sauce all over the noodles, and with tongs, turn until the noodles are evenly coated.

In a medium-size bowl, combine the cucumber, rice wine, red pepper flakes, the remaining ½ teaspoon salt and the remaining sesame oil, and stir well. Allow to marinate for about 15 minutes.

In a small bowl, mix red onion with 2 tablespoons of the lime juice, and allow the onions to macerate and mellow, 10 to 15 minutes.

In a medium-size mixing bowl, combine the melon, a sprinkling of sugar, and 1 tablespoon of the lime juice. Stir well. Taste for salt. The fruit should be a little bit salty; this is intentional. If the flavor is faint, add a pinch of salt. Stir in the macerated onions and their juices.

With tongs, lift the cucumber mixture out of its marinade and transfer to the seasoned noodles; turn the mixture until well combined. Taste a noodle. Does it have good, well-balanced flavor? If not, ask yourself what the noodles need—salt, fat, or acid—and season accordingly and gradually.

Add the melon mixture to the noodles, and with salad hands or tongs, give the salad a good toss. Add the herbs and garnish with peanuts, if using.

Makes 4 to 6 servings

STUFFED BELL PEPPERS   (DO) (GF) (XTRA)

These beauties are decidedly unlike the ground beef-filled, army-green oddities that were all the rage in the '70s. (Remember the canned tomato soup draped on top as the sauce?)

Instead, the peppers are sweet, sun-kissed shades of yellow, orange, and red, and the meat takes the day off without incident. At their peak in late summer and early fall, bell peppers make festive one-dish containers for a mix of seasonal veg and herbs, with nutty grains of quinoa doing a bang-up job as both starchy connector and protein-rich stand-in. What follows is a mere template for the filling; feel free to play and experiment with various flavor combinations, using the recipe as a guide.

P.S. The filling is outrageously delicious all by its lonesome, almost a meal unto itself.

In keeping with the bell pepper theme, the main dish is paired up with romesco sauce, an intoxicating roasted red pepper spread from Spain that is divine smeared on your favorite toast.

INGREDIENTS

Salt

½ cup red or white quinoa, rinsed in a sieve, or rice, pearl barley, or instant couscous

4 yellow, orange, or red bell peppers, sliced in half lengthwise, without removing stems

3 tablespoons olive oil

¼ cup red onion or shallots, diced

½ fresh chile pepper of choice, seeded and minced (omit if you want less heat)

2 to 3 cloves garlic, chopped finely

1½ cups fresh (from 2 medium-size ears) or frozen corn kernels, or 1 (15-ounce) can chickpeas, drained and rinsed

HERE'S WHAT YOU DO:

Preheat the oven to 400°F.

In a small saucepan, bring 1 cup of water to a boil for the quinoa. (The water amounts will differ for other starch options; prepare according to package instructions.)

Add a pinch of salt, and then add the quinoa. Stir, then cover and simmer over low heat until the grains are tender and begin to look starry and luminescent, about 15 minutes. Turn off the heat and set aside.

Carefully remove the seeds and membranes of the peppers. In a large saucepan, bring 6 cups of water and 1 teaspoon of salt to a lively simmer (not a rolling boil). Add the pepper halves (submerge the peppers cut side first) and simmer until slightly tender, about 5 minutes. Using tongs, remove the peppers and drain any excess water. Transfer to a baking dish for later.

In a large skillet, heat 2 tablespoons of the oil. Add the onion and chile pepper (if using), and cook over medium heat for 3 minutes, until slightly softened. Add the garlic, corn, and greens, plus 2 tablespoons of water, and cook until the greens are wilted, about 5 minutes.

STUFFED BELL PEPPERS

INGREDIENTS

continued

4 cups spinach, washed well, stemmed, and roughly chopped, or equal amounts of chard or tender kale, stemmed

¼ cup chopped fresh cilantro, flat-leaf parsley, or basil

Salt and ground black pepper

½ cup feta cheese, crumbled (or queso fresco, ricotta, or goat cheese—or no cheese at all)

½ lemon (optional finishing touch)

HERE'S WHAT YOU DO:

continued

Stir in the herbs and quinoa and mix everything together until well combined. Taste for salt and pepper, and season as you see fit.

Fill the peppers with the filling and dot with cheese (if using).

Drizzle the remaining oil over the peppers and bake for about 20 minutes.

Serve hot or at room temperature, squeezing the lemon over the top, if you wish.

Makes 4 servings

ROMESCO SAUCE

This almond, garlic, and roasted pepper-scented puree hails from Catalan, in the northeastern part of Spain, along the Mediterranean coast. You can spread it on grilled bread, use it as a dip for roasted veg, or eat it right from the spoon. Don't worry if you don't have all the peppers listed below; if red bell peppers are all you get, this elixir, er sauce, will still make you swoon. A note on peppers: Ancho chiles are dried poblanos, which will yield a sweeter, almost raisin-y result; fresh roasted poblanos will deliver more smoke.

INGREDIENTS

1 (1-pound) loaf country-style
  bread
¼ cup olive oil
2 red bell peppers, roasted,
  peeled, and seeded (See page
  194 for roasting tips.)
3 dried ancho chile peppers,
  soaked for 1 hour, drained,
  seeded, and roughly chopped,
  or 2 fresh poblano chile
  peppers, roasted, peeled, and
  seeded (either is optional but
  really nice)
1 small piece fresh serrano or
  jalapeño pepper (½ to 1 inch
  long), seeded and minced
4 cloves garlic, minced
½ cup almonds and/or hazelnuts,
  roasted
2 to 3 plum tomatoes, peeled and
  seeded (I use canned whole
  plum tomatoes, drained)
2 teaspoons red wine vinegar or
  lemon juice
½ teaspoon salt
¼ teaspoon cayenne
¼ teaspoon smoked paprika
  (optional; particularly useful in
  absence of poblano or ancho
  chile peppers)

HERE'S WHAT YOU DO:

In a skillet, fry one 1-inch slice of the bread (crusts removed) in 1 tablespoon of the oil over medium heat until golden on both sides, about 5 minutes. Remove from the pan and allow to cool. Place all the peppers in the bowl of a food processor, along with the garlic, nuts, and the fried bread slice. Use the "pulse" button to insure that mixture does not overpuree; you want some texture.

Add the tomatoes, then the remaining oil and vinegar. The mixture will emulsify quickly. Add the salt and cayenne, and smoked paprika, if appropriate. If the mixture is too thick, add 1 to 2 tablespoons of water. The mixture should be thick but also have a slightly liquidy quality. Taste for salt, heat, and acid and season accordingly.

Slice one to two pieces of the remaining bread per serving and grill or toast to serve with romesco. Gets better on the second and third day; keeps for about five days.

Makes about 2 cups

SUSAN'S EGGPLANT STACK

GF

This is a souped-up version of the recipe that sparked the idea for this book project. One night, a few years ago, my mom (Susan) called me up, asking for advice on what to do with the eggplant and tomato she had picked up from the local farm stand earlier that day. She was hoping to cook something low-fat and yet satisfying for her longtime companion, the original Mister Sausage, who was recovering from a recent heart attack.

In years past, I had watched the dude lap up an entire stick of butter with his lobster tail in one sitting. If I was going to have anything to do with dinner on this particular night, the menu would be heavy on the veggies, hold the artery cloggers, please.

In response, I rattled off a few random thoughts about grilling the eggplant, slicing her beloved tomatoes, and layering the produce on top of each other to create a stack. She had basil and some feta, so they would be included, too. As I hung up, I thought how the old girl might just pull this off.

And she did. And Mikey—I mean Mister Sausage—liked it.

The version that follows is a triple-layer "club sandwich" of eggplant rounds, sliced tomato, and grilled onion, with basil pesto between each layer. Meaty enough to cut into with a steak knife, Susan's stack works equally well tucked into a soft bun, for the best-looking Big Mac–like creation you ever did see.

KITCHEN NOTES: While the eggplant is leaching, make the pesto. While the eggplant is roasting, prep the other components of the stack.

Note on leaching: Sprinkling salt on sliced eggplant helps release its high water content, a process called leaching. For this dish, leaching helps dry out the eggplant and minimize the oil needed to lubricate it while cooking.

INGREDIENTS

Cooking spray, for greasing the baking pan

2 medium-size globe eggplants (about 1 pound each)

Salt, for leaching

½ medium-size red or Vidalia onion, sliced through the root

8 slices smoked mozzarella, Gouda, provolone, or cheddar cheese

¼ to ½ cup basil pesto (details follow)

2 to 3 vine-ripened tomatoes, at least 3 inches wide

HERE'S WHAT YOU DO:

Note: The eggplant and onion may be grilled or roasted.

Preheat the oven to 400°F or prepare your grill. Thoroughly grease two baking trays with cooking spray.

Slice the eggplant into ½-inch rounds. Place the eggplant on a rack in a single layer and sprinkle salt on top to help release the water content. Allow to leach for about 15 minutes.

With a towel, pat the eggplant dry.

continues

SUSAN'S EGGPLANT STACK

HERE'S WHAT YOU DO:

continued

Place the eggplant rounds on in a single layer on both trays. Roast for 15 minutes, then remove from the oven, turn, and roast the second side for an additional 10 minutes, for a total of 25 minutes.

Meanwhile, place a cast-iron skillet over medium heat and place the onion half on it, cut side down. Allow to char for 5 minutes, then transfer the skillet to the oven and roast for 12 to 15 minutes. The onion will be somewhat charred and softened. Remove from the oven and set aside.

(On the grill: Using a brush, grease the grate. Grill using the direct method, making sure the eggplant does not burn. After 7 to 10 minutes, turn and grill on the second side. Grease the onion and cook on the grill for 3 minutes on each side.)

Transfer all but eight eggplant rounds to a plate. Place a slice of cheese on each remaining eggplant round and heat on your heat source of choice for 2 minutes, allowing the cheese to melt. Remove from the heat.

STACK ASSEMBLY:

You can build your stack any way you see fit; my recommendations are: Each serving gets two stacks. Each stack contains three eggplant rounds (one with cheese), three applications of pesto (¼ to ½ teaspoon each, to taste), two slices of tomato, and one onion.

The order that has proven reliable:

Eggplant, pesto, tomato

Pesto, eggplant, onion

Tomato, pesto, eggplant/cheese

Build stacks on a platter or on individual dinner plates. Serve with a steak knife.

Makes 4 servings. Amounts can be halved.

SUSAN'S EGGPLANT STACK

INGREDIENTS:

Basil Pesto

2 heaping cups fresh basil leaves

¼ cup pine nuts, walnuts, or almonds

1 to 2 cloves garlic

½ cup olive oil

¼ to ½ teaspoon salt

¾ cup grated Parmigiano-Reggiano cheese

HERE'S WHAT YOU DO:

Bring 2 cups of water to a boil and add the basil leaves. Blanch for 15 seconds, then remove from the pot with a skimmer or a pair of tongs. Transfer to a bowl of ice-cold water. This will shock the basil and intensify its brilliant shade of green.

Extract the basil from the water and squeeze it dry as much as possible with your hands.

Place the nuts and the garlic in the bowl of a food processor or heavy-duty blender and whiz until pulverized. Add the basil and process until mixture is well combined. While the machine is running, gradually add the oil, until well blended. You may need to stop and scrape the sides of the bowl a few times for thorough blending.

Transfer the pesto to a small bowl and stir in the cheese. Add ¼ teaspoon of the salt and taste, adding more as you see fit.

Makes 1 cup. You will have about half for leftovers that can go to good use in a bowl of pasta.

MINTY CHICKPEAS

INGREDIENTS

1 (15-ounce) can chickpeas, rinsed and drained

¼ to ½ cup mint, chopped

2 to 3 scallions, white and light green parts only, minced

Zest and juice of ½ lemon

1 tablespoon olive oil

½ teaspoon salt

¼ teaspoon ground chile pepper, nothing too hot (Aleppo or New Mexico)

HERE'S WHAT YOU DO:

In a medium-size mixing bowl, combine all the ingredients and stir.

Makes 4 servings

ZUCCHINI & CORN-STUDDED ORZO

Orzo may be one of the smallest members of the pasta *famiglia*, but don't underestimate its diminutive nature. Its ricelike shape and size is perfect for a hot summer supper; you get your fix of pasta but without the bulk of orzo's bigger-boned relatives.

In keeping with the small-is-beautiful theme, I pair it with compatibly sized grated zucchini and onion and in-season corn kernels, a veritable edible high-five to summer.

For a little extra treat, try the roasted peppers bundled around a tangy filling of goat cheese and walnuts.

KITCHEN NOTES: Roast the peppers first or in advance and keep in the fridge. While the orzo cooks, fill the peppers.

INGREDIENTS

1 tablespoon salt

2 cups orzo pasta

3 tablespoons olive oil

1 large zucchini, grated coarsely (about 2 cups)

½ medium-size onion, grated coarsely

2 tablespoons butter, or equal amounts olive oil

1 medium-size ear corn, shucked and kernels removed

HERE'S WHAT YOU DO:

Bring 8 cups of water and 2 teaspoons of the salt to a boil. Add the orzo, cooking until al dente, 8 to 9 minutes. Drain and transfer to a wide serving bowl. Drizzle with olive oil to keep lubricated.

Gather the grated vegetables into your hands, in small bunches if necessary, and squeeze out any water, until nearly dry.

In a 10- or 12-inch skillet, heat the butter over medium-high heat. Add the grated veg mixture and lower the heat, stirring with a wooden spoon to minimize burning. Cook for 5 minutes by itself, then add the corn kernels, garlic, thyme, red pepper flakes, and remaining salt. Stir until well combined, and cook for an additional 5 minutes; it's okay if the mixture develops a little crust.

continues

ZUCCHINI & CORN-STUDDED ORZO

INGREDIENTS
continued

1 clove garlic, sliced thinly

3 sprigs fresh thyme and/or oregano, or 1½ teaspoons dried

¼ teaspoon red pepper flakes

½ cup fresh mint leaves, finely chopped

½ cup fresh basil leaves, cut into chiffonade

Squeeze of ½ lemon

¼ cup grated Parmigiano-Reggiano cheese

Ground black pepper

½ to 1 cup cherry or grape tomatoes, for garnish

HERE'S WHAT YOU DO:
continued

Transfer the cooked veg to the pasta bowl, and stir into the orzo, until everything is thoroughly combined. Add the mint and basil leaves and the lemon, mix, then stir in the cheese. Taste for salt and pepper. Garnish with the tomatoes.

Serve hot or at room temperature.

Makes 4 to 5 servings

GOAT CHEESY ROASTED PEPPERS

GF

INGREDIENTS

3 medium-size red bell peppers
½ cup goat cheese
⅓ cup toasted walnuts, finely
    chopped
½ cup fresh basil leaves, cut into
    chiffonade
Olive oil, for drizzling
Squeeze of ½ lemon

HERE'S WHAT YOU DO:

Preheat the oven to 400°F. Place the peppers on a baking sheet, whole with their stems attached.

Roast for 40 minutes.

While the peppers roast, make the filling. Place the goat cheese in a small bowl, and with a spoon, stir to soften and "whip." Stir in the walnuts.

Transfer the peppers to a sealed container or bag so that they can sweat and loosen their skins. After 15 minutes, remove the stems and seeds, which should easily give way. With your hands, remove the skins to the best of your ability; don't rinse, as this zaps away the roasted goodness.

Cut the peppers into two or three sections, depending on size. Measure out 1 teaspoon of goat cheese filling and tuck inside a pepper section that you may wrap or fold around it.

Garnish the peppers with the basil, a drizzle of olive oil, and a lemony squeeze. Can be made in advance.

Makes 4 to 6 servings

Fall . . .

. . . makes us wake up and smell the coffee.

Back to school, the grind and reality. We resume the lightning-speed pace of our lives and fill the calendar. For a short time, we have the best of both produce worlds; the last hurrah of summer crops and the debut of underground morsels hinting at the seasonal transition.

There's a chill in the air when the sun goes to bed, a call for supper warmer-uppers such as red lentil dal with cumin-fried onions and twice-baked sweet potatoes. Yet we also race to eat every last tomato before the first frost, a perfect opportunity for a swan song pot of ratatouille, bursting with the last bit of sun.

With the rustle of leaves under our feet, it's time to let go of the past and embrace the here and now: Halloween shades of squash, ruffly leaves of roasted kale, blood red beets tucked into a cheesy tortilla, and pears ripening for a salad of hearty greens.

RATATOUILLE

Too often, the idea of ratatouille is better than it tastes, as many cooks often overcook this veg mélange into cafeteria mush. The secret to keeping it bright and fresh tasting is to cook and season the veg separately before they all come together in a stew pot. This dish is a wonderful way to celebrate the late summer harvest. Ratatouille pairs extremely well with either couscous (page 78) or quinoa salad (page 79).

INGREDIENTS

1 large globe eggplant
   (about 1 pound), or 3 thinner
   Asian eggplants
Salt for leaching eggplant
5 tablespoons olive oil
2 medium-size onions, halved
   and sliced thinly (about
   2 cups)
3 red or yellow bell peppers,
   seeded and julienned
   (about 2½ cups)
4 to 6 cloves garlic, minced
1 large yellow or green zucchini,
   cut into half-moons
   (about 2½ cups)
Ground black pepper
6 medium-size fresh vine-ripe
   tomatoes (about 3 cups),
   or 1 (28-ounce) can plum
   tomatoes
1 to 2 sprigs of fresh thyme, or
   1 teaspoon dried
1 teaspoon dried oregano
Chopped fresh basil and/or
   parsley, for garnish
To serve: couscous (page 78)
   or gluten-free quinoa with
   chickpeas and herbs (page 79)

HERE'S WHAT YOU DO:

Preheat the oven to 450°F.

Cut the eggplant into ½-inch cubes (You'll end up with 5 to 6 cups). Sprinkle with salt and allow to drain on a rack for about 30 minutes. (This step, called leaching, is not mandatory, but it does help to release water.)

Pat the eggplant dry with a towel. Toss with 2 tablespoons of the oil and place on a baking sheet in a single layer.

Roast for 15 minutes; the eggplant will brown a bit and get perfume-y. You'll also notice that the eggplant will shrink substantially, resulting in about 2 cups.

Remove from the oven and set aside.

For the rest of this dish, you'll need a large skillet as well as a deeper saucepan or pot with a lid, which we'll refer to as the "casserole."

In the large skillet, heat 2 tablespoons of oil over medium heat. Add the onions and cook until tender, about 5 minutes. Stir in the peppers and a generous pinch of salt; cook until the peppers are softened, 5 to 7 minutes.

Stir in half of the garlic and cook for another minute, then transfer to the casserole.

Heat the remaining the tablespoon of oil in the skillet and add the zucchini plus salt and pepper to taste and cook over medium-high heat, until the zucchini is tender but still bright, 5 minutes. Stir in the remaining garlic, then mix into the vegetables in the casserole.

Roughly chop or mash the tomatoes with a potato masher as you see fit (I like to give them a head start before cooking), then add to the

RATATOUILLE

HERE'S WHAT YOU DO:

continued

casserole, along with the thyme and oregano. The mixture should be thick; the tomatoes will release their juices when heated. If the mixture seems too thick, however, add a few tablespoons of water. Stir everything well, cover, and cook over medium-low heat, 12 to 15 minutes.

Meanwhile, prepare the couscous or quinoa (see page 78 or 79).

The ratatouille should be fragrant, the veggies tender but still bright. Taste for salt and pepper, and season accordingly. Remove the herb sprigs, if using. Stir in the basil and parsley just before using.

Serve over ½ cup of couscous or quinoa. Will keep in the fridge for about 5 days.

Makes 6 servings

TWICE-BAKED SWEET POTATOES

This is the kind of meal I yearn for as summer makes room for fall, when the days are still warm, but as soon as the sun sets, the air has a distinct crispness that wasn't there just a few weeks ago.

For me, the seasonal transition is always bittersweet, as I mourn the loss of bright sun yet revel the arrival of autumn produce, which is altogether varied, versatile, and downright stunning.

Two of my favorite fall ingredients are sweet potatoes and pears, so this two-dish combo is my way of embracing the season. At first glance, this menu may seem lean, but you gotta trust me on this one. With the addition of tahini, the roasted sweet potato flesh, which gets pureed with charred onions, is a real mouthful, both creamy and rich.

INGREDIENTS

4 medium-size sweet potatoes
  (about 12 to 16 ounces each)
Vegetable oil, for brushing
2 medium-size onions
8 tablespoons tahini
4 to 6 cloves garlic, chopped
Juice of 2 lemons
2 teaspoons cayenne or smoked
  paprika
2 teaspoons salt

HERE'S WHAT YOU DO:

Preheat the oven to 400°F.

Inspect the sweet potatoes for blemishes and trim with a knife as necessary. Prick all with a fork, and with a silicone or pastry brush, lightly oil the exterior surface. Place in a baking dish or on a baking tray. Roast until fork tender, about 1 hour.

Meanwhile, cut the onions in half through the root and remove the skins. Place all four onion halves, cut side down, on a dry griddle or cast-iron skillet, over medium heat. Roast for about 8 minutes, checking periodically to make sure the onion is charring but not completely blackening. With a brush, oil the onions and then either transfer the skillet to the oven or transfer them to the baking dish, right beside the sweet potatoes.

When the sweet potatoes are fork tender, remove them and the onions from the oven. Lower the oven temperature to 325°F.

With a sharp knife and with the protection of an oven mitt or pot holder, make a vertical incision in the midline of each sweet potato to allow steam to release and help speed up the cooling process. Allow the sweet potatoes and onions to cool, about 10 minutes.

TWICE-BAKED SWEET POTATOES

HERE'S WHAT YOU DO:

continued

Meanwhile, set up a food processor with the blade attachment. Alternatively, you may use a food mill.

With a teaspoon, scoop out the flesh from the sweet potato, leaving behind a small amount on the bottom to help minimize any tearing of the skin, then transfer to the bowl of the food processor. Add the onions, tahini, and garlic. Puree. Add the lemon juice and your pepper of choice, plus the salt. Taste, and adjust the seasoning as you see fit.

If using a food mill, mill the onions and garlic along with sweet potato, add the lemon and seasonings, and puree.

Transfer the seasoned puree to a small mixing bowl. With a spoon or rubber spatula, carefully refill the sweet potato skins with the puree and return to the baking dish.

Reheat for about 10 minutes and eat hot.

Makes 4 servings. Amounts may be halved for smaller servings.

PEAR-ARUGULA SALAD

GF

INGREDIENTS

4 to 5 cups arugula (about
   1 bunch), washed thoroughly,
   dried, and trimmed as needed

⅛ teaspoon salt, plus more to
   taste

1 tablespoon juice from a lemon,
   lime, or grapefruit

2 ripe Bartlett pears, trimmed as
   needed and sliced thinly

½ cup of your favorite blue
   cheese, chopped or crumbled

½ cup toasted walnuts or pecans,
   chopped

¼ cup toasted sunflower seeds
   (optional but really nice)

Extra-virgin olive oil that you love

HERE'S WHAT YOU DO:

Place the arugula in a wide salad bowl. Sprinkle with the ⅛ teaspoon of salt, and with tongs or salad hands, turn to ensure even coverage. Add the citrus juice, and turn with the tools to distribute evenly and moisten.

Add the pears, cheese, nuts, and seeds (if using) and gently toss all the ingredients until well integrated. Drizzle the oil over the salad (a trickle, not a rainfall), gently toss again, and taste for salt-acid-fat balance.

Makes 4 servings. Amounts may be halved for smaller servings.

ROASTED BEANS, GREENS, & SQUASH RINGS **GF** **V**

When I discovered delicata squash a few years ago, I felt as if I had hit the autumn produce jackpot. Unlike its winter squash brethren, the oblong delicata is thin and thin-skinned, which means it cooks in a fraction of the time. When sliced into rings and roasted, its creamy flesh—often compared to a cross of sweet potato and corn—caramelizes yet takes on a delightfully surprising "meaty" texture that warrants a steak knife.

Paired with garlicky, rosemary-scented white beans and a bed of kale, this is one gorgeous fall trio that can be on the table in just under 45 minutes.

KITCHEN NOTES: While roasting the squash, prepare the beans and kale. Unlike other varieties of winter squash, which vary greatly in size and weight, the delicata consistently weighs just under a pound and is about 7 inches long. On average, it yields about twelve rings. Have a second squash on hand just in case, and if you don't need it, delicata keep really well in a cool place for a few months.

INGREDIENTS

1 to 2 delicata squash, cut into ½-inch rings, seeds and strings removed

1 tablespoon vegetable oil

½ teaspoon salt

1 (15-ounce) can cannellini or great northern beans

2 to 3 cloves garlic, minced

Needles from 1 to 2 sprigs rosemary, chopped finely

¼ teaspoon pepper flakes

¼ teaspoon ground black pepper

Juice of ½ lemon or lime

4 to 5 cups Lacinato (a.k.a. Dinosaur), Red Russian, or green curly kale leaves (about 1 bunch), washed thoroughly and dried

¼ cup olive oil

HERE'S WHAT YOU DO:

Preheat the oven to 400°F.

Place the squash in a single layer on a baking tray or in an ovenproof dish. Estimate three or four squash rings per serving; cut into the second squash if necessary. Pour the oil into a small dish. With a silicone or pastry brush, apply the vegetable oil to both sides of squash rings, sprinkling both sides with ¼ teaspoon of the salt as well.

Place in the oven and bake the first side for 10 minutes.

With tongs or a fork, turn the squash rings to their second side. Return the squash to oven and bake for another 10 to 15 minutes, or until fork tender. Remove from the oven and set aside. The skin will soften and is edible (and quite delicious).

Pour the beans into a colander and rinse thoroughly under cold water. Transfer to a flat surface—such as a platter, piece of parchment paper, or a baking tray—to dry for a few minutes.

Prepare the kale: With a knife, remove and discard the stems. Finely chop the leaves and transfer to a large mixing bowl.

In a small mixing bowl, combine the beans with the garlic, rosemary, pepper flakes, black pepper, the remaining ¼ teaspoon of salt, and the citrus juice and stir.

continues

ROASTED BEANS, GREENS, & SQUASH RINGS

Drizzle the oil over the kale, and with tongs, toss to combine. Add the bean mixture and toss to thoroughly coat. Taste a piece of kale for salt, and adjust the seasonings if need be.

Transfer the kale mixture to a baking dish and roast in the oven, tossing with tongs after 5 minutes. Roast for an additional 3 to 5 minutes. Remove from the oven.

Spoon the kale mixture onto a plate and place the squash rings all around. They will stand up and beg for a steak knife.

Makes 4 servings. Amounts can be doubled easily.

Kale Chips,
page 57

Tempeh Hoagie-letta, pages 55–56

West Indian-Style
Channa Wrap, pages 52-53

Polenta Squares with Puttanesca Sauce
& Broccoli Raab, pages 162–164

Twice-Baked Sweet Potatoes, pages 112–113

Shepherd's Pie with Chard-Lentil Filling, pages 171–174

Chesapeake Bay-Style
Chickpea "Crabcakes," pages 69–70

Susan's Eggplant Stack, pages 101–103

Pepita-Crusted Tofu Cutlets, pages 128–129
Dino-Mash, page 130

Tofu Barbecue, pages 92–93

Slurpy Pan-Asian Noodles, pages 175–176

Ratatouille,
pages 110–111

Romesco with bread
and almonds, page 100

Pizza with Good Ole
Marinara and Mozzarella
(and Arugula and Lemon,
If You're Smart) Topping,
page 182

Blue Corn Cakes ★ Roasted Red Pepper Sauce ★ Whipped Feta

BLUE CORN CAKES

GF

Inspired by the blue corn pancakes that are a weekend breakfast favorite at our casa, I've come up with a savory version that works great for supper. This is a really thin pancake that can either be rolled into a crepe or made into a short stack; either way, you'll swoon over the gorgeous splashes of color, when purpley blue meets fiery red-orange.

KITCHEN NOTES: Make the red pepper sauce and whipped feta before you prepare the batter. If you're not up to whipping your own feta (or you're not a feta fan), Boursin cheese will give a similar texture and flavor profile. And if you're pressed for time, buy prepared roasted peppers; but I'm telling you, it's worth making a batch of your own for keeping on hand in the fridge.

Tools: 6- or 7-inch nonstick crepe or omelet pan

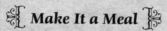

Make It a Meal

Is your appetite bigger tonight than anticipated? Consider a versatile side to round out your plate. Mix-and-matching encouraged! See Make It a Meal sidebar on page 26.

continues

ROASTED RED PEPPER SAUCE

INGREDIENTS

2 red bell peppers, roasted (For details for roasting peppers, see page 194.)

1 clove garlic, chopped

1½ teaspoons balsamic or sherry vinegar

1½ tablespoons olive oil

¼ teaspoon salt

¼ teaspoon dried oregano (optional)

HERE'S WHAT YOU DO:

With a blender or food processor, puree the peppers and garlic until smooth. Add the vinegar, oil, salt, and oregano (if using) and taste. Add more salt as needed. The puree should not be soupy; it should have some body. Set aside until ready to serve.

Makes about ¾ cup, just enough for the final dish

WHIPPED FETA

As mentioned in the recipe notes, you may substitute Boursin cheese (available in the dairy section of the supermarket) for a similar texture and flavor profile.

INGREDIENTS

¼ pound feta, removed from its brine

Juice of ½ lemon

¼ teaspoon dried oregano

¼ teaspoon black pepper

2 tablespoons olive oil

HERE'S WHAT YOU DO:

Place the feta in the bowl of a food processor or blender and whip until smooth, about 90 seconds. Add the remaining ingredients and whiz until well blended.

Makes about ½ cup. Amounts may be doubled if you like the flavor and want to use in sandwiches or omelets.

CORN CAKES

INGREDIENTS

1 cup plus 2 tablespoons blue cornmeal

½ teaspoon salt

½ teaspoon sugar

1¼ cups whole milk

1 large egg, beaten

2 tablespoons butter, melted

⅛ cup scallions (about 3 scallions), cleaned, white and light green parts only, diced finely

¼ cup roasted almonds, chopped, for garnish

HERE'S WHAT YOU DO:

In a small mixing bowl, combine the cornmeal, salt, and sugar and stir well.

In a separate mixing bowl, whisk the egg into the milk. Whisk in the butter when it is slightly cooled. Fold the liquid ingredients into the dry, then whisk vigorously with a fork. Add the scallions and whisk. You will have a total of 2 scant cups of batter. Pour the batter into a liquid measure with a spout.

Heat a nonstick skillet over medium-high heat.

Cook the batter in ¼-cup increments. Typically, I pour from the larger measuring cup to a smaller cup to maintain the consistency of size and thickness. You may need to stir the batter occasionally, as the cornmeal tends to settle to the bottom.

Pour one measure of batter into the skillet, lower the heat to medium, and cook on the first side until the batter starts to dry and get bubbly around the edges, about 90 seconds. Carefully turn onto the second side and cook for an additional 90 seconds.

Transfer to a plate and cook the remaining cakes. It's okay to stack on top of one another.

TO SERVE:

In a small saucepan, warm the red pepper sauce over low heat, about 90 seconds. Alternatively, heat in a microwave for about 30 seconds. Add 1 to 2 tablespoons of water if the sauce needs thinning.

As short stack: Top each cake with a teaspoon of room-temperature cheese. Ladle the red pepper sauce on top or around the cakes. Garnish with almonds.

As crepes: Spread 1 teaspoon of cheese in the middle of each cake, then fold in half or completely roll up, seam side down. Ladle the sauce on top, garnishing with almonds.

Note: These are best eaten right away, as the cornmeal toughens quickly; you may reheat, but do so in a low oven, with a foil cover, or in a dry skillet for 30 seconds.

Makes 8 cakes/crepes, enough for 3, possibly 4 servings

MUSHROOM-SPINACH SCRAMBLE

This one-skillet wonder is inspired by a legendary dish—Joe's Special—from Original Joe's, an old-school San Francisco landmark. As is the case with iconic recipes, there are many variations on this diner-style scramble of eggs, spinach, and ground beef. In the KOD version, mushrooms are the "meat" of this matter, which, according to my mushroom-loving recipe testers, do a bang-up job. Special? Hell, yes.

KITCHEN NOTES: Get the potatoes going first, so they are in the oven while you prepare the scramble.

INGREDIENTS

2 bunches spinach (9 to 10 cups), washed thoroughly and stemmed as needed (chard, stems removed, works equally well)

3 tablespoons vegetable oil

1 medium-size onion, chopped finely, or 2 shallot bulbs, minced

1 to 2 cloves garlic, chopped finely

1 pound mushrooms, sliced thinly (Choose oyster, porcini, shiitake, or cremini, depending on availability and preference.)

1 to 2 sprigs fresh thyme, or 1 teaspoon dried

½ teaspoon salt

¼ teaspoon cayenne

6 large eggs, beaten lightly and seasoned with black pepper and salt to taste

½ to ¾ cup grated Parmigiano-Reggiano cheese (optional)

HERE'S WHAT YOU DO:

Have ready a bowl of ice water. Bring about 6 cups of water to a rolling boil with 1 tablespoon of salt in a large saucepan. In batches, cook the spinach for about 60 seconds, then immediately transfer to the bowl. Squeeze out the excess water, then coarsely chop the spinach. (Alternatively, you may steam the spinach.)

Heat the oil over medium-high heat in a 10- or 12-inch skillet with a lid. Add the onion and cook until slightly softened, about 5 minutes, followed by the garlic, for 60 seconds. Add the mushrooms and thyme, and allow to brown and shrink a bit, up to 10 minutes. Stir occasionally (and add a few tablespoons of water, if necessary) to keep from sticking to the pan. Add the salt and cayenne.

Add the spinach, stirring until well combined with the mushrooms and aromatics. Pour in the eggs, tilting the skillet until they cover the surface of the skillet. Lower the heat to medium-low, cover, and cook, without stirring, for 6 to 8 minutes, or until the eggs are just set.

Remove the lid from the skillet, add the cheese (if using), and stir everything together, so that eggs break up and are scrambly.

Serve hot with a few slices of crusty bread or roasted potatoes (details follow).

Makes 4 hearty servings

ROSEMARY-GARLIC ROASTED POTATOES

INGREDIENTS

4 medium-size thin-skinned
    potatoes (I'm partial to Yukon
    Gold and Yellow Finn)
    (about 1½ pounds), peeled
    and trimmed as needed,
    and quartered
1 to 2 cloves garlic, minced
1 to 2 sprigs fresh rosemary,
    minced, or 1 teaspoon dried
1 teaspoon salt
Ground black pepper
1 to 2 tablespoons olive oil

HERE'S WHAT YOU DO:

Preheat the oven to 400°F.

Place the potatoes in a medium-size mixing bowl with the garlic,
rosemary, salt, and black pepper as you see fit. Add 1 tablespoon of
the oil, and with your hands, slather the potatoes, making sure that
they're well coated with the seasonings and aromatics. If they seem
less than well lubricated, add the remaining oil.

Transfer the potatoes to a baking dish or baking sheet large enough
for them to roast in a single layer with plenty of room around them.
Cook for 30 minutes, then give the potatoes a good toss to ensure
even cooking. Return to the oven and continue to roast for an additional 10 minutes, or until fork tender.

Makes 4 servings

BRAISED WINTER SQUASH WITH BLACK BEAN SAUCE & BOK CHOY Ⓥ

When seemingly impenetrable chunks of winter squash meet an aromatic broth of ginger, garlic, and Asian black bean sauce, something magical happens—and fast. Within 30 minutes, rock-hard squash transforms into velvety morsels. But don't mistake surrender for wimpiness—this little stew's got gusto.

Every time I make this dish, I'm always surprised (and delighted) at how quickly it comes together. In fact, the squash preparation (peeling, chopping, and seeding) may take longer than the actual cooking time; and while the squash simmers, the coconut rice is in progress.

Made from fermented black beans, Asian black bean sauce is pungent, spicy, and worth keeping on hand to zip up sauces and marinades.

INGREDIENTS

3 tablespoons vegetable oil

¼ cup shallots (about 2 bulbs' worth), minced

2 cloves garlic, minced

1 (1 x 1-inch) hunk ginger, peeled and minced

1 tablespoon Asian black bean–garlic sauce

3 to 4 cups winter squash, peeled and cut into 1- or 2-inch chunks (recommended: kabocha, Hubbard, or butternut)

HERE'S WHAT YOU DO:

In a deep skillet or wok with a lid, heat the vegetable oil over medium heat and add the shallots. Cook until softened, stirring occasionally, about 5 minutes. Add the garlic and ginger and cook for 1 minute or so, then add the black bean sauce. Stir to keep from sticking.

Add the squash and stir to coat with the aromatics, 2 to 3 minutes. Meanwhile, in a small bowl, combine the rice wine, soy sauce, and sugar. Stir until the sugar is dissolved. Add to the squash and bring to a lively simmer. Add enough liquid so that the vegetables are barely covered. Cover and cook until the squash is just about fork tender, 15 minutes.

Meanwhile, prepare the coconut rice (details follow).

BRAISED WINTER SQUASH WITH
BLACK BEAN SAUCE & BOK CHOY

INGREDIENTS

continued

2 tablespoons Shaoxing rice wine or dry sherry (if alcohol is an issue, omit)

2 tablespoons soy sauce

½ teaspoon granulated sugar

1 cup water or vegetable stock

1 large bunch bok choy or 6 bunches of baby bok choy (about 6 cups), cleaned thoroughly and trimmed as needed, and cut into 2-inch pieces

Sesame oil, for drizzling

1 teaspoon sesame seeds or gomasio (optional garnish)

HERE'S WHAT YOU DO:

continued

Remove the lid and place the bok choy on top of the squash mixture. Drizzle the bok choy with the sesame oil. Return the lid and allow to "steam" until the bok choy arrives at your desired doneness, at least 3 minutes.

Serve hot, over the coconut rice.

Makes 4 servings

COCONUT RICE

INGREDIENTS

1 cup uncooked long- or
  medium-grain rice
¾ cup water
¾ cup unsweetened coconut milk
  (about half of a 14-ounce can)
Pinch of salt

HERE'S WHAT YOU DO:

In a medium-size saucepan, combine the rice and water and bring to
a boil over medium-high heat. Add the coconut milk and salt, stir,
lower the heat to low, and cover. Cook at a simmer for 12 minutes,
without lifting the lid. Turn off the heat and leave the rice alone for
10 minutes. Serve hot.

Makes 4 side-dish servings

Roasted Eggplant–Lentil Caviar on Oversized Crostini ★ Pistachio-Raisin Rice Pilaf

ROASTED EGGPLANT–LENTIL CAVIAR ON OVERSIZED CROSTINI

XTRA **V**

Confession: Originally conceived as a stuffed eggplant, this recipe almost ended up on the editing floor. Instead, I've held onto the best part—a silky lemon and garlic–infused eggplant puree studded with earthy lentils—and spread the love on slabs of country-style toast for killer crostini. A simple stovetop pilaf, scented with a cinnamon stick, turns this snack into supper.

KITCHEN NOTES: Get the eggplant into the oven first. While it roasts, prepare the lentils. While the lentils are cooking, prepare the rice. Speaking of lentils, the French *lentilles du Puy*, which have a more refined texture, are my preference, but they're not always available. Use what you can find in your local market.

INGREDIENTS

2 medium-size eggplant, sliced lengthwise

2 to 4 cloves garlic, smashed

Juice of 1 lemon

2 tablespoons olive oil

1 teaspoon salt

¼ teaspoon cayenne

1 cup prepared lentils (details follow)

1 loaf country-style bread (about 1 pound), cut into ½-inch slices (estimate 2 slices per serving)

Optional but nice garnishes: Extra-virgin olive oil you really love, ½ cup crumbled feta, ¼ cup chopped fresh parsley

HERE'S WHAT YOU DO:

Preheat the oven to 400°F.

Place the eggplant halves on a baking sheet, cut side up, and roast until extremely tender, 40 to 45 minutes.

Remove from the oven and allow the eggplant to cool at least 10 minutes. With a fork (and maybe a spoon), scoop out the flesh and transfer to the bowl of a food processor. Lower the oven temperature to 375°F.

Puree with the garlic, lemon juice, olive oil, salt, and cayenne. Transfer to a medium-size bowl and mix in 1 cup of the lentils (the rest is cook's treat), until well combined.

Place the bread in a single layer on a baking sheet and toast for about 5 minutes, or until the bread is slightly dried out but not crisp. (You may also do this on top of the stove on a grill pan or directly over the coals of a grill.)

Remove the toast from the heat source. Apply ¼ cup of eggplant-lentil caviar to each slice, and with a knife, smear until evenly distributed. Garnish with olive oil, feta, and parsley (if using).

Estimate 2 toasts per serving, paired with a fluffy mound of rice pilaf (details follow).

Makes 4 servings

ROASTED EGGPLANT–LENTIL CAVIAR ON OVERSIZED CROSTINI

LENTIL CAVIAR

INGREDIENTS

1 tablespoon vegetable oil

½ cup diced onion

¼ cup diced carrot

1 sprig thyme, or ½ teaspoon dried

½ cup brown or green dried lentils, rinsed

2 tablespoons red wine that you enjoy drinking (optional)

¾ to 1 cup water

¼ to ½ teaspoon salt

HERE'S WHAT YOU DO:

In a large saucepan, heat the oil over medium heat and add the onion, carrot, and thyme. Cook for about 5 minutes, until the aromatics slightly soften. Add the lentils and stir to coat. Add the red wine and bring up to a lively simmer. The wine will reduce a bit. Add ¾ cup of the water, return to a lively simmer, then lower the heat, cover, and cook until tender to the bite, about 40 minutes, adding up to ¼ cup of the water if the lentils begin to dry out as they cook.

Add ¼ teaspoon of the salt, taste, then add the remaining salt if needed.

Makes 1½ cups

PISTACHIO-RAISIN RICE PILAF

INGREDIENTS

¼ cup unsalted shelled
   pistachios

2 tablespoons vegetable oil
   or butter

½ cup diced onion

1 cup uncooked basmati rice

1¾ cups water

1 cinnamon stick

½ teaspoon salt

⅓ cup raisins (golden raisins are
   prettier, but Thompson raisins
   do the job just fine)

HERE'S WHAT YOU DO:

Place the pistachios in a dry skillet over medium heat and toast for about 90 seconds, keeping a close eye to make sure they don't burn. This can also be done on a baking sheet in a 300°F oven for 5 minutes.

Let the pistachios cool, then chop coarsely.

In a medium-size saucepan with a lid, heat the oil over medium heat and add the onion. Cook until slightly softened, about 5 minutes.

Add the rice and stir to coat with the onions and oil. Toast for 1 to 2 minutes, until fragrant and translucent. Add the water, cinnamon stick, and salt and bring to a boil. Lower the heat to low, cover, and cook for 12 minutes, without lifting the lid.

Lift the lid and sprinkle the raisins on top of the rice, allowing the steam to plump them up. Return the lid and allow the rice to rest for 8 to 10 minutes.

Stir in the nuts, as well as raisins, and serve hot.

Makes 4 side-dish servings

PEPITA-CRUSTED TOFU

Although a high-protein flavor chameleon, tofu is typically a hard sell with the meat set. I'd be lying if I told you it tastes like chicken, and its squishy marshmallow-like texture takes some time getting used to. But a meatless cookbook without tofu? That just didn't seem right.

As a culinary writing fellow at the Writer's Colony at Dairy Hollow in Eureka Springs, Arkansas, I dreamed up this dish with the tofu-reticent in mind. The magic flavor element is a pumpkin-seed pesto seasoned with garlic and cilantro, an irresistible combo that delivers both herby tang and nutty richness. As for the texture kinks, the tofu is sliced into thin "cutlets," which facilitate a toothy crust when baked in the oven. The result: the "most chickeny" tofu that did ever pass my lips.

Do try it with the Dino-Mash, my take on colcannon, the classic Irish mashed potato and cabbage dish, updated with Lacinato (a.k.a. Dinosaur) kale.

KITCHEN NOTES: The first thing you should do is roast the garlic for the Dino-Mash, as it will take 50 minutes.

INGREDIENTS

1 (14-ounce) package fresh extra-firm tofu, preferably organic
1½ cups raw, unsalted pepitas
2 to 3 cloves garlic, peeled
¾ cup fresh cilantro, chopped roughly
¾ teaspoon salt
½ fresh chile pepper of your choice, seeded and chopped roughly (I like things on hot side, so I use ¼ habanero)
⅓ cup soy sauce
1 teaspoon sesame oil
Cornstarch, for dredging
Vegetable oil, for brushing

HERE'S WHAT YOU DO:

Drain the tofu: Remove from the package and place on a dinner plate. Place a second plate on top of the tofu and weigh it down with a something heavy, such as a can of food. Allow to sit for about 20 minutes. (While the tofu drains, you can make the pesto.)

In the bowl of a food processor or wide-mouthed blender, place the pepitas. Pulverize, using the "pulse" button. *Do not puree into a paste*; you're looking for texture.

Add the garlic, cilantro, salt, and chile pepper, and continue to process, using the "pulse" function.

Taste and smile. This stuff is really good, and if you're not careful, you could end up eating it all and forget about the tofu. Transfer to a shallow mixing bowl.

With a sharp (serrated is even better) knife, cut the tofu into ½-inch cutlet-like slabs. (You should get eight to ten pieces.) Transfer to a dish deep and wide enough to accommodate all the slabs in a single layer.

PEPITA-CRUSTED TOFU

HERE'S WHAT YOU DO:

continued

Preheat the oven to 350°F.

Pour the soy sauce and sesame oil, if using, over the tofu and allow to marinate for at least 15 minutes, making sure you turn the tofu once to ensure even coverage of the marinade.

Place about ¼ cup of cornstarch in a small, wide bowl.

Dredge a tofu cutlet in the cornstarch. Dust off any excess.

With a silicone or pastry brush, apply oil to both sides of the cutlet.

Place in the pepita mixture, and with your hands, press on both sides of tofu. The pepita mixture will adhere and look a bit like a mosaic.

Transfer to a baking dish large enough to hold all the tofu in a single layer, being careful of the pepita crust. Repeat these steps for the remaining tofu cutlets.

Bake for 30 minutes, carefully turning onto the second side with a spatula or tongs after the first 15 minutes.

Meanwhile, prep the Dino-Mash (recipe details follow).

Remove from the oven and serve hot or at room temperature.

Makes 4 servings

DINO-MASH

This pretty mash is completely dairy free yet manages to be creamy and full-flavored, with the help of starchy cooking water and a head of roasted garlic.

INGREDIENTS

1 head garlic

Olive oil for slathering, plus ¼ cup

2 pounds Yukon Gold, Yellow Finn, or red-skinned potatoes (4 or 5 medium-size), scrubbed, trimmed, and peeled as necessary

2 teaspoons salt

2 cups Lacinato kale, stemmed and chopped finely

¼ teaspoon ground black pepper

HERE'S WHAT YOU DO:

Preheat the oven to 400°F.

Trim the top of garlic and pull away the outermost skin. With your hands, lightly rub the garlic with oil and place in a small roasting dish. Cover with foil.

Roast the garlic until the cloves are fork tender (but not burned), about 50 minutes. Check for doneness at 40 minutes. (A kitchen timer is helpful.)

Meanwhile, prepare the potatoes: Quarter and place in a medium-size saucepan with 4 cups of water. The water should just barely cover the potatoes. *This is important.*

Add the salt. Cover the saucepan and bring to a boil. Lower the heat to medium. Cook for 25 minutes, place the kale on top of the potatoes, replace the lid, and allow the kale to steam for 5 minutes. Test the potatoes with a fork for doneness. Remove from the heat.

Squeeze the garlic flesh from the cloves into a large mixing bowl. With tongs or a strainer, transfer the potatoes and kale to the mixing bowl, reserving the cooking liquid.

With a hand masher, mash the potatoes and kale, focusing on the potatoes at first, ensuring that they're smooth, ladling in their cooking liquid as necessary (you'll use some, but likely not all). Use a wooden spoon to combine all of the ingredients. Add the remaining ¼ cup of oil and black pepper, stir, then taste for salt, adding more as needed.

Eat hot.

Makes 4 servings

THAI-STYLE RED CURRY TEMPEH

Coconut curry is a whole lot easier than it sounds, and for this version, we go nice and easy, using a prepared curry paste available in most supermarkets and quick-cooking vegetables of your choice.

The unique piece of this dish is the addition of pan-fried tempeh, my savory toothsome friend featured elsewhere in the book (see page 55 for details). The tempeh adds both texture and protein and melds beautifully with the red curry gravy.

KITCHEN NOTES: Make the rice first so that it's ready to go when the curry is.

Pan-fry the tempeh before preparing the veg and seasonings, all of which should be ready for action before turning on the stove. Smile; you're about to have a tongue-dancing experience!

INGREDIENTS:

Tempeh

1 (8-ounce) package tempeh
(See page 19 for brand
recommendations.)

4 tablespoons soy sauce

1 teaspoon sesame oil

Juice of ½ lime

2 to 3 tablespoons vegetable oil,
for pan-frying

Salt

HERE'S WHAT YOU DO:

Slice the tempeh into triangles and then make those triangles thinner by slicing in half lengthwise, so that you end up with about eighteen ½-inch-thick triangles. (You can also slice the tempeh into strips, but triangles make a prettier presentation.)

Place the tempeh in a shallow baking dish big enough for it to lie in a single layer. Combine the soy sauce, sesame oil, and lime juice and pour over the tempeh. Allow to marinate for about 10 minutes.

In a skillet, heat 2 tablespoons of the vegetable oil over medium heat. Remove the tempeh from marinade and pan-fry until crispy on both sides. You may need to fry it in batches. Add the remaining oil if necessary, to keep the pan lubricated.

Transfer to paper towels and sprinkle lightly with salt. Set aside.

THAI-STYLE RED CURRY TEMPEH

INGREDIENTS:

Curry

2 tablespoons vegetable oil

½ cup minced shallots (1 to 2 shallot bulbs, depending on size)

1 (2 x 1-inch) hunk fresh ginger, peeled and minced (about 1 tablespoon)

2 to 3 tablespoons red curry paste (3 tablespoons yields a fairly hot result; 2 tablespoons is the lower end of medium-hot)

1 (15-ounce) can unsweetened coconut milk (I prefer full-fat and not "lite")

4 teaspoons brown sugar

1 tablespoon soy sauce

Zest of ½ lime

About 3 cups of fairly quick-cooking vegetables, such as 1 small red bell pepper, julienned; 1 to 2 medium-size carrots, peeled and cut into 2-inch-long matchsticks; 1 cup cauliflower florets; 1 Japanese eggplant, sliced lengthwise and cut into half-moons; and/or 1 cup thinly sliced mushrooms

4 cups cooked jasmine or basmati rice, made from 1⅓ cups uncooked rice (For how to cook rice, see page 203.)

Optional garnishes: Chopped cilantro and/or Thai basil; ¼ cup chopped unsalted peanuts or cashews

HERE'S WHAT YOU DO:

In a deep skillet or wok, heat the oil over medium heat. Add the shallots and ginger and cook until softened, about 4 minutes. Add the curry paste, coating the aromatics. Cook over medium-low heat for about 90 seconds, stirring continuously.

Pour in half of the coconut milk and stir to combine. Cook over medium-low heat until the coconut milk is at a lively simmer, about 2 minutes. Add the brown sugar, soy sauce, lime zest, and the remaining coconut milk, and cook for 2 minutes, lowering the heat to keep at a simmer.

Add the vegetables and stir to combine. Check the liquid level: If the liquid is below the solid ingredients, gradually add water, a tablespoon or two at a time.

Cover and cook over low heat for 10 to 12 minutes, stirring occasionally, until the vegetables are fork tender. You'll notice that the sauce has thickened.

Spoon about ¾ cup of cooked rice into each bowl, followed by a ladleful or two of the curry mixture, then a few tempeh triangles. Dress with your choice of garnishes and eat hot.

Makes about 5 servings

RED LENTIL DAL WITH CUMIN-FRIED ONIONS & WILTED SPINACH

V **XTRA** **KIDDO**

The inspiration for this little gem comes from South Asia, where dal—a "stew" of dried beans or legumes—is a dietary mainstay and protein source. In this version, red lentils, in their gorgeous coral glory, are front and center, with ginger, garlic, and cinnamon doing a bang-up job of flavoring the pot (and perfuming the kitchen).

Thicker than a soup yet not quite a stew, this dal is difficult to pigeonhole. A potage, perhaps? And when the dal is topped off with a colorful, aromatic layer of wilted spinach, cumin-scented onions, and sweet tomatoes, words do fail to describe the experience you're about to have.

For dipping every last morsel (and you will want to dip and sop), the same dough I use for pizza (see page 135) is shaped here into individual-size flatbreads.

KITCHEN NOTES: Make the dough for the flatbreads first. While the dough is rising, prepare the ingredients for the soup. When the dough has doubled, put the soup on the stove. While the soup is simmering, bake the flatbreads. You can also make the dough in advance and keep it in the fridge or freezer, then bring to room temperature and bake while the soup is simmering.

INGREDIENTS

2 cups dried red lentils, rinsed

6 cups water

1 (1 x 1-inch) hunk fresh ginger, peeled but left whole

¼ teaspoon ground turmeric

2 cloves garlic, 1 peeled but left whole, the other chopped

1 cinnamon stick (optional but really nice)

½ bunch spinach (about 2 cups), washed thoroughly, stemmed, dried, and chopped coarsely

1¼ teaspoons salt

3 tablespoons vegetable oil

HERE'S WHAT YOU DO:

Place the rinsed lentils in a heavy-bottomed pot and add water (it will cover the lentils, plus a little extra.). Add the ginger, turmeric, whole garlic clove, and the cinnamon stick (if using).

Bring to a lively simmer, then lower the heat, cover, and cook the lentils at a gentle simmer for about 30 minutes.

Remove the ginger, garlic, and cinnamon stick. If the lentils have not pureed on their own to your liking, run a whisk through the pot a few times and, within seconds, they will be completely pureed. Add the salt, taste, then add more as needed.

Add the spinach, give it a quick stir, and return the cover to the pot. The spinach will wilt quickly.

continues

RED LENTIL DAL WITH CUMIN-FRIED ONIONS & WILTED SPINACH

INGREDIENTS

continued

1½ teaspoons cumin seeds
1 medium-size onion, sliced in
  half and then into half-moons
¼ teaspoon cayenne
1 dozen grape or pear tomatoes,
  halved lengthwise (best when
  in season)
A squeeze of ½ lemon (optional)

HERE'S WHAT YOU DO:

continued

Meanwhile, in a 9- or 10-inch skillet, heat the oil over medium heat and add the cumin seeds. Cook briefly (15 seconds), then add the garlic and onions. Cook over medium heat, allowing the onions to brown at the edges, at least 5 minutes. Add the cayenne and tomatoes (if using), stir to coat, and taste for salt, adding if you feel the need.

Transfer the fried onion mixture to the dal, stir, and serve. If using, squeeze the lemon over the dish as a last-minute flavor spritz.

Makes about 6 servings

INDIVIDUAL FLATBREADS

INGREDIENTS

1 cup water

1 (¼-ounce) envelope active dry yeast, or 2¼ teaspoons from a jar

Pinch of sugar

About 3 cups all-purpose flour

1 teaspoon salt, plus more for sprinkling

1 tablespoon olive oil

Cornmeal, for dusting the pans

4 tablespoons (½ stick) butter, melted

HERE'S WHAT YOU DO:

Heat the water until its temperature reaches 100°F—this is not even close to boiling!—and pour into a small bowl. Sprinkle the yeast, sugar, and 1 tablespoon of the flour over the water. With a fork, stir until dissolved. Cover the bowl and allow it to sit at room temperature until the mixture is slightly foamy, about 15 minutes.

In a large bowl (think wide and shallow versus tall and narrow), combine 1 cup of the flour, the salt, and the olive oil and stir with a rubber spatula or heavy wooden spoon. Add the yeast mixture and stir until just mixed. Add the remaining flour, ½ cup at a time, stirring between flour additions. You are looking for a soft, sticky dough that is just pulling away from the sides of the bowl. Depending on the weather (humidity, heat), the amount of flour used will vary between 2½ and 3½ cups total. It's unnecessary to use the maximum amount.

Lightly dust a work surface with flour and pour the mixture out of the bowl onto the work surface.

Begin kneading the dough in the following manner: punch gently but firmly, fold in half, and turn (rotate 15 minutes on your imaginary clock, or one-quarter turn). Make *punch-fold-turn* your mantra until your dough becomes a smooth, soft, springy ball, as smooth as a baby's bottom. The entire process should take about 6 minutes.

Lightly oil a large bowl and place the dough in the bowl, turning to coat. Cover the bowl with a towel or plastic wrap and place in a warm spot, away from drafts. (Alternatively, place in a lightly greased soup pot with a lid.) Let rise until doubled, about 1 hour.

Cut the dough into six pieces. Work only with what you plan to bake, and refrigerate or freeze leftover dough for another time.

Preheat the oven to 500°F.

Wipe the work surface clean of dough scraps, then dry thoroughly before rolling out the dough. Dust the work surface with flour. Gently press the dough into a thick disk. After every few motions, rotate the dough one-quarter turn. With a rolling pin or your hands, roll out the dough from center, continuing to rotate, being careful not to tear the dough, until you have formed a circle 4 to 6 inches across.

continues

INDIVIDUAL FLATBREADS

HERE'S WHAT YOU DO:

continued

Dust a pizza pan, stone, or bottom side of a baking sheet with cornmeal, for texture. Carefully lift the dough onto the baking surface. (You will likely be able to fit two dough circles on one inverted baking tray.)

In a small saucepan, melt the butter over medium-low heat. As the milk solids rise, skim off with a slotted spoon. Try to remove as much as you can, for a fairly clarified butter.

With a silicone or pastry brush, apply the clarified butter to the surface of each dough circle. Sprinkle salt on top.

Bake until the dough makes a hollow sound when you tap the crust and is golden in color. A 4- to 6-inch round will take about 6 minutes. The bottom of the crust should be golden. Transfer to a kitchen towel to keep warm until serving.

Makes 6 pieces

STUFFED SHELLS WITH LENTIL RAGOUT & SPINACH

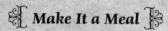

I've been a longtime fan of the lentil, but in the course of exploring more meat-free options, I've become even more impressed by the itty-bitty pulse that could. For the stuffed shells, an Italian-American classic typically stuffed with ground beef and heaps of ricotta, I throw caution to the wind and let the lentils take over. They don't just do the job; they will wildly surpass your expectations, behaving with heft and grace, as if they should have been in that sauce all along.

KITCHEN NOTES: Boil the water for the pasta while preparing the lentils. While the shells are cooking, put the lentils on the stove. While the shells are cooling, put together the ragout.

> ### ❧ Make It a Meal ❧
>
> Is your appetite bigger tonight than anticipated? Consider a versatile side to round out your plate. Mix-and-matching encouraged! See Make It a Meal sidebar on page 26.

INGREDIENTS

1 small cinnamon stick (or break a larger one in half)

¼ medium-size onion, peeled but left intact, plus ½ onion, minced

½ cup dried brown or green lentils

3½ teaspoons salt

½ package dried jumbo pasta shells (about 20 pieces)

3 tablespoons olive oil

1 medium-size carrot, peeled and diced

1 celery stalk, diced

HERE'S WHAT YOU DO:

Prepare the lentils: Bring 1 cup of water to a boil with cinnamon stick and the intact ¼ onion in a small saucepan. Add the lentils, cover, and lower the heat to low. Cook for 25 minutes. Discard the cinnamon and onion. Add ½ teaspoon of the salt and stir.

In a large saucepan, bring 3 quarts of water to a boil. Add the shells and 2 teaspoons of the salt and cook for 12 minutes; the shells will still be a little tacky. Drain and transfer to a baking sheet to cool. Untangle the shells to prevent sticking.

Preheat the oven to 350°F.

Prepare the ragout: In a large saucepan, heat the oil over medium heat and add the carrot, celery, the minced ½ onion, and garlic. Stir and cook until softened, about 8 minutes.

continues

STUFFED SHELLS WITH
LENTIL RAGOUT & SPINACH

INGREDIENTS

continued

3 cloves garlic, minced

¼ cup red wine

1 sprig fresh thyme, or
½ teaspoon dried

2½ cups tomato puree (nearly
an entire 28-ounce can)

¼ teaspoon cayenne

Ground black pepper

4 cups spinach, washed
thoroughly, stems removed
and finely chopped
(about 1 bunch)

Optional but tasty toppers: ¼ cup
grated Parmigiano-Reggiano
and ¼ cup smoked mozzarella
cheese, grated, or smoked
provolone or Gouda

HERE'S WHAT YOU DO:

continued

Add the wine and thyme, allowing the wine to reduce for about 2 minutes. Add the tomato puree and cayenne, stir to combine, and cook over low heat for 10 to 15 minutes. Add the lentils and cook for an additional 5 to 10 minutes. Add the remaining 1 teaspoon of salt and the black pepper, and taste, adding more as you see fit. Discard the thyme sprig, if using fresh.

Stir in the spinach, turn off the heat, and cover.

Ladle a small amount of ragout into a square or rectangular baking dish (9 x 13 inches works great). Line up the shells in dish, then with a small spoon, fill each shell with the ragout. Top off the shells with a ladleful of ragout, followed by your choice of cheeses (if using).

Bake for 30 minutes. The cheese will bubble a bit, but the shells should be pretty tender.

Makes 4 to 5 servings

BEETS & GREENS QUESADILLAS

XTRA **KIDDO**

Until I met Devra Gartenstein, I kept beets out of my kitchen. In addition to writing meatless cookbooks, Devra owns and operates a quesadilla and tamale stand at several Seattle farmers' markets. One Sunday morning at the market, I queued up and ordered one of her seasonally inspired quesadillas, completely unaware that I was eating beets. Someone please give this woman a genius grant. I am thrilled to share a home-cook version of Devra's basic quesadilla recipe, with her blessing—and plenty of beets.

If you like to dip your quesadilla wedges, you'll love the roasted red pepper soup, which is completely dairy free and thickened with potatoes.

KITCHEN NOTES: Make the soup first. While it's simmering, proceed with preparing the quesadillas. I love the handheld stick blender for these kinds of soups; you can puree on the spot in the pot!

To really make the quesadillas sing, the onion and beets have to be sliced super thin. Use a mandoline or slicer blade attachment in your food processor to yield the best results. The recipe calls for 8-inch tortillas, but feel free to use the larger 10-inch variety; just add 20 percent more filling and cheese to accommodate.

INGREDIENTS

1 tablespoon vegetable oil

½ medium-size onion, sliced
  thinly

1 unpeeled beet, sliced very thinly

1 bunch (4 to 5 cups) beet greens
  and/or chard, chopped finely
  (I omit the chard stems, but
  this is a personal preference)

1 teaspoon chili powder, mild
  or hot

HERE'S WHAT YOU DO:

Heat the oil in a 10- or 12-inch skillet. Add the onion and beet, and cook over medium-high heat for about 6 minutes, stirring often.

Add the greens, chili powder, cumin, oregano, salt, and water, and stir until the spices and salt are well distributed. Cook over medium heat for 2 to 3 minutes, or until the vegetables are soft and all the water has evaporated.

Transfer the cooked vegetables to a bowl, then wash and dry the skillet. Heat the clean skillet over medium-low heat and grease lightly with cooking spray.

continues

BEETS AND GREENS QUESADILLAS

INGREDIENTS

continued

HERE'S WHAT YOU DO:

continued

½ teaspoon ground cumin

½ teaspoon dried oregano

½ teaspoon salt

2 tablespoons water

Cooking spray

6 (8-inch) or 3 (10-inch) whole wheat, tomato-, or spinach-flavored flour tortillas

1 heaping cup grated Monterey Jack or cheddar cheese

Other veggie options depending on season and cook's preference: 1 small zucchini, 1 cup green cabbage, carrot rounds, Lacinato kale, sliced mushrooms, and/or parsnips

Lay a tortilla in the pan, then spread about 2 tablespoons of cheese over half of the tortilla. Cover the cheese with 2 to 3 heaping tablespoons of the cooked vegetables. Spread another tablespoon of cheese over the vegetables, then fold the tortilla in half and flip it with a spatula. Cook for 1 to 2 minutes on each side, until the tortilla is nicely browned and the cheese is melted through.

Repeat with the remaining tortillas, cheese, and vegetables. Cut each quesadilla into four wedges with a knife or pizza cutter.

Makes 6 servings. Quesadillas can be assembled in advance and reheated within 24 hours

ROASTED RED PEPPER SOUP

INGREDIENTS

3 medium-size red bell peppers
2 tablespoons vegetable oil
1 medium-size onion, chopped
1 clove garlic, smashed
1 pound potatoes
   (about 3 medium-size),
   peeled and quartered
1 to 2 sprigs fresh thyme
3 cups water
1 teaspoon salt
2 ounces bourbon (optional but
   nice)
¼ teaspoon cayenne
¼ teaspoon smoked paprika
A few lemon wedges (optional)

HERE'S WHAT YOU DO:

Preheat the oven to 400°F.

Remove and discard the stems and tops of the peppers and place on a baking sheet. Roast until blistered and charred, 30 to 40 minutes.

Remove the peppers from the oven and place in a sealed bag or container, to help remove stubborn skins, for at least 15 minutes.

With your hands or with the help of a paring knife, remove the seeds, veins, and skins, but do not rinse the peppers. Chop coarsely and set aside.

In a medium-size saucepan over medium heat, heat the oil, then add the onion and garlic. Cook until the onion is slightly softened, about 5 minutes. Add the potatoes, thyme, water, and salt. Bring to a lively simmer, then lower the heat, cover, and cook until the potatoes are fork tender, 15 to 20 minutes.

Remove the thyme, add the peppers and bourbon (if using), and stir in the cayenne and smoked paprika.

Puree until smooth and free of lumps; taste for salt and season as needed.

Return the soup to the saucepan and reheat.

Serve hot, with lemon wedges, if desired, for a finishing touch.

Makes 4 servings

Winter . . .

Baby, it's cold outside.

When the ground is frozen solid and local produce choices are few, meatless seems hard to do. But hang onto your New Year's hat and step up to the stove; winter is tailor made for stirring the pot—of beans (Hoppin' John, black bean–sweet potato chili) and braises (veg curry 'n' dumplings), the culinary equivalent of wooly socks. It's the green light to crank up the oven for casseroles (brocco mac & cheese) and savory pies of all shapes and sizes (shepherd's pie with chard-lentil filling, potpie with cheddar crust), warming both the belly and the spirit.

BLACK BEAN–SWEET POTATO CHILI   **XTRA** **DO**

When I began developing hearty Meatless Mondays recipes, I asked both meat eaters and vegetarians what kinds of recipes they'd like to see, and the overwhelming response was black bean chili. Here's my version, with a fair amount of spice, smokiness, and just enough tomato flavor to add tang without overwhelming acidity. Sweet potatoes lend color, texture, and immune-boosting beta-carotene, which we all can use during the coldest, darkest months of the year. In the course of my testing, I've determined that dried beans deliver the tastiest results with a texture that holds up for several days. Remember how chili gets better the next day? This version is no exception.

Skillet corn bread (page 148) is a knockout partner, but so are warmed-up corn tortillas or a simple pot of rice.

KITCHEN NOTES: I highly recommend dried beans over canned for this dish and urge you to give them a chance, even just once. I've tested this recipe both ways and the texture and flavor of the dried-bean version are infinitely more satisfying.

INGREDIENTS:
Simple Pot of Black Beans

1 pound (2 cups) dried black beans
2 cloves garlic, peeled and smashed
1 teaspoon salt

HERE'S WHAT YOU DO:

Place the beans in a soup pot and cover with water, plus a few inches. Soak for at least 4 hours or overnight at room temperature. (If your kitchen is very warm, place the beans in the fridge to minimize chances of fermentation.) Drain. You now have 4 cups of soaked beans.

Return the beans to the pot, add 4½ cups water to cover, plus the garlic. Bring to a boil, and cook at a hard boil for 5 minutes. Skim off any scum that rises to the top.

Lower the heat to a simmer and cook, covered, for at least 1 hour, until the beans are tender to the bite. The cooking time will depend on the age of the beans—older beans take longer. Meanwhile, begin working on the sauce (details follow), which takes about 30 minutes and will be ready by the time the beans are done.

Season the beans with the salt and remove the garlic cloves.

BLACK BEAN–SWEET POTATO CHILI

INGREDIENTS:

Sauce

1 medium-size sweet potato (12 to 16 ounces), peeled and cut into ½-inch cubes (2 to 2½ cups)

3 tablespoons vegetable oil

1 medium-size onion, chopped finely

4 cloves garlic, minced

1 tablespoon ground cumin

⅛ teaspoon ground cinnamon

1 teaspoon dried oregano

½ teaspoon cayenne

1 teaspoon smoked paprika

½ teaspoon salt

2 to 2½ cups tomato puree

2 tablespoons tomato paste, dissolved in ¼ cup water

2 chipotle chiles in adobo sauce, minced

Possible garnishes: Chopped fresh cilantro, squeeze of lime, grated cotija or Monterey Jack cheese, chopped scallions, sour cream

HERE'S WHAT YOU DO:

Have ready a bowl of ice water. Bring about 3 cups of water to a boil in a medium-size saucepan and add the sweet potato. Return to a boil, cover, and cook for 2 minutes. With a skimmer or sieve with a handle, remove the sweet potato from the pot and transfer to the bowl. Drain and set aside.

Heat the oil in a deep skillet over medium heat and add the onion. Cook until softened, about 6 minutes. Add the garlic, followed by the cumin, cinnamon, oregano, cayenne, smoked paprika, and salt and stir to combine. The mixture will be pasty. Add the sweet potato, stirring to coat with the aromatics and spices. Cook for an additional 3 to 5 minutes over medium-low heat, allowing the ingredients to get acquainted with one another.

Add 2 cups of the tomato puree and increase the heat to medium, bringing to a lively simmer. Stir in the tomato paste mixture and chipotle chiles, lower the heat, and cook until well blended, about 10 minutes, stirring regularly to keep from sticking and burning.

Pour the sweet potato mixture into the beans and stir to combine. Simmer over medium-low heat until you are satisfied with the overall consistency and texture of the chili, about 30 minutes. If the mixture seems too thick, feel free to stir in more tomato puree or water.

Serve with your choice of garnishes by itself, over rice, or with tortillas or corn bread.

Makes at least 6 servings

SMOKIN' HOPPIN' JOHN   XTRA DO

Although delicious at any time of year, Hoppin' John, a classic Southern combo of black-eyed peas and rice, is traditionally eaten on or around New Year's Day. According to the story told by slaves brought to the Americas from Africa, black-eyed peas represent coins, clearing the way for fortune and prosperity in the new year. Diehards have long served up their Hoppin' John with pork for salt and smoke, but I've discovered that the meat is far from necessary, particularly if you've got a chipotle chile and a little smoked paprika on hand. It's so satisfying I reckon you'll forget about the p-o-r-k.

A note on the peas: I really like the results with frozen peas, which make this dish completely doable on a weeknight. For those who prefer working with dried peas, see the Plan B course of action following the recipe. As you may have noticed, I'm not recommending canned black-eyed peas for this dish, as I find them too mushy from the get-go.

INGREDIENTS

2 tablespoons vegetable oil

1 medium-size onion, chopped coarsely

2 cloves garlic, minced

1 cup uncooked medium- or long-grain rice

½ teaspoon smoked paprika

1 (20-ounce) bag frozen black-eyed peas

2 to 3 cups water or unsalted vegetable stock

¼ cup beer you like to drink (optional)

1 chipotle chile in adobo sauce, minced

1 teaspoon salt or soy sauce (Smoked salt is also nice here; use sparingly.)

Optional fixins and garnishes: Chopped scallions, halved grape tomatoes, chopped fresh parsley, shredded cheddar, hot sauce

HERE'S WHAT YOU DO:

Over medium heat, heat the oil in a large saucepan or heavy-bottomed pot. Add the onions and garlic and cook until the onions are slightly softened, about 5 minutes.

Add the rice and stir to coat with the aromatics. Allow to toast for 1 minute. Add the smoked paprika and stir to coat.

Add the peas, followed by 2 cups of water, the beer (if using), and the chipotle chile. (If not using beer, add ¼ cup of water in its place.) Bring to a lively simmer, lower the heat to low, cover, and cook for 25 minutes without lifting the lid. At 25 minutes, check the rice for both doneness and moisture. The rice and peas should be moist, but not super soupy. If the mixture is too dry, add additional liquid, a few tablespoons at a time, up to 1 cup. Return the lid and allow to cook for an additional 5 to 7 minutes.

Add the salt or soy sauce, stir, and taste, adding more as you see fit.

Serve hot with any or all fixins (you can even set it up as a fixins bar so folks can dress their Hoppin' John as they wish).

Makes about 6 servings

SMOKIN' HOPPIN' JOHN

Plan B: Hoppin' John with Dried Peas

▌ The big difference with Plan B is soaking and cooking the peas before you do anything else.

YOU'LL NEED:

2 cups dried black-eyed peas,
  soaked for at least 2 hours in
  enough water to cover, and
  drained
1 teaspoon salt

HERE'S WHAT YOU DO:

In a large stockpot, combine the soaked peas and about 4 cups of water. Bring to a lively simmer over medium-high heat. Cook at a hard boil for about 5 minutes, then lower the heat, cover, and simmer, until the beans are tender to the bite. This could take up to 1 hour.

Season with the salt and add more as needed. Going forward, you use the same ingredients as listed for the frozen pea version, just in a slightly different order.

Add the minced chipotle and smoked paprika and stir to combine.

Add the rice, plus 1 additional cup of water, plus the beer (if using), return the lid, and cook for 20 minutes over medium-low heat, without lifting the lid.

Meanwhile, in a skillet, heat the oil over medium heat and cook the onion and garlic until slightly softened, about 5 minutes. Season with salt and pepper.

Lift the lid off the bean pot. The rice and peas should be moist, but not super soupy. Add the onion mixture. Stir to combine and taste for salt and other seasonings.

Serve as originally suggested.

SKILLET CORN BREAD

My husband is from Kentucky, and he swears corn bread ain't corn bread if it contains even a smidgen of sugar. I played around with several versions of this Southern classic, and this Yankee girl has decided that a little bit of sugar goes a long way in the chemistry department. You don't taste the sugar in the recipe below, but it helps to balance out a fairly salty and acidic batter. If, like him, you remain unconvinced, keep the batter sugar free and go on your merry way. Life is too short to be quibbling over a teaspoon of sugar.

KITCHEN NOTES: I highly recommend using a cast-iron skillet. Of course you can use a baking dish, but the results will be denser and cakier. On that note, a smaller (9-inch) skillet will yield cakier results; a larger (11- or 12-inch) skillet will deliver thinner, crisper results. Bottom line: Any way you do it will be delicious.

INGREDIENTS

1½ cups cornmeal (preferably stone ground, which yields more character)

½ teaspoon salt

1 teaspoon baking soda

1 teaspoon baking powder

1 teaspoon sugar (optional)

2 tablespoons butter

1 large egg, beaten lightly

1½ to 2 cups buttermilk

HERE'S WHAT YOU DO:

Preheat the oven to 450°F.

In a medium-size mixing bowl, combine the cornmeal, salt, baking soda, baking powder, and sugar (if using).

Place the butter in a skillet and heat in the oven until the butter just begins to bubble, 3 to 5 minutes.

Meanwhile, add the egg to the dry ingredients and then pour in 1½ cups of the buttermilk. With a fork, whisk together, then switch to using a wooden spoon to combine. If the batter seems dry, add more buttermilk (which lends a custardy result).

Remove the skillet from the oven and immediately pour the batter on top of the sizzling butter. Return to the oven. Bake until golden on top, 15 to 20 minutes.

Remove from the oven, slice the corn bread into wedges, and dig in, with or without butter or honey (or if you live in the South, sorghum syrup!).

Makes 6 servings

KOD'S QUICKIE COLLARDS

Ⓥ

Most folks assume you need to set aside hours to cook up a pot of greens, and I'm urging you not to believe the hype. Many of us grew up eating green vegetables cooked until no longer recognizable, which is probably why they tasted so terrible. When trimmed of the tough ribs and stems (which do take a long time to soften), collard leaves need just about 30 minutes in a seasoned liquid to relax and make you forget all about the traditional ham hock—and unrecognizable veg—of yesteryear.

KITCHEN NOTES: The greens may be sandy and require a few washings. The reason behind the smaller strips is so the collards can cook more quickly (ergo the "quickie" claim).

INGREDIENTS

3 tablespoons vegetable oil

1 medium-size onion, chopped finely

2 cloves garlic, minced

½ small fresh chile pepper of your choice, seeded and diced, or ½ teaspoon crushed red pepper flakes (fresh will yield spicier results)

1 teaspoon smoked paprika

2 pounds collard greens, trimmed of stems and middle ribs and cut into 2 x 4-inch strips (about 6 cups)

4 cups water or veg stock (Rapunzel no-salt bouillon cubes are a personal favorite)

Soy sauce

Ground black pepper

Cider vinegar (optional)

HERE'S WHAT YOU DO:

In a heavy-bottomed pot, heat the oil over medium heat. Add the onion, garlic, and chile pepper and cook until the onion is translucent, about 5 minutes. Stir in the smoked paprika; it's okay for the mixture to be pasty.

Add the greens to the pot and allow to wilt. Using a pair of tongs, turn the greens and coat with the aromatics. Add the liquid gradually—to barely meet the level of the greens. If the greens are properly submerged and you have leftover liquid, reserve it for later if necessary. Bring to a lively simmer, then lower the heat and coax the greens into submission.

Cook until the greens arrive at your desired tenderness. They may be done in 25 minutes, but it's okay to go until 40 minutes or so. See what you think.

Season with soy sauce (go gradually and taste), pepper, and if using, a spritz of cider vinegar.

Makes 4 to 5 side-dish servings

BROCCO MAC & CHEESE

KIDDO

This Southern comfort classic makes room for a wholesome addition of broccoli, the green spear that so many picky eaters love to hate (you know who you are).

If you're thinking this will be a DIY replica of the goopy stuff from the infamous blue box, think again. This is the real deal, with a proper Mornay sauce that screams *cheese*, not *cheez*.

I love teaming this dish with stewed tomatoes and braised collard greens (page 149), two quintessentially Southern sides. The tomatoes cut the fat in the mac and the mac sops up all those savory juices, both red and green.

A FEW MEAL-PLANNING TIPS: Make the mac first. While it's in the oven, whip up the collard greens. The stewed tomatoes, which take a mere 12 minutes to throw together, can be done just before serving. If the mac is done early, turn off the oven, cover the dish with foil, and keep warm in the oven.

INGREDIENTS

2 cups elbow macaroni

2¼ teaspoons salt

1 teaspoon vegetable oil

1 to 1½ cups broccoli florets (depending on your love for broccoli)

3 tablespoons butter

3 tablespoons all-purpose flour

2½ cups whole or low-fat milk

1½ teaspoons dry mustard

¼ teaspoon ground black pepper

¼ teaspoon freshly ground nutmeg

¼ teaspoon cayenne

2½ cups grated cheese (cheddar, Gruyère, aged Gouda)

¼ to ½ cup dried bread crumbs (seasoned with ¼ teaspoon dried thyme and ½ teaspoon salt)

HERE'S WHAT YOU DO:

Preheat the oven to 350°F. Grease the sides of a 3-quart glass or ceramic baking dish (or two smaller baking dishes).

Bring 2 quarts of water and 1 teaspoon of the salt to a boil. Cook the macaroni until al dente, about 5 minutes. Using a strainer, skimmer, or sieve with a handle, remove the pasta from the water in batches and transfer to a colander. (Do not pour away the cooking liquid; you will need it to cook the broccoli.) Drain the pasta and transfer to a mixing bowl. Drizzle the vegetable oil over the pasta and toss to coat, so that the pasta stays lubricated while it waits.

Add the broccoli to the boiling water, and cook 3 for 4 minutes, then drain. Allow the broccoli to cool slightly, then cut into smaller pieces if necessary. You want it to be comparable in size to the macaroni.

Season the broccoli with ¼ teaspoon of the salt. Combine the broccoli with the macaroni and stir for even distribution. Transfer to the greased baking dish.

In a medium-size saucepan, melt the butter over medium-low heat. Add the flour, and with a wooden spoon, stir quickly to combine and form a roux. Continue to stir, and cook for about 1 minute, making

BROCCO MAC & CHEESE

HERE'S WHAT
YOU DO:

continued

sure that any flour lumps disappear. The roux will be a golden yellow color.

Add the milk, mustard, remaining 1 teaspoon of salt, pepper, nutmeg, and cayenne and stir to combine. Cook over medium-low heat, stirring regularly with a wooden spoon to make sure the milk does not scald, until the mixture is thickened. The mixture is ready when you can run a prominent streak along the back of the spoon with your finger. Add the cheese, and stir or whisk constantly until the mixture is smooth and free of lumps.

Pour the cheese sauce over the macaroni mixture to cover evenly. Top it off with the bread crumbs.

Place the dish in the oven and bake for about 30 minutes, until the cheese begins to bubble at the edges. To crisp up the bread crumb topping, place the dish under the broiler for about 1 minute. Remove from the oven and allow to cool slightly.

Makes about 6 servings

STEWED TOMATOES

INGREDIENTS

1 to 2 tablespoons olive oil

½ medium-size onion, chopped

1 to 2 cloves garlic, minced

½ bell pepper, seeded and chopped finely

1 (15-ounce) can whole or crushed plum tomatoes, including juices

Hot sauce of choice

Salt and ground black pepper

¼ cup of chopped fresh herbs (e.g., parsley or thyme in the winter, basil in the summer) (optional)

HERE'S WHAT YOU DO:

Pour the oil into a medium-size saucepan and heat over medium heat. Add the onion, garlic, and bell pepper and cook until the onion is somewhat softened, about 4 minutes. Add the tomatoes and stir to combine. Bring to a lively simmer, then lower the heat and cook at a simmer, covered.

Within 10 minutes or so, the tomatoes will start to soften and break down; use the back of a wooden spoon to help the process. Cook until the mixture reaches your desired consistency and season to taste with hot sauce and salt and pepper. If the tomatoes were packaged with salt, season sparingly.

Makes about 2 cups

WINTER VEG & CILANTRO "CURRY" WITH DUMPLINGS

The inspiration for this one-pot extravaganza is a chicken cilantro curry from Indian cooking doyenne Madhur Jaffrey. I've recreated her spicy green gravy to team up with a mix of root vegetables, which surrender into melty, aromatic morsels. Whiffs of the pot are strongly encouraged.

The crown jewel is a cloak of savory dumplings, an unlikely element atop Indian-spiced fare, but it really works, elevating this dish to meat-loving levels.

KITCHEN NOTES: It's a good idea to get all the mise en place done before firing up the pot.

INGREDIENTS:

Curry

¼ cup vegetable oil

1 medium-size onion, sliced in half through the root, and then sliced in thin half-moons

1 (2 x 1-inch) hunk fresh ginger, peeled and smashed in a mortar and pestle or pureed with ¼ cup water

5 cloves garlic, minced

½ habanero pepper, seeded and diced (for less spicy results, omit or reduce amount)

2 teaspoons ground cumin

1 teaspoon ground coriander

½ teaspoon ground turmeric

¼ teaspoon cayenne (for less spicy results, omit or reduce the amount)

1 teaspoon salt

HERE'S WHAT YOU DO:

In a deep stovetop casserole or Dutch oven, heat the oil over medium heat. Add the onion and cook until golden brown, about 12 minutes. It's okay if the onions get a little crispy, but don't let them burn. With a pair of tongs, remove the onions and set aside.

Add the ginger and you'll notice a sizzling reaction; with a wooden spoon, scrape any cooked-on bits at bottom of pan. Add the garlic, chile pepper, spices, and salt, and stir vigorously; the mixture will be somewhat pasty.

Return the onions to the pot and add the vegetables. With a wooden spoon, toss to coat and cook for 1 to 2 minutes over medium heat. Add the cilantro, lemon juice, and at least 2 cups of water. You want the liquid to barely cover the mixture.

Bring to a lively simmer, then lower the heat, cover, and simmer until vegetables are almost fork tender, 35 to 40 minutes. You're still looking for a little bit of a bite.

Meanwhile, make the dumplings: In a medium-size mixing bowl, combine the flour, baking powder, oregano, salt, and pepper.

In a smaller bowl, whisk the egg with the milk, butter, and minced onion (if using), until the egg is well integrated. Pour into the dry ingredients, and with a fork, stir gently so that the dough is just blended. It's okay if a few flour flecks are visible. The batter should be somewhat wet and sticky. Cover with plastic wrap and refrigerate for 30 minutes.

Preheat the oven to 400°F.

continues

WINTER VEG & CILANTRO "CURRY" WITH DUMPLINGS

INGREDIENTS

continued

4 cups vegetables, including any
    combination of the following:
Cauliflower, cut into florets
Sweet potato, cut into 1-inch
    pieces
Turnip, cut into ½-inch cubes
Butternut squash, peeled,
    seeded, and cut into
    1-inch pieces
2 bunches (about 3½ cups)
    cilantro, thoroughly washed,
    trimmed, and finely chopped
Juice of 1 lemon
Salt

INGREDIENTS:
Dumplings

1 cup all-purpose flour
2 teaspoons baking powder
1 teaspoon dried oregano
¾ teaspoon salt
¼ teaspoon ground black pepper
1 egg
½ cup milk
2 tablespoons butter, melted
¼ cup finely minced onion
    (optional)

HERE'S WHAT YOU DO:

continued

Taste the stew for salt and add as you see fit, and add more water if it looks dry.

Remove the dumpling batter from the fridge, and using two table-spoons, scoop the batter from bowl, using one spoon as the scoop and the other as the scraper to drop dumplings directly onto the stew.

Once the dumplings are added, bake the stew, uncovered, until the dumplings are golden, about 20 minutes. Remove from the oven, al-low to cool for a few minutes, and transfer with a spoon into bowls.

Makes about 6 servings

PENNE WITH TEMPEH, CARAMELIZED SHALLOTS, & GOAT CHEESE

XTRA

This dish marks my first foray into tempeh a few years ago and remains a mainstay at our casa. Short pasta gets the royal treatment, with cooked-down shallots, oozy goat cheese, and pan-fried tempeh that will make you wonder why you waited so long to try it. A serious goodie on a cold night. No penne in the house? No worries; this dish likes rotini, farfalle, and ziti, too.

INGREDIENTS

2 tablespoons soy sauce

2 teaspoons Dijon mustard

1 teaspoon sesame oil

1 clove garlic, minced

Juice of ½ lime

1 teaspoon hot sauce of choice (optional)

1 (8-ounce) package soy tempeh, cut into 1-inch strips

Vegetable oil, for pan-frying

2 to 3 shallot bulbs, sliced thinly (about ½ cup)

A few sprigs' worth of fresh thyme leaves, picked from stems

Salt and ground black pepper

12 ounces short pasta, such as penne, rotini, or ziti

3 ounces soft goat cheese

3 tablespoons grated Parmigiano-Reggiano cheese

A small handful of fresh flat-leaf parsley, chopped roughly

**Makes 4 hearty servings.
Reheats beautifully.**

HERE'S WHAT YOU DO:

Marinate the tempeh: In a small bowl, combine the soy sauce, mustard, sesame oil, garlic, lime juice, and hot sauce (if using). Place the tempeh in a shallow dish in a single layer and pour the marinade on top, ensuring complete coverage. Let the tempeh sit in marinade at room temperature for a minimum of 20 minutes, or in the fridge for up to several hours.

Remove the tempeh from the marinade and gently pat with paper towels to minimize splattering when frying in the hot oil.

Pour the oil to a depth of ¼ inch into a wide skillet and heat over medium heat. The oil is hot enough when it surrounds the tempeh with bubbles.

Gently add the tempeh and turn with tongs or a fork, until golden brown on both sides, about 3 minutes. Add more oil as necessary and allow to heat sufficiently before adding more tempeh. Transfer the tempeh to paper towels to drain and allow to cool slightly. Sprinkle with salt.

Lower the heat and add shallots. (Add more oil if need be, but be careful, you don't want shallot mixture to be overly greasy.) Cook over medium-low heat, so they soften, sweeten, and reduce but not brown, about 15 minutes. Add the thyme and salt and pepper to taste. Remove from heat.

Meanwhile, boil water for the pasta and prepare according to the package instructions.

Crumble the tempeh into small pieces and add to the shallot mixture, stirring to combine.

In the bottom of a serving bowl, place the goat cheese. Drain the pasta when ready (saving a few ounces of pasta water just in case the end result needs thinning) and pour into the bowl over the goat cheese. With two wooden spoons, coat the pasta with the melting goat cheese. Add the tempeh mixture and the parsley, stirring gently until well combined. Garnish with Parmigiano-Reggiano, if you like.

Serve hot.

GUMBO Z'HERBES (GREEN GUMBO)   XTRA DO

No matter your house of worship or whether you believe in a higher power, if you're ever been to New Orleans, you know that food is a religion unto itself, and that everyone is a devoted believer.

And if you've been there, you've likely had the pleasure of tucking into a bowl of gumbo, a feat of great gastronomic proportions traditionally brimming with seafood, chicken, or andouille sausage.

Unless, of course, it's Lent.

The morning after Mardi Gras, the most famous party of the year, is Ash Wednesday, the first day of Lent, a forty-day season of abstinence and reflection. For those who observe, this means doing without an object of pleasure or luxury, which, for many, means meat.

Enter Gumbo z'Herbes, a.k.a. green gumbo, a hearty stew made with the roux and all the fantastic Creole fixins but without a drop o' meat. But I'll bet you my weight in King Cake that you'll have a hard time believing there's no meat in here.

> **KITCHEN NOTES:** Get everything cleaned, chopped, and ready to go before you even touch that stovetop. There are four major components: stock (which can be made in advance), roux, trinity, and greens, which all come together in a soup pot. Make the stock first so that it's ready to go right after you've made the roux.
>
> The total active cooking time is about 90 minutes, including at least 45 minutes of preparation, so you may consider making this a day in advance, and simply reheat. Besides, this is the kind of dish that gets better on the second and third day.

Gumbo Stock

If you can't bear the thought of making your own stock, I like stock made from Rapunzel brand vegetable bouillon cubes, which actually tastes like vegetables.

INGREDIENTS

2 leeks, cleaned thoroughly, trimmed, and roughly chopped, or 1 large onion, unpeeled and quartered

3 cloves garlic, peeled but left whole

10 black peppercorns

A small handful of stripped parsley stems

4 cups cold water

HERE'S WHAT YOU DO:

Place all the ingredients in a large saucepan. Bring to a lively simmer, then lower the heat and cook over medium-low heat for 30 minutes. Strain, return to saucepan, and keep at a low simmer.

GUMBO Z'HERBES (GREEN GUMBO)

Roux

INGREDIENTS

½ cup (1 stick) butter or
   vegetable oil
½ cup all-purpose flour

HERE'S WHAT YOU DO:

In a large soup pot that will eventually encompass the entire gumbo, heat your choice of fat over high heat just until either smoke rises from the oil or the butter begins to actively bubble. Lower the heat to medium, add the flour, and stir with a tall, heavy-duty wooden spoon to completely blend.

Prepare to stand by the pot for at least 15 minutes (and as long as 30 minutes), constantly stirring the mixture as it changes color from blond to brown. The color you're looking for is a burnt orange, on its way to a shade of chocolate. You can go as dark as you like; the darker the roux, the more intense flavor, but it depends on patience and persistence.

Trinity

One of the foundations of classic French cooking is *mirepoix*, a mixture of diced carrots, onions, and celery, which is used to flavor sauces and soups. Its influences are felt deeply in Creole cooking, whose mirepoix is called the "Holy Trinity"—a mix of onion, celery, and bell pepper.

INGREDIENTS

½ medium-size onion, chopped
½ green bell pepper, seeded and
   chopped
2 celery stalks, chopped
2 to 3 cloves garlic, minced

HERE'S WHAT YOU DO:

Remove the roux from the heat and add the trinity, plus the garlic. Stir to combine, return the pan to medium heat, and cook until softened, about 10 minutes.

Slowly add the simmering stock to the roux, while stirring. Bring to a lively simmer, cover, and keep at a simmer.

continues

GUMBO Z'HERBES (GREEN GUMBO)

Gumbo seasonings and greens

INGREDIENTS

Fresh thyme leaves, picked from
   about 4 stems, or 1½
   teaspoons dried
1 teaspoon dried oregano
½ teaspoon cayenne
½ teaspoon smoked paprika
1 chipotle chile in adobo sauce,
   diced (add 1 more if you
   like heat)
¼ teaspoon white pepper
   (traditional for Creole cooking,
   but optional, in my opinion)
2 pounds (about 8 cups) mixed
   greens, cleaned, stemmed and
   roughly chopped, of any
   combination: collard, mustard,
   turnip, beet, kohlrabi, sweet
   potato, carrot tops, kale,
   chard, sorrel, dandelion,
   chicory—I recommend using
   at least three different kinds of
   greens
1½ to 2 teaspoons salt
Ground black pepper
4 cups cooked jasmine or
   basmati rice, made from
   1⅓ cups uncooked rice
   (For how to cook rice, see
   page 203)

HERE'S WHAT YOU DO:

Stir the thyme, oregano, cayenne, smoked paprika, chipotle chile, and white pepper (if using) into the roux-enriched stock.

Stir in the greens, which will gradually wilt and shrink. When the greens are wilted, add the salt gradually, and taste, adding more as you see fit, plus black pepper. Cook the gumbo over medium-low heat for about 40 minutes, until the greens reach your desired tenderness.

Serve over the rice.

Makes 6 to 8 servings

NONNA CATERINA'S PASTA E FAGIOLI (DO) (XTRA)

I used to work with Gio (short for Giovanni), whose parents are first-generation immigrants from Sicily. A few years ago, Gio was kind enough to share his mama's recipe for pasta e fagioli, a cross between a bean soup, stew, and sauce, with a little pasta thrown in for good measure.

Essentially, this version is a three-legume affair, simply seasoned with modest ingredients, then slightly diluted so that the pasta can cook in the beans.

What I like best about this dish is its "cook to order" quality—once cooked, the beans can be portioned out to accommodate the pasta quantity of your choice. Too many beans, you say? Freeze 'em for later.

INGREDIENTS

1 cup dried pinto beans

1 cup dried green or yellow split peas

2 tablespoons olive oil, plus more for seasoning

1 cup diced onion

4 carrots, washed, peeled, and diced

4 celery stalks, washed and diced

1 teaspoon dried oregano

¼ teaspoon cayenne

1 cup dried green lentils

4 cloves garlic—2 whole, 2 minced

2 sprigs fresh thyme, or 1 teaspoon dried

Parmigiano-Reggiano cheese rind (optional but nice)

1½ teaspoons salt

Ground black pepper

About 4 ounces pasta per serving (spaghetti broken into fourths; ditalini, which are shaped like short little tubes; or Spanish fideos)

HERE'S WHAT YOU DO:

Place the beans and peas (but not the lentils) in a soup pot and cover with water, plus a few inches. Soak for at least 4 hours or overnight at room temperature. (If your kitchen is very warm, place the beans in the refrigerator to minimize chances of fermentation.)

Drain the beans and set aside.

Place a heavy-bottomed soup pot over medium heat and heat 2 tablespoons of the oil. Add the onion, half of the carrots, and half of the celery. Cook over medium-low heat until the onions soften slightly and are aromatic, about 5 minutes. Stir in the oregano and cayenne.

Add the drained beans and lentils. With a wooden spoon, coat the beans with the aromatics and oil. Then cover the mixture with 4 to 6 cups of water (add 4 cups first, then add more water if the beans are not covered).

Add the whole garlic, thyme, and Parmigiano-Reggiano rind (if using). Bring to a boil and allow to cook at a rolling boil for 5 minutes. Lower the heat to a simmer and cover the pot.

Meanwhile, in a blender or food processor, puree the remaining carrots and celery, plus the minced garlic, adding a small amount of water (about ¼ cup) to moisten the mixture. Stir into the bean mixture.

Cook the mixture until tender to the bite, 45 to 60 minutes. Add the salt and pepper, taste, and add more as you see fit.

continues

NONNA CATERINA'S PASTA E FAGIOLI

INGREDIENTS

continued

¼ cup fresh parsley, chopped
    finely
Zest of 1 lemon
Grated Parmigiano-Reggiano
    cheese, for garnish (optional)

HERE'S WHAT YOU DO:

continued

ASSEMBLING YOUR PASTA E FAGIOLI:

For each serving, measure out 1 cup of the beans (4 servings = 4 cups).

For four servings, bring 4 cups of water (with ½ teaspoon of salt) to a boil. Stir in the beans, cover the pot, and allow the mixture to come to a boil. Add the pasta, stir to combine, and cover. Cook until the pasta is al dente, 9 to 11 minutes, but pay attention to the water level and add more water if the bean mixture is getting dry.

While the pasta cooks, prepare parsley and lemon zest for garnish.

Serve in individual bowls. Sprinkle with the parsley and lemon zest and add a drizzle of olive oil and grated Parmigiano-Reggiano (if using).

Once completely cooled, the beans can be frozen and then reheated and assembled with a new batch of pasta.

Makes at least 8 servings

WILTED GREENS IN A SKILLET VINAIGRETTE

INGREDIENTS

2 to 3 scallions, white and light
   green parts only, minced
2 tablespoons lemon juice
2 teaspoons Dijon mustard
¼ teaspoon salt
3 tablespoons olive oil
1 bunch (4 to 5 cups) quick-
   cooking greens (spinach,
   chard, tatsoi, lamb's quarters,
   frisée), washed thoroughly,
   dried, and stemmed

HERE'S WHAT YOU DO:

In a small mixing bowl, combine the scallions, lemon juice, mustard, salt, and olive oil and whisk with a fork until the salt is dissolved.

Pour the vinaigrette into a shallow skillet, at least 10 inches across, over medium heat. Tilt the pan, if necessary, to make sure the vinaigrette completely covers the surface. Add the greens, and with tongs, turn until well coated with the vinaigrette. Cook until wilted, 2 to 3 minutes.

Serve hot.

Makes 4 side-dish servings

POLENTA SQUARES WITH PUTTANESCA SAUCE & BROCCOLI RAAB

Sun-colored cornmeal is the basis of a porridge called polenta that has an amazing capacity and versatile nature. Cooked polenta (which everyone should try at least once) can be molded and cut into shapes, baked, pan-fried, or grilled. By itself, it's humble, unmemorable fare, but it's amazing how a little sauce and green veg can turn her into the belle of the ball.

This is hearty chow with a real pretty face.

KITCHEN NOTES: As with preparing risotto, this recipe requires your presence by the stovetop for about half an hour. As soon as polenta is poured into the baking sheet to set up, start the puttanesca sauce. Wait until polenta is baked to cook the broccoli raab, which takes less than 5 minutes.

INGREDIENTS:

Polenta Squares

7 cups water

2 teaspoons salt

2 cups stone-ground medium-grind cornmeal (also sold as corn grits or polenta)

½ cup grated Parmigiano-Reggiano cheese

Leaves picked from about 3 sprigs fresh thyme, or 1 teaspoon dried

2 tablespoons butter (optional but nice)

HERE'S WHAT YOU DO:

With cooking spray or an oil-dipped silicone brush, grease an aluminum baking sheet with a rim (about 13 x 18 inches or a similar size).

In a large heavy-bottomed pot, bring the water and salt to a boil. Drop the cornmeal into the pot a handful at a time, while whisking constantly and making sure the water continues to boil. It may take 3 to 5 minutes to complete this process.

As the cornmeal thickens, lower the heat and switch from a whisk to a heavy-duty wooden spoon. The polenta will become dense and may gurgle and erupt; stir regularly and you'll keep the eruptions to a minimum. The polenta will lighten up, and, as it approaches 30 minutes' cooking time, will begin to pull away from the sides of the pot.

Turn off the heat, add the cheese and thyme, and stir to combine. If using, stir in the butter at this time.

Preheat the oven to 350°F.

Pour the polenta onto prepared baking sheet, and with a rubber spatula, smooth out until it completely fills the pan. Allow it to cool, and set up/harden, 10 to 15 minutes.

Bake the polenta for 15 to 20 minutes, and longer if you want a crispier top crust. Turn off the heat and leave in the oven while your puttanesca sauce comes together.

POLENTA SQUARES WITH
PUTTANESCA SAUCE & BROCCOLI RAAB

INGREDIENTS:

Puttanesca Sauce

2 tablespoons vegetable oil

1 medium-size onion, diced

4 cloves garlic, minced

¼ teaspoon red pepper flakes or
   ground cayenne

½ teaspoon smoked paprika
   (optional but nice)

¼ cup red wine

2 cups tomato puree

2 tablespoons tomato paste
   dissolved in 4 tablespoons of
   water

Pinch of sugar

½ to ¾ cup good-quality pitted
   kalamata olives, chopped
   (amount depends on your olive
   preference)

¼ cup capers (optional)

Salt

Small handful of chopped fresh
   parsley (optional)

HERE'S WHAT YOU DO:

Heat the oil in a deep skillet over medium heat and add the onion. Cook until soft, about 5 minutes, then add the garlic and spices. Stir to combine and cook for about 1 minute.

Add the red wine and bring to a lively simmer, allowing to reduce, 1 to 2 minutes. Add the tomato puree and stir everything together. Once the mixture has returned to a lively simmer, add the tomato paste mixture and the sugar.

Lower the heat, add olives and capers (if using), and cook for 20 minutes. The sauce will reduce a bit. Taste first before seasoning with salt (olives and capers are salty). Turn off the heat and add the parsley.

continues

POLENTA SQUARES WITH PUTTANESCA SAUCE & BROCCOLI RAAB

INGREDIENTS:
Quickie Broccoli Raab

1 teaspoon salt, plus more
    to taste
1 bunch broccoli raab (also sold
    as rapini), washed and
    trimmed as needed
2 tablespoons olive oil
1 to 2 cloves garlic, smashed

HERE'S WHAT YOU DO:

Have ready a bowl of ice water. Bring 4 cups of water in a medium-size saucepan to a rapid boil. Add 1 teaspoon salt. Add the broccoli raab and cook for about 90 seconds. With tongs, remove from the pot and place in the bowl.

Drain and chop roughly.

Heat the oil in a skillet over medium heat and add the broccoli raab, turning with tongs. Add the garlic and allow it to season the oil and veg. Cook for about 2 minutes. Season with salt to taste.

ASSEMBLY

Cut the polenta into squares or triangles. Place one or two pieces on each plate. Spoon the sauce on top and finish with a few pieces of broccoli raab.

Makes 6 servings

GO-WITH-THE-FLOW POTPIE WITH CHEDDAR-BISCUITY CRUST

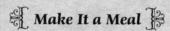

For several years, I've had a version of this recipe in my files, and over time I have revisited and revised the filling, much like a work in progress. To that end, I've come up with a filling that gives you both structure and room to experiment, so you can create your own works of art!

KITCHEN NOTES: There are three elements to this dish: crust, filling, and gravy. Make the crust first. Even though it requires little resting time, it's good to get it out of the way and have it ready to go when time to assemble the pie. You can make the crust in advance, but use it the same day, as the milk and cheese are perishable.

❧ Make It a Meal ❧

Is your appetite bigger tonight than anticipated? Consider a versatile side to round out your plate. Mix-and-matching encouraged! See Make It a Meal sidebar on page 26.

INGREDIENTS:

Crust

1 cup all-purpose flour

2 teaspoons baking powder

½ teaspoon salt

¼ teaspoon cayenne or ground chile pepper of choice

¼ teaspoon dry mustard

¼ teaspoon ground black pepper

½ teaspoon garlic powder, or 1 clove garlic, minced

3 tablespoons cold butter, diced (I've also done this with Earth Balance nondairy spread)

½ cup grated cheddar cheese

½ cup whole or 2% milk

HERE'S WHAT YOU DO:

You can make the dough in a food processor or completely by hand.

In the bowl of a food processor, combine the flour, baking powder, salt, cayenne, dry mustard, black pepper, and garlic powder. Use the "pulse" function to blend.

Add the butter and cut into the flour mixture so that it is integrated, with the texture of coarse meal. Add the cheese and pulse just a few times. Add the milk gradually, just until the dough holds together. It will be wet and sticky. Scoop out the dough into a bowl and cover with plastic wrap. Place in the fridge to relax for about 15 minutes.

By hand: Combine the dry ingredients in a large bowl. When adding the butter, cut it in with the tips of your fingers to achieve a coarse meal texture. With a rubber spatula, fold in cheddar, then add just enough milk for the dough to hold together.

Cover with plastic wrap and allow to relax in the fridge for about 15 minutes.

continues

GO-WITH-THE-FLOW POTPIE WITH CHEDDAR-BISCUITY CRUST

INGREDIENTS:

Filling

1½ teaspoon salt

2 medium-size thin-skinned waxy potatoes (Yukon Gold, Yellow Finn, red-skinned), peeled and cut into 1-inch cubes (about 2 cups)

A total of 4½ cups of additional vegetables, in any combination: denser longer-cooking options—cauliflower florets, diced sweet potato, parsnip, rutabaga or turnip, cubed winter squash; quicker-cooking options—thinly sliced mushrooms, fennel, bok choy, leeks

2 to 3 tablespoons vegetable oil

½ medium-size onion, diced (½ cup)

1 to 2 stalks celery, sliced thinly (about ¼ cup)

1 medium-size carrot, peeled and diced (¼ cup)

3 cloves garlic, minced

2 sprigs fresh thyme, or 1 teaspoon dried

¼ teaspoon ground black pepper

1 teaspoon dried oregano

Optional flavor zingers: 1 ounce white wine, 1 tablespoon soy sauce or sherry vinegar, or a few glugs of your favorite hot sauce

HERE'S WHAT YOU DO:

In a saucepan, bring 6 cups of water and 1 teaspoon of salt to a boil. Add the potatoes and other veg of the longer-cooking category and return to a boil. Cover and parboil for 5 minutes. Do this in batches if necessary, removing the veg with a skimmer or sieve and transferring to a medium-size bowl.

In a large skillet (12- to 14-inch wide is ideal), heat the oil and add the onion, celery, and carrot. Cook over medium heat until softened, about 6 minutes. Add the garlic and your selection of quick-cooking veg, plus the thyme, and cook for 3 to 6 minutes, depending on volume. Turn regularly with tongs to keep from sticking. Add the remaining ½ teaspoon of salt and pepper.

Add the parboiled long-cooking veg, turning with tongs until well mixed. Add the oregano, plus any of the optional flavor zingers at this time, cooking at a simmer for up to 2 minutes.

Taste for salt and season as you see fit. Turn off the heat.

GO-WITH-THE-FLOW POTPIE WITH CHEDDAR-BISCUITY CRUST

INGREDIENTS:

Gravy

2 cups potpie stock (Rapunzel no-sodium bouillon cubes are great in a pinch; DIY stock details follow)

2 tablespoons butter

2 tablespoons all-purpose flour

½ teaspoon salt

Ground black pepper

Note: if you're using commercial stock, check label for sodium before adding salt to your gravy.

HERE'S WHAT YOU DO:

Warm the stock in a medium-size saucepan and keep at a simmer. In another medium-size saucepan, melt the butter over medium-low heat. As the butter melts, add the flour, stirring vigorously until it is integrated with the fat. Continue to stir until the roux is a shade of blond, about 2 minutes.

Gradually pour the stock into the roux and stir to make sure the flour does not clump. Stir in the salt and pepper, taste, and reseason as you see fit.

ASSEMBLE THE PIE:

Preheat the oven to 350°F.

Grease a 9-inch pie plate or a baking dish of similar proportions.

Spoon the filling into prepared pan, then pour the gravy over the veggies.

Remove the dough from fridge and place on a lightly floured work surface. If the dough has been refrigerated for more than 1 hour, allow to warm up for at least 5 minutes.

Dust the top of the dough with flour, and with a rolling pin or your hands, gently roll or press into a circle about 10 or 11 inches across. If the dough resists because it's cold, let it relax for another few minutes. Gently lift the dough circle off the work surface and drape on top of the filling, trimming any excess and pinching the edges.

With a paring knife, make X incisions on top of dough to allow steam to release. Bake until the dough turns a golden color and the filling is bubbling, about 45 minutes.

Serve while hot.

Makes about 6 servings

Potpie Stock

INGREDIENTS

1 leek, cleaned thoroughly, trimmed of root and cut into fourths (dark green part can be used), or 1 medium-size onion, unpeeled and quartered

1 stalk celery, cleaned and cut into thirds

3 cloves garlic, peeled but left whole

10 black peppercorns

3 cups cold water

HERE'S WHAT YOU DO:

Place all the ingredients in a large saucepan. Bring to a lively simmer, then cook over medium-low heat for 30 minutes. Strain.

Makes about 2½ cups. (You may have a smidge left over.)

SICILIAN-STYLE ROASTED CAULIFLOWER WITH PASTA

DO **XTRA**

For years, I stayed away from cauliflower, as I had experienced it exclusively raw, which is funky, gritty, and hard to swallow. But I no longer despair because now I know what happens when those chalky-white florets spend some time in a hot oven. They transform into cream—well, not quite—but heady, almost sweet morsels that have changed my cauliflower tune forever. Wait till you get a load of this cauli combo—wine-soaked raisins, garlic, and pine nuts—tossed with short pasta.

INGREDIENTS

1 cup dark raisins

1 cup white wine you enjoy drinking

1 head white, green, or purple cauliflower (about 1 pound), cleaned, trimmed, and cut loosely into florets

2 to 3 tablespoons olive oil (use more if necessary)

1½ teaspoons salt

Ground black pepper

¼ cup pine nuts or chopped walnuts

4 cloves garlic, smashed

¼ to ½ cup plain bread crumbs

8 to 12 ounces short pasta, such as penne, farfalle, or gemelli

¼ to ½ cup grated Parmigiano-Reggiano cheese (optional but nice)

¼ cup chopped fresh parsley

HERE'S WHAT YOU DO:

Preheat the oven to 400°F.

In a small bowl, soak the raisins in the wine until they plump up, about 15 minutes.

Place the cauliflower in a 9 x 13-inch baking dish or something of similar size. Pour the olive oil on top of the florets, and with your hands, toss until the florets are generously slathered with oil. Season with ½ teaspoon of the salt and pepper to taste.

Add the raisins and wine, nuts, and garlic, and with your hands, mix to combine. Sprinkle bread crumbs generously on top.

Bake uncovered until fork tender, 40 to 45 minutes. After 20 minutes, check the liquid level; if the wine is completely evaporated, add a few tablespoons of water to keep the raisins from burning.

Meanwhile, bring at least 6 cups of water to a boil and add the remaining 1 teaspoon of salt. Add the pasta and cook until al dente, about 10 minutes. Drain and pour into a serving bowl. Pour the cauliflower and trimmings over the pasta and stir to combine.

Add Parmigiano-Reggiano, if using, and garnish with parsley.

Makes 4 servings

STIR-FRIED CABBAGE & CUMIN (OR CARAWAY)

What a delightful surprise is this zippy little number, a mouthful of crunch and seed-popping flavor from an ordinary head of green cabbage. Although caraway is a traditional cabbage partner, cumin seeds deliver zesty change to the old equation.

KITCHEN NOTES: With a paring knife, remove the core from the bottom of the cabbage, then cut the cabbage into more manageable chunks before slicing into julienne strips. The inner white layers tend to be tougher, FYI.

INGREDIENTS

3 tablespoons vegetable oil

2 cloves garlic, left whole but peeled and smashed slightly

1 medium-size head green cabbage, cored and julienned (5 to 6 cups)

1 medium-size leek, cleaned, white and light green parts only, sliced in half lengthwise and into half-moons

½ teaspoon salt

½ teaspoon cumin seeds, or 1 teaspoon caraway seeds

HERE'S WHAT YOU DO:

Heat the oil in a wide skillet or wok over medium-high heat. Add the garlic to flavor the oil, stirring to minimize burning. Add the cabbage and leek and stir immediately (or turn with tongs) until the veg are completely coated with oil. Add the salt and continue to stir the mixture to keep it from burning; you'll notice that the cabbage will reduce by about one-third.

After 5 minutes, the cabbage should be tender with slight crunch; cook for a few minutes longer (8 to 9 minutes, total) if you prefer a softer result. Just before you turn off the heat, add the seeds and stir to combine, allowing them to warm up and release their flavor.

Makes 4 servings

SHEPHERD'S PIE WITH CHARD-LENTIL FILLING `GF`

Looking for cozy cookin'? Dog-ear this page pronto. Curled up under a blanket of garlicky mashed is a lentil-chard filling that totally hits the spot. But wait, there's more: Your hunk o' pie gets extra love with a sultry caramelized onion gravy.

KITCHEN NOTES: Although this is a four-pot affair, it need not feel like a three-ring circus. First item of business: Get the lentils on the stove. While they're simmering, work on the onion gravy. While the gravy simmers, boil the potatoes for the mashed topping. Everything comes together in a pie plate.

❧ Make It a Meal ☙

Is your appetite bigger tonight than anticipated? Consider a versatile side to round out your plate. Mix-and-matching encouraged! See Make It a Meal sidebar on page 26.

INGREDIENTS

- 1 cup wine-braised lentils (details follow)
- 1½ cups onion gravy (details follow)
- 2 pounds medium-size potatoes (4 to 5 potatoes; my favorites are Yukon Gold or Yellow Finn), washed, trimmed/peeled as needed, and cut into quarters
- 2 teaspoons salt
- 3 cloves garlic, peeled but left whole
- 5 tablespoons olive oil
- Ground black pepper

HERE'S WHAT YOU DO:

Grease a 9-inch pie plate.

Fill a medium-size saucepan with 4 cups of water, and add the potatoes and salt. The water should just barely cover the potatoes. *This is important.*

Cover and bring to a boil. Add the whole garlic. Return the lid and cook until fork tender, about 30 minutes.

Preheat the oven to 350°F.

With a slotted spoon or skimmer, transfer the potatoes and garlic to a large mixing bowl and mash with a hand masher. Stir in the reserved cooking liquid as necessary to moisten the potatoes. Add 3 tablespoons of the olive oil and stir in vigorously with a wooden spoon. Taste for salt, pepper, and texture and season and stir accordingly; mashed potatoes should be smooth and well seasoned.

continues

SHEPHERD'S PIE WITH CHARD-LENTIL FILLING

INGREDIENTS

continued

3 to 4 cups chard (from 1 bunch),
    washed, stemmed, and
    chopped finely into "ribbons"
1 clove garlic, chopped roughly
¼ teaspoon freshly grated
    nutmeg
¼ cup grated Parmigiano-
    Reggiano cheese

HERE'S WHAT YOU DO:

continued

In a large skillet, heat the remaining olive oil over medium heat and cook the chard with the chopped garlic, until wilted, 3 to 5 minutes, regularly tossing with tongs to cook evenly. Stir in the nutmeg and season with more salt to taste, if needed. Transfer to a medium-size bowl.

Portion out 1 cup of the lentils (the rest is cook's treat) and stir into the chard until well combined.

Assemble the pie: Transfer the chard mixture to the greased pie plate. Top with the mashed potatoes, and with a rubber spatula, smooth the mash so that it's evenly distributed and completely covers the surface. Top off with grated Parmigiano-Reggiano.

Place the dish in the oven and heat through, 20 to 25 minutes. During the final 2 minutes of cooking, set the oven to the broil setting to brown the cheesy-mashed top.

Remove from the oven, slice into wedges, and eat hot with a ladleful of onion gravy.

Makes about 6 servings

SHEPHERD'S PIE WITH CHARD-LENTIL FILLING

INGREDIENTS:

Wine-Braised Lentils

1 tablespoon vegetable oil

½ cup onion, diced

¼ cup carrot, peeled and diced

1 sprig fresh thyme, or
   ½ teaspoon dried

½ cup dried brown or green
   lentils, rinsed (the smaller
   French *lentilles du Puy*, with a
   more refined texture, are my
   preference, but they're not
   always available. Use what you
   can find in your local market.)

2 tablespoons red wine you enjoy
   drinking

¾ to 1 cup water

¼ to ½ teaspoon salt

HERE'S WHAT YOU DO:

In a small saucepan, heat the oil over medium heat and add the onion, carrot, and thyme. Cook for about 5 minutes, until slightly softened. Add the lentils and stir to coat. Add the red wine (if using) and bring to a lively simmer. The wine will reduce a bit. Add ¾ cup of the water, return to a lively simmer, then lower the heat, cover and cook until fork tender, about 40 minutes. Check and add a little extra water if need be, to keep the lentils from drying out completely. Stir in ¼ teaspoon of the salt, taste, and add the remaining salt, if needed.

Makes 1½ cups. If you love these lentils, amounts may be doubled for a big pot that will keep for days and pair up seamlessly with your favorite grain.

SHEPHERD'S PIE WITH CHARD-LENTIL FILLING

INGREDIENTS:

Onion Gravy

3 tablespoons butter

2 cups onions, sliced thinly into half-moons

1 or 2 sprigs fresh thyme

1 tablespoon balsamic vinegar

2 cups water

1 tablespoon cornstarch dissolved in 1 tablespoon water

½ teaspoon salt

Pinch of sugar

1 teaspoon soy sauce

HERE'S WHAT YOU DO:

In a deep skillet, melt the butter over medium heat and add the onions and thyme. With tongs, toss to coat the onions with the butter and cook over medium-low heat, until softened, reduced, and jam-like, about 25 minutes.

Add the balsamic vinegar, stir, and cook for an additional 5 minutes.

Add the water and bring to a lively simmer. Reduce by half, about 15 minutes. Stir in the cornstarch mixture and cook for an additional 5 minutes; the gravy will continue to reduce. Stir in the salt and sugar, and taste. Finish off with the soy sauce.

Turn off the heat, cover, and gently reheat at a simmer, just before serving with pie.

Makes approximately 1½ cups

SLURPY PAN-ASIAN NOODLES

XTRA **KIDDO** **V**

Hang up the phone, put down the carry-out menu, and make these seriously chops-licking noodles instead. You'll probably have to duke it out over who gets lunch leftovers (if there are any left in the wok). By no means is this dish authentically Chinese or Japanese, but a tribute to both cuisines, incorporating ingredients and flavor combinations that have become favorites in my own kitchen. This is a one-pot meal, with ample slurping ops for four to five servings, but you can easily halve the amounts for two-plus eaters.

KITCHEN NOTES: The recipe calls for udon noodles, thick wheat-flour Japanese noodles that come in 8-, 9-, and 12-ounce packages and are available in most conventional supermarkets and Asian groceries. Weigh or measure out the noodles before cooking. While you're out shopping, look for Shaoxing rice wine, from China. Gluten-free option: 100 percent buckwheat noodles.

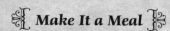

Make It a Meal

Is your appetite bigger tonight than anticipated? Consider a versatile side to round out your plate. Mix-and-matching encouraged! See Make It a Meal sidebar on page 26.

INGREDIENTS

16 to 18 ounces udon noodles

⅔ cup soy sauce

8 teaspoons Shaoxing rice wine, or dry sherry, sake, or vermouth

1 tablespoon hoisin sauce

6 tablespoons vegetable oil

1 (2 x 1-inch) hunk fresh ginger, peeled and minced

6 cloves garlic, minced

½ fresh chile pepper of choice, seeded and minced (optional)

HERE'S WHAT YOU DO:

Cook the noodles in at least 8 cups of boiling water. The noodles will be ready in 8 to 9 minutes. Don't overcook; they will get really mushy and gross. Drain and rinse under running cold water. Set aside.

Measure the soy sauce and set aside 2 tablespoons. In a small bowl, combine remaining soy sauce, rice wine, and hoisin sauce. Stir until the hoisin is dissolved.

In a wok, heat the oil over medium-high heat. Cook the ginger, garlic, and chile pepper (if using), stirring with a wooden spoon to keep from sticking, about 30 seconds.

Add the carrots and pepper (which take a bit longer to cook than the bok choy), and cook for 2 to 3 minutes.

continues

SLURPY PAN-ASIAN NOODLES

A total of approximately 10 cups
   of quick-cooking veg; my
   suggestions follow:
2 to 3 medium-size carrots,
   peeled and cut into 2-inch
   matchsticks
2 red, orange, or yellow bell
   peppers, seeded and julienned
6 bunches (about 6 cups) baby
   bok choy, thoroughly rinsed
   and sliced into 1-inch pieces
   (Larger bok choy or another
   kind of choy is perfectly fine;
   the baby choy yields the
   mildest and most tender
   results, in my opinion.)
Other veg options: chopped green
   beans, snow peas, shredded
   cabbage, small broccoli
   florets, thinly sliced
   mushrooms

1 tablespoon gomasio
2 teaspoons sesame oil
Optional garnishes: 3 chopped
   scallions and ¼ cup chopped
   cilantro

Add the bok choy, and with tongs, toss to mix with the other vegeta-bles; it will shrink quickly and soften. Cook for about 2 minutes.

Season the vegetables with remaining 2 tablespoons of soy sauce and the gomasio. Transfer to a medium-size bowl.

Pour the soy sauce mixture into the wok and heat over medium heat. It will quickly come to a lively simmer. Add the drained noodles, and with tongs, coat with the sauce. Gently stir the mixture until the noo-dles are hot, at least 2 minutes.

Return the vegetables to the wok and stir everything together until well combined. Drizzle with sesame oil, and if using, top off with your desired garnishes.

Serve immediately while hot.

Makes 4 to 5 servings

Wild Cards
Menus for All Seasons

The following four menus are appropriate at any time of the year, whenever you've got a hankering. Although seasonal variations are offered, the choice is all yours.

PIZZA DOUGH

KIDDO

When I asked my pal Jim if he'd like to try out my recipe for pizza dough, he warned me that unless chocolate chip cookies are on the menu, he and baking don't mix. I believe the word *fail* came up several times in our conversation.

His arm reasonably twisted, Jim took on my pizza dough challenge like a champ, this time with a directive to bake his pie not on a pizza stone but on an inverted baking sheet.

Within 24 hours, he resurfaced. The e-mailed verdict: "OKAY DUDE I MADE PIZZA!!!!!! I FREAKIN DID IT AND IT WAS SOOOOOO YUMMY."

What Jim is trying to say is, if his doughy thumbs can make pizza dough, yours can, too. Consider making a batch of dough in advance, keep in the fridge, and a two-pizza supper can be ready in about 40 minutes.

INGREDIENTS

1 cup water
1 (¼-ounce) envelope active dry yeast, or 2¼ teaspoons from a jar
Pinch of sugar
About 3 cups all-purpose flour
1 teaspoon salt
1 tablespoon olive oil
Cornmeal, for dusting pans

Makes 2 small (10- to 12-inch) pizzas or 1 large (16-inch) pizza

---

HERE'S WHAT YOU DO:

Heat the water until its temperature reaches 100°F—this is not even close to boiling!—and pour into a small bowl. Sprinkle the yeast, sugar, and 1 tablespoon of the flour over the water. With a fork, stir until dissolved, cover the bowl, and allow it to sit at room temperature until the mixture is slightly foamy, about 15 minutes.

In a large bowl (think wide and shallow versus tall and narrow), place 1 cup of the flour, the salt, and the olive oil and stir to combine with a rubber spatula or heavy wooden spoon. Add the yeast mixture and stir until just combined. Add the remaining flour, ½ cup at a time, stirring between flour additions. You are looking for a soft, sticky dough that is just pulling away from the sides of the bowl. Depending on the weather (humidity, heat), the amount of flour used will vary between 2½ and 3½ cups total. It's unnecessary to use the maximum amount.

Lightly dust a work surface with flour and pour the mixture out of the bowl onto the work surface.

Begin kneading the dough in the following manner: punch gently but firmly, fold in half, and turn (rotate 15 minutes on your imaginary clock, or one-quarter turn). Make *punch*, *fold*, *turn* your mantra until your dough becomes a smooth, soft, springy ball, as smooth as a baby's bottom. The entire process should take about 6 minutes.

PIZZA DOUGH

Lightly oil a large bowl and place the dough in the bowl, turning to coat. Cover the bowl with a towel or plastic wrap and place in a warm spot, away from drafts. (Alternatively, place in a lightly greased soup pot with a lid.) Let rise until doubled, about 1 hour.

At this point, the risen dough may be wrapped in plastic and refrigerated (or frozen) for later use. (Thaw frozen dough in the fridge and allow chilled dough to warm at room temperature for at least 15 minutes before rolling and shaping.)

Meanwhile, make the filling (details follow).

For two pizzas, cut the ball of dough in half and work with one half at a time. (Alternatively, you can make one 16-inch-diameter pizza. Just make sure you have a pan wide enough.)

Preheat the oven to 500°F.

Wipe the work surface clean of dough scraps, then dry thoroughly before rolling out the dough. Dust the work surface with flour. With your hands, gently press the dough into a thick disk. After every few motions, rotate the dough one-quarter turn. With your hands or a rolling pin, roll out the dough from the center, continuing to rotate, being careful not to tear the dough. Roll to your pizza's desired thinness and shape. At this point, I like to use a tape measure or ruler to help keep track of width. My preference is a 12-inch circle, about ¼ inch thick, but it's cook's choice. If rectangular pizza is your thing, go for it.

Dust a pizza pan, stone, or bottom side of a baking sheet with cornmeal, for texture. Fold your dough in half and carefully lift onto the baking surface. Adjust the shape of the dough and begin adding the toppings of your choice (I like to make a dough border by folding the edges and making a thumb indentation all around). A final addition of a sprinkling of salt just before baking is recommended.

Bake until the dough makes a hollow sound when you tap the crust and is golden in color. A 12-inch pie takes 12 to 15 minutes, but varies by oven. The bottom of crust should be golden.

Transfer the pizza to a cutting board and cut into slices with a serrated knife or pizza slicer.

continues

GOOD OLE MARINARA & MOZZARELLA (AND ARUGULA AND LEMON, IF YOU'RE SMART) TOPPING

This topping is dedicated to my dear friend Tai, who encouraged me several years ago to try pizza her way: as soon as it comes out of the oven, garnish the pizza with raw arugula, a squeeze of lemon, and a drizzle of olive oil. The girl's a genius; her peppery salad idea with an ad hoc vinaigrette takes this plain ole marinara topping to a new level.

The amounts below are enough for two 10- or 12-inch pizzas. If you plan on making one pizza, you may halve amounts accordingly.

INGREDIENTS

2 cups tomato puree (straight from a jar, or whole tomatoes from a 28-ounce can that you puree yourself)

1 clove garlic, smashed

1 teaspoon dried oregano

1 teaspoon tomato paste

½ teaspoon salt (Note: taste the puree before adding, if it was processed with salt)

Ground black pepper

¼ teaspoon red pepper flakes (optional)

2 cups shredded mozzarella cheese (You may also use fresh mozzarella balls or bigger pieces that you slice yourself. Estimate about 1 pound in water for both pies.)

½ cup grated Parmigiano-Reggiano cheese

Optional but really good add-ons: ½ bunch (about 2 cups) arugula, cleaned and dried; squeeze of ½ lemon; a drizzle of olive oil

HERE'S WHAT YOU DO:

Pour the tomato puree into a medium-size saucepan and heat over medium heat. Add the garlic, oregano, and tomato paste. Stir to make sure the paste has been absorbed into the puree.

Bring to a simmer (this helps sauce reduce a bit), then lower the heat and stir to make sure the sauce is not sticking. The sauce can be ready in 15 minutes or can simmer for longer, up to ½ hour. It will reduce by about one-fourth, which gives you at least ¾ cup of puree per pizza.

Taste for salt and season accordingly, and add the black pepper and/or red pepper flakes. Remove the garlic clove.

Ladle the sauce into middle of dough circle, and with a rubber spatula, spread until the surface is completely covered. Place the mozzarella (1 cup per 12-inch pizza) on top of the sauce. Remember, the cheese will spread as it melts in the oven, so don't worry if it seems as if your pizza is not amply covered with cheese.

Place in the oven and bake as directed for the pizza dough.

When the pizza is done, garnish it with Parmigiano-Reggiano and, if using, the arugula. Squeeze the lemon all over the greens and/or drizzle with olive oil if you wish. Now go eat!

APPLE, BLUE CHEESE, & CARAMELIZED ONION TOPPING

This is a rich filling. The amounts below are enough for one 12-inch pizza. Double if you are making two pizzas.

INGREDIENTS

2 tablespoons vegetable oil

1 tablespoon butter (or forego the butter and use oil only)

2 medium-size onions, cut in half through the root, and sliced thinly into half-moons

1 teaspoon dried thyme, or 1 sprig fresh

½ teaspoon salt

1 large, firm apple that rocks your world, peeled, quartered, and cut into ½-inch slices (avoid juicy apples such as Honeycrisp, Macintosh, and Empire)

Needles from 1 sprig fresh rosemary, chopped finely

⅓ cup of your favorite blue cheese (keep in fridge until ready to use)

¼ cup grated Parmigiano-Reggiano (optional)

HERE'S WHAT YOU DO:

Caramelize the onions: In a 10-inch skillet, heat the oil, and butter if using, over medium heat and add the onions. Stir in the thyme and allow the onions to shrink and sweeten. Cook over medium-low heat, occasionally stirring to keep from burning. In 30 minutes, the onions will gradually darken and soften. Stir in the salt and turn off the heat. You'll have just about 1 cup of onions.

In a small bowl, combine the apples and rosemary, until well mixed.

To assemble the pizza, spread the onions on the surface of the dough, until it is completely covered. Remove the blue cheese from the fridge and break into small pieces and "dot" the pizza.

Top the pizza with the apple mixture and drizzle with olive oil.

Place in the oven and bake as directed for the pizza dough recipe.

Garnish with Parmigiano-Reggiano just before serving.

MUSHROOM-ROSEMARY TOPPING

Before I developed a pesky mushroom allergy, I loved them on pizza, particularly when paired with rosemary and onion. Make this so I can live vicariously through you!

KITCHEN NOTES: The amounts below make enough for two small (10- to 12-inch) pizzas or 1 large (16-inch) pizza.

INGREDIENTS

3 tablespoons olive oil

1 pound mixed mushrooms, sliced thinly

½ medium-size red onion, or 1 large shallot bulb, sliced thinly

1 to 2 cloves garlic, minced

Needles from 1 sprig fresh rosemary, chopped finely, or 1 teaspoon dried

½ teaspoon salt

Ground black pepper

2 cups of any of the following cheeses: mozzarella (shredded or sliced thinly), smoked mozzarella (sliced thinly), fontina (sliced thinly)

½ cup grated Parmigiano-Reggiano cheese

HERE'S WHAT YOU DO:

Heat the oil in a large skillet over medium heat. Add the mushrooms and cook over medium heat, allowing to brown, 5 to 7 minutes. Add the onion, stirring to mix with the mushrooms, and cook for about 3 minutes.

Stir in the garlic and rosemary and cook for 1 to 2 minutes, adding 2 tablespoons of water if the mixture is sticking. Add the salt and season with the pepper to taste.

Cover the dough with your choice of cheeses, followed by the mushroom topping.

Place in the oven and bake as directed for the pizza dough recipe.

Garnish with Parmigiano-Reggiano just before serving.

VEGGIE FRIED RICE BOWL

We've all been there: Tonight's the night you've got just 20 minutes to put dinner on the table, and the box of cereal is looking better as the clock ticks.

With some cold cooked rice on hand (make a pot the night before), you can put that cereal to shame and whip up the bestest and fastest food there is.

Should greasy take-out containers come to mind, let it go. This version defies old stereotypes and delivers light, bright results, a wokful of colorful veg that still have their crunch and chile peppers that still have their punch. In a hectic household, this dish is a dream, which is why it's earned year-round, go-to status in our kitchen.

KITCHEN NOTES: This dish requires cold cooked rice, so plan to make ahead, at least 4 hours in advance. Chop and prep all ingredients before even thinking of turning on the wok.

INGREDIENTS

2 tablespoons vegetable oil

3 teaspoons sesame oil

2 large eggs, beaten (Plan B: ½ cup toasted chopped cashews)

½ cup shallots, diced (about 2 bulbs)

Fresh chile peppers, seeded and minced (Use what works best for your heat tolerance; I start with ½ teaspoon and add more depending on my mood.)

1 tablespoon minced garlic (2 to 3 cloves)

1 cup diced carrots (about 2 carrots) or chopped fresh green beans

½ cup diced red bell pepper

4 cups cold cooked rice (about 1⅓ cups uncooked rice)

1 cup mixed celery, diced, and baby bok choy, chopped into 1-inch pieces, or use one or the other

¼ cup soy sauce

¼ cup chopped fresh cilantro, for garnish

HERE'S WHAT YOU DO:

Heat a wok (I use a 14-inch flat-bottomed variety) or deep skillet over high heat.

Place 1 tablespoon of the vegetable oil, 1 teaspoon of the sesame oil, and the eggs in the wok. Tilt the wok so that the eggs cover the entire surface, making it thin as a pancake. Cook for about 45 seconds; the egg will set quickly. With a thin-edged flipper or tongs, fold the egg in half and transfer to a cutting board. Cut into thin strips.

Add the remaining tablespoon of vegetable oil, followed by the shallots, chile pepper, and garlic and stir-fry for about 20 seconds. Add the carrots and bell pepper, lower the heat to medium, and stir-fry for an additional 2 to 3 minutes, until the mixture begins to soften.

Add the rice and the celery mixture. With a wooden spoon, break up any clumped rice as needed. Add the soy sauce and stir well, and cook for an additional 3 minutes or so. Stir in the egg strips.

Turn off the heat. Stir in the cilantro, if using, and drizzle the remaining 2 teaspoons of sesame oil.

Note: You may make this dish without eggs. If so, eliminate the teaspoon of sesame oil at the beginning of the recipe and proceed with 2 tablespoons of vegetable oil, going straight to adding the vegetables and aromatics. Stir in the cashews just at the end, before serving.

Makes three to four 2-cup servings

GRILLED CHEESE & SOUP FOR ALL SEASONS

When life throws you daggers, sometimes the only thing that'll save the day is a grilled cheese sandwich. A few years ago, while working at washingtonpost.com, I wrote a piece called "The Tao of Grilled Cheese," which explains the "You had me at hello" allure of this universally beloved sandwich: "The most simple and humble of hot sandwiches is what makes me feel most at home, when time stands still, when I think of nothing but the alchemy that results from two slices of ordinary bread, a few hunks of cheese and the heat of a skillet. It is the grilled cheese that has walked alongside me throughout my life."

So I present my grilled cheese, jazzed up with a little Dijon mustard and olive oil in place of butter. Naturally, soup is on the menu, because when there's grilled cheese, there's soup, just like when we were kids. There are three to choose from, depending on the season, and all can be made in advance.

GRILLED CHEESE TEMPLATE

INGREDIENTS FOR 1 SANDWICH

2 slices bread (white, rye, whole wheat, pumpernickel, or raisin)

1 to 2 ounces of your favorite cheese, sliced thinly (cheddar, Gruyere, Havarti, Monterey Jack, Gouda, or Gorgonzola, to name a few)

1 teaspoon Dijon mustard

2 to 3 teaspoons olive oil

Optional flavor zingers: Pickled peppers or cucumbers, thinly sliced red onion, sliced tomato

Suggested crispy accompaniment: kale chips (page 57)

HERE'S WHAT YOU DO:

Arrange the cheese on one piece of bread. On the second slice, spread the mustard. Add any optional flavor zingers at this time. Place the mustard-coated slice on top of cheese-covered slice and press together.

Over medium heat, heat the oil in a small skillet or on a griddle, tilting so that the oil is evenly distributed. Place the sandwich in the skillet and cook until golden brown on the bottom, 3 to 4 minutes, adjusting the heat if the oil begins to smoke.

With a spatula, turn the sandwich onto its second side, and weigh down top with a sandwich press or a small lid (what's important is the weight). This helps facilitate the melting of the cheese before the bread begins to burn. Cook until the sandwich has arrived at desired melty gooiness and the second side is golden brown.

Slice in half and eat while hot.

POTATO-LEEK-PARSLEY PUREE

Ⓥ

INGREDIENTS

2 cloves garlic, peeled

1 leek, cleaned thoroughly, root
and dark green top removed,
and sliced into ½-inch rounds

4 medium-size potatoes (such as
Yukon Gold or Yellow Finn),
cleaned, quartered, and rid of
blemishes

2 teaspoons salt

2 sprigs fresh thyme

6 black peppercorns

½ cup fresh flat-leaf parsley,
chopped

Ground black pepper

HERE'S WHAT YOU DO:

In a medium-size saucepan, combine the garlic, leek, potatoes, salt, and thyme. Place the peppercorns in cheesecloth or an herb sachet and add to the pot. Cover the ingredients with just enough water to barely cover the vegetables. This is important.

Bring to a lively simmer and cook until the potatoes are tender, about 15 minutes. Do not cover, or the beautiful green leeks will turn an ugly army brown. Take off the heat. Remove the peppercorn bundle.

With a handheld stick blender, puree the contents of the pot until well blended. Alternatively, puree in a blender or food processor, in batches. Add the parsley and you will see beautiful green flecks transform the soup. Season with the pepper to taste.

Serve immediately. Can also be made in advance and reheated. Nice when served with crusty bread or croutons.

Makes 4 servings

BROCCOLI SOUP

V

INGREDIENTS

3 tablespoons vegetable oil

1 leek, cleaned, root and dark green woody top removed, sliced thinly

1 medium-size onion, peeled and chopped

2 cloves garlic, peeled and minced

2 medium-size potatoes, cleaned, peeled of blemishes and quartered

1 pound broccoli, florets and stems, chopped into 1-inch chunks

2 teaspoons salt

A few sprigs fresh thyme, or 1 teaspoon dried

About 6 cups water or veg stock

½ teaspoon curry powder, or more to taste

Pinch of cayenne

Ground black pepper

Optional add-ons: Toasted slabs of country bread rubbed with garlic; a sprinkling of Parmigiano-Reggiano cheese

HERE'S WHAT YOU DO:

Heat the oil in a medium-size saucepan over medium heat. Add the leek and onion and cook until the onion is slightly softened, about 7 minutes. Add the garlic and cook for 1 minute.

Add the potatoes, broccoli, and salt, then enough of the water to barely cover the vegetables. Add the thyme, if using. Bring to a boil, then lower the heat and cook at a simmer, until the veggies are fork tender, about 20 minutes.

Remove the thyme sprigs from the pot and take the pot off the heat. With a handheld stick blender, puree the soup directly in the pot. Alternatively, puree in a blender or food processor, in batches. (Pass the puree through a food mill, if you have one, for an even finer result.)

Return the puree to the pot and season with the pepper and spices. Stir to combine. Simmer over low heat until ready to serve and add the optional add-ons at that time.

Makes 4 servings

CREAMY TOMATO SOUP

INGREDIENTS

1 tablespoon butter

2 tablespoons olive oil

1 large onion, chopped

3 to 4 cloves garlic, minced

2 teaspoons ground cumin

1 teaspoon ground coriander

2 tablespoons all-purpose flour

5 large vine-ripe tomatoes, cored
   and quartered

A few sprigs fresh thyme,
   or 1 teaspoon dried

2 cups water or stock

1 teaspoon salt

Ground black pepper

¼ to ½ cup half-and-half or
   heavy cream

10 to 12 fresh basil leaves,
   cut into chiffonade

HERE'S WHAT YOU DO:

Melt the butter in a heavy-bottomed pot over medium heat, then add the oil. Add the onion and cook until slightly softened, about 7 minutes. Add the garlic and cook for 2 minutes, stirring to keep it from burning. Add the spices and stir to coat, then add the flour and quickly stir; the mixture will foam slightly. Add the tomatoes, then enough liquid to barely cover. Bring to a lively simmer, then lower the heat, cover, and cook at a simmer, about 30 minutes, until the tomatoes are soft. Remove the thyme sprigs and allow the tomato mixture to cool for 5 minutes. Puree the mixture in a food processor or with a handheld stick blender.

Pass the pureed mixture through a food mill to eliminate the skins and seeds. (Alternatively, you can blanch the tomatoes early in the process to remove the skins, and remove the seeds with a spoon before adding to the pot with the other ingredients.)

Return the puree to the pot and add the salt and season with pepper to taste. Add the half-and-half gradually, tasting for richness; add more if desired. Reheat at a simmer until ready to serve.

Garnish with the basil chiffonade.

Makes 4 servings

CANNED BEANS & RICE: A TEMPLATE MEANT TO BE TWEAKED

> In addition to the beloved grilled cheese and soup combo, another perennial favorite at our casa is beans and rice on the fly. In less time than it takes to watch the evening news, you can have supper on the table, and a complete protein at that.
>
> In the spirit of efficiency and on-the-fly improv, I offer a template to work from, with lots of room to play and experiment with flavors and seasonings. See page 13 for my thoughts on canned versus dried beans.

THE BEANS:

1 (25-ounce) can or 2 (15-ounce) cans black, red kidney, cannellini, or pinto beans, drained and rinsed thoroughly before cooking

THE AROMATICS AND SEASONINGS:

2 tablespoons vegetable oil
½ medium-size onion or shallot, and/or 2 cloves garlic, minced
Other options: For white beans, 1 small diced carrot; for black beans, ½ bell pepper, diced

HERBS AND SPICES:

Black beans: 1 teaspoon ground cumin, ¼ teaspoon cayenne, 1 teaspoon dried oregano
White beans: Needles from 1 sprig rosemary, minced, ¼ teaspoon cayenne, ½ teaspoon paprika
Kidney, pinto or red beans: 1 teaspoon dried thyme, ¼ teaspoon cayenne, ¼ teaspoon ground cinnamon

OTHER NECESSARY BASICS:

Cooked rice (see page 203)
Your favorite hot sauce

POSSIBLE FIXINS, GARNISHES, AND TOPPERS:

Shredded cheese, thinly sliced red onions, a fried egg, chopped fresh parsley or cilantro, a squeeze of lemon or lime, pickled peppers.

CANNED BEANS & RICE:
A TEMPLATE MEANT TO BE TWEAKED

HERE'S WHAT YOU DO:

Heat the oil in a medium-size saucepan over medium heat. Add the onion and/or shallot, and/or garlic and cook until the onion is softened slightly, about 5 minutes. If using the carrot or the bell pepper, add now to the mixture and cook for an additional 3 minutes.

Add the beans, along with your choice of the herbs and spices, stir to mix well, and bring to a lively simmer. Cover and cook over low heat for about 15 minutes. The beans will reduce and thicken a bit.

Taste for salt and season accordingly. Add a glug of your favorite hot sauce.

Measure ½ cup of cooked beans per serving, with equal amounts of rice.

Makes 4 to 5 servings

Kitchen Tricks for Your Sleeve

You may recognize many of the following recipes and technique tidbits from various menus throughout the book. Here, they're offered as stand-alone, all-purpose flavor enhancers that work well in a variety of kitchen scenarios. After all, no matter how long we've been cooking, we all can use a few more tricks.

HOW TO ROAST A BELL PEPPER

Preheat the oven to 400°F. Place the pepper on a baking sheet, whole, with its stem attached.

Roast for 40 minutes.

Transfer the pepper to a sealed container or bag so that the pepper can sweat and loosen its skin. After 15 minutes, remove the stem and seeds, which should easily give way. With your hands, remove the skin to the best of your ability; don't rinse, as this zaps away the roasted goodness.

---

1 medium-size pepper yields about 1 cup roasted

HOW TO ROAST A HEAD OF GARLIC

Preheat the oven to 375°F.

Trim the top of the garlic and peel away the outermost layer of skin. Pour a small amount of vegetable oil into the palm of your hand and slather the garlic. Place in a small dish, cover with foil, and roast until the cloves are soft, 30 to 40 minutes.

Remove from the oven and allow to cool slightly, about 10 minutes. With one hand at the root, use the other hand to squeeze out the garlic pulp, which should emerge easily.

HOW TO CUT UP A PINEAPPLE

Cut off the bottom first to create a flat surface, making the cutting easier and safer; then slice off the top.

From top to bottom, slice away the tough exterior, including the brown prickly things.

Using the core as a focal point, visualize the pineapple as a four-sided object. Place the blade of a sharp knife on the fleshy edge of the core and slice from top to bottom. You should have four large hunks of pineapple, with only the core remaining.

HOW TO SLICE KERNELS OFF A CORN COB

Husk the corn thoroughly, including the interior silk. Lay the corn on a work surface.

Use one hand to anchor the corn, and the other hand to place the edge of a sharp, wide knife against the kernels. Move the blade away from your anchoring hand, in a horizontal direction, allowing the kernels to fall as they are cut.

HOW TO CHIFFONADE

The literal translation for "made of rags" in French, this term refers to shreds or ribbonlike strips of leafy greens (kale, chard) or delicate, easily bruised herbs (basil, mint, sage). How to: Stack the leaves, roll up like a cigar, and slice with a sharp chef's knife (or snip with kitchen shears) on a diagonal.

HOW TO MAKE YOUR OWN BREAD CRUMBS

It's important to use dry, not stale or moldy bread for bread crumbs.

Cut or tear the bread into 1-inch pieces in preparation for the food processor (you could do some damage to your food processor with a large hunk of dry bread). If the crusts are too hard, remove them. Pulverize until the crumbs achieve your desired texture, and season with dried herbs, salt and pepper, and/or Parmigiano-Reggiano cheese. Store in an airtight container in the fridge. If you'd like the bread crumbs to have a drier, toastier texture, spread them on a baking tray and toast at 250°F for about 10 minutes. Store as you would fresh bread crumbs.

SIMPLE POT OF DRIED BEANS

This method applies to several varieties of beans—black turtle, white cannellini, pinto, and red and white kidney—but doesn't apply to chickpeas (which take longer to soak and cook) and lentils (which don't require soaking and take less time to cook).

A note on dried beans: The more local the source, the better. They are undoubtedly fresher, have more flavor, and will cook quick more quickly. Unfortunately, there's no telling how old the beans in those bags on supermarket shelves are. Check to see if your local supermarket or co-op sells beans in bulk, which tend to be fresher.

INGREDIENTS

1 pound (2 cups) dried beans
2 cloves garlic, peeled and
   smashed
1 teaspoon salt

HERE'S WHAT YOU DO:

Place the beans in a soup pot and cover with water, plus a few inches. Soak for at least 4 hours or overnight at room temperature. (If your kitchen is very warm, you may want to place in the refrigerator to minimize chances of fermentation.) Drain.

Return the beans to the pot, add 4½ cups water to cover, plus the garlic. Bring to a boil and cook at a hard boil for 5 minutes. Skim off any scum that rises to the top.

Lower the heat to a simmer and cook, covered, for at least 1 hour, until the beans are tender to the bite. The cooking time will depend on the age of the beans—older beans take longer. Season the beans with the salt and remove the garlic cloves.

From here, you can take the beans to the next level, with various sauces and veg add-ons, as detailed throughout the book.

Makes 4 cups

SIMPLE MARINARA SAUCE

▌ This should not be confused with raw tomato sauce, using in-season fresh tomatoes.

INGREDIENTS

2 cups tomato puree (from a jar, or whole tomatoes from a 28-ounce can that you puree yourself)

1 clove garlic, smashed

1 teaspoon dried oregano

1 teaspoon tomato paste

½ teaspoon salt
(Note: Before adding salt, taste the puree, particularly if it was already processed with salt.)

Ground black pepper

¼ teaspoon red pepper flakes (optional)

HERE'S WHAT YOU DO:

Pour the tomato puree into a medium-size saucepan and warm over medium heat. Add the garlic, oregano, and tomato paste. Stir to make sure the paste has been absorbed into the puree.

Bring to a lively simmer (this helps the sauce reduce a bit), then lower the heat and stir to make sure the sauce is not sticking. The sauce can be ready in 15 minutes or can simmer for longer, up to ½ hour. It will reduce by about one-fourth.

Taste for salt, and then add as you see fit, plus the black pepper and/or red pepper flakes to taste. Remove the garlic clove.

Makes about 1½ cups

CARAMELIZED ONIONS

GF

INGREDIENTS

4 tablespoons (½ stick) butter
5 cups onion (about 3
   medium-size onions),
   sliced into half-moons
A handful of sprigs of fresh thyme
Salt and ground black pepper

HERE'S WHAT YOU DO:

In a 10- or 12-inch skillet, melt the butter over medium heat and add the onions. Add the thyme sprigs. Cook over medium-low heat, stirring every 5 minutes and adjusting the heat to ensure that the onions are cooking evenly and not burning. Gradually the onions will soften, shrink, and sweeten, becoming caramelized and jamlike in about 1 hour.

Season with salt and pepper to taste, remove the thyme sprigs, and allow to cool.

Makes 1 to 2 cups, depending on how long you allow the onions to cook

LEMON-GARLIC VINAIGRETTE

INGREDIENTS

Juice of 1 medium-size lemon
(about 3 tablespoons)

¼ teaspoon salt

1 clove garlic, smashed or
pulverized using a mortar and
pestle or mini-chopper

4 tablespoons olive oil

Optional add-ons: 1 tablespoon
of minced shallots, 1 teaspoon
Dijon mustard, fresh thyme
or oregano leaves (picked
from stems)

HERE'S WHAT YOU DO:

Pour the lemon juice into a small bowl. Add the salt and whisk with a fork until dissolved. Taste. It should be somewhat salty. Whisk in the garlic. Drizzle in the oil, whisking with the other hand, to emulsify.

Shallot version: Add in place of or in concert with the garlic.

Mustard version: Whisk in before the oil.

Herby version: Whisk in just before serving.

**Makes enough to properly dress 4 cups
of raw lettuce or mixed greens**

LIME-CILANTRO COMPOUND BUTTER

INGREDIENTS

1 stick butter, softened enough to
    be pliable
1 small shallot bulb, minced
    (about 1 tablespoon)
Zest of 1 lime
¼ cup fresh cilantro leaves,
    chopped finely
½ teaspoon salt
⅛ teaspoon cayenne
⅛ teaspoon smoked paprika
    (optional but really nice)

HERE'S WHAT YOU DO:

Place the butter in a medium-size mixing bowl and add the remaining ingredients. With your hands and then with a rubber spatula, mix until the ingredients are well blended and distributed. Taste and modify according to your preferences. Season before the butter sets up in the fridge or freezer.

Roll the butter into a log, then wrap in plastic wrap, followed by parchment paper, if you have it. Refrigerate for short-term use or freeze for up to one month. Remove from the fridge/freezer and slice as needed.

Makes about ¼ cup

TAHINI SAUCE

INGREDIENTS

1 cup tahini, stirred well before
    using
¼ to ½ cup lemon juice
1 to 2 cloves garlic, mashed
1 teaspoon salt
½ cup water

HERE'S WHAT YOU DO:

In a medium-size bowl or a food processor, mix together all the ingredients and blend until smooth; add extra water if necessary to make a pourable sauce. Taste for salt and lemon and add more if need be.

Keeps in the fridge for a few days.

Makes about 2 cups

PICO DE GALLO

INGREDIENTS

4 plum (a.k.a. Roma) tomatoes, sliced in half lengthwise

3 to 4 scallions, cleaned, roots removed, white and light green parts only

¼ cup fresh cilantro, chopped finely

½ jalapeño chile pepper, seeded, deveined, and minced

Juice of ½ lime

½ teaspoon salt

HERE'S WHAT YOU DO:

With a teaspoon or your fingers, remove the seeds from tomato halves and shake out any accumulating juices. Cut each tomato half into julienned strips, then dice the strips. Place in a small bowl by themselves and allow to rest for 10 minutes to release any remaining juice and seeds.

Thinly slice and then mince the scallions. Transfer to a medium-size bowl and add the cilantro, jalapeño, and lime juice. Drain the tomatoes, then combine with the other ingredients. Stir to well, then add the salt. Stir again, taste, and adjust both the salt and lime as you see fit. The flavors should feel fresh in the mouth.

Eat same day the salsa is prepared.

Makes about 1½ cups

RELIABLE STOVETOP RICE THAT EVEN MY HUSBAND CAN MAKE

INGREDIENTS

1 cup long- or medium-grain
   white rice
1⅓ cups water
Pinch of salt

HERE'S WHAT YOU DO:

In a medium-size saucepan with a lid, combine the rice, water, and salt, and bring to a boil over medium-high heat. Cover, lower the heat to low, and cook at a simmer for 12 minutes, without lifting the lid. Turn off the heat and leave the rice alone for 10 minutes.

Makes 3 cups

Coconut Variation: Combine ¾ cup of water with ¾ cup of rice and bring to a boil. Add ¾ cup of unsweetened coconut milk (about half of a 13-ounce can), plus the salt, stir, and cook exactly the same way as the plain rice.

ROASTED BROCCOLI PICK-UP STICKS

INGREDIENTS

1 pound broccoli, separated into florets (ideal length: 3 inches)

1 (2 x 1-inch) hunk fresh ginger, peeled and minced

1 to 2 cloves garlic, minced

½ teaspoon salt

¼ teaspoon cayenne or smoked paprika

3 tablespoons olive oil

HERE'S WHAT YOU DO:

Preheat the oven to 400°F.

Place all the ingredients in a large mixing bowl. With your hands, mix until the broccoli is well coated. The broccoli should glisten with oil; if it seems dry, feel free to add a wee bit more oil. Taste a floret for salt and add more if needed. Transfer the broccoli to a baking tray and place in the oven.

Roast until fork tender, 15 to 16 minutes. Serve warm or at room temperature.

Makes 4 side-dish servings

Cauliflower Variation

INGREDIENTS

1 head cauliflower, separated into florets

3 tablespoons olive oil

½ teaspoon salt

½ teaspoon ground coriander

¼ teaspoon ground cinnamon

¼ teaspoon cayenne

¼ teaspoon ground ginger

HERE'S WHAT YOU DO:

Preheat the oven to 400°F.

Place all the ingredients in a large mixing bowl. With your hands, mix until ¾ cauliflower is well coated. The cauliflower should glisten with oil; if it seems dry, feel free to add a wee bit more oil. Taste a floret for salt and spices and add more if needed. Transfer the cauliflower to a baking tray and place in the oven.

Cook for 30 to 32 minutes, which will yield fork-tender florets with a slight bite. Cook for an additional 8 minutes if you're looking for softer results.

Makes 4 side-dish servings

PESTO FOR ALL SEASONS

Arugula Variation

INGREDIENTS

2 bunches arugula
(about 8 cups), washed
thoroughly, stemmed, and
spun dry

2 tablespoons olive oil

3 cloves garlic, sliced thinly

½ teaspoon red pepper flakes
(add up to 1 teaspoon if you
like heat)

¼ cup walnuts (optional)

½ teaspoon salt

Ground black pepper

HERE'S WHAT YOU DO:

Divide the arugula between two bowls.

Heat 1 tablespoon of the olive oil in a 10-inch skillet over medium heat and add the garlic and half of the arugula. With tongs, turn the arugula to coat with the oil; it will wilt (and shrink) rather quickly. Cook for about 2 minutes.

Transfer the wilted arugula and garlic to the bowl of a food processor. Add the remaining uncooked arugula, pepper flakes, and nuts (if using) to the food processor, in batches if necessary. Whiz until the mixture is an emerald green puree. Add the remaining oil and whiz for another minute or so. Add the salt and whiz for a few seconds. Taste, and add more as needed. Add pepper as you see fit.

Makes 1½ cups

Basil Variation

INGREDIENTS

2 heaping cups basil leaves

¼ cup pine nuts, walnuts, or almonds

1 to 2 cloves garlic

½ cup olive oil

½ to ¾ cup grated Parmigiano-Reggiano cheese

¼ to ½ teaspoon salt

HERE'S WHAT YOU DO:

Here's what you do:

Bring 2 cups of water to a boil and add the basil leaves. Blanch for 15 seconds, then remove from the pot with a skimmer or a pair of tongs. Transfer to a bowl of ice cold water. This will shock the basil and intensify its brilliant shade of green.

Extract the basil from the water and squeeze it dry as much as possible with your hands.

Place the nuts and the garlic in the bowl of a food processor or heavy-duty blender and whiz until pulverized. Add the basil and process until the mixture is well combined. While the machine is running, gradually add the oil, until creamy and well blended. You may need to stop and scrape the sides of the bowl a few times for thorough blending.

Transfer the pesto to a small bowl and stir in the cheese. Add ¼ teaspoon of the salt, taste, and add more as you see fit.

Makes about 1 cup

PESTO FOR ALL SEASONS

Kale Variation

INGREDIENTS

¼ to ½ cup chopped walnuts

4 cups Lacinato (a.k.a. Dinosaur) kale, stems removed, chopped coarsely

1½ to 2 teaspoons salt

2 cloves garlic, minced

½ cup olive oil

½ cup grated Parmigiano-Reggiano cheese

Ground black pepper

HERE'S WHAT YOU DO:

Toast the chopped walnuts in a dry, heavy skillet over high heat, stirring constantly, until they start to brown and become fragrant. Alternatively, place on a baking sheet and toast at 325°F for about 5 minutes. Keep an eye on the nuts—they burn quickly and will become bitter!

Bring 8 cups of water to a boil. Add 1 teaspoon of the salt, then add the kale. Cook, uncovered, until tender, about 10 minutes. Remove from the pot and drain.

In a blender or food processor, combine the garlic, walnuts, and drained kale and whiz until well mixed. Pour in the oil in a steady stream, and pulse until combined. Add ½ teaspoon of the salt, pulse, then taste. Add the remaining ½ teaspoon of salt if necessary.

Transfer the pesto to a medium-size bowl and stir in the cheese and pepper.

Keeps really well in an airtight container in the fridge, for up to a week.

Makes about 1 cup

Garlic Scape Variation

INGREDIENTS

⅓ cup walnuts
1 cup garlic scapes
    (about 8 or 9 scapes), top
    flowery part removed, cut into
    ¼-inch slices
¾ cup olive oil
¼ to ½ cup grated Parmigiano-
    Reggiano cheese
½ teaspoon salt
Ground black pepper

HERE'S WHAT YOU DO:

Toast the chopped walnuts in a dry, heavy skillet over high heat, stirring constantly, until they start to brown and become fragrant. Alternatively, place on a baking sheet and toast at 325°F for about 5 minutes. Keep an eye on the nuts—they burn quickly and will become bitter!

Place the walnuts and the scapes in the bowl of a food processor and whiz until well combined and somewhat smooth. Slowly drizzle in the oil and process until integrated. With a rubber spatula, scoop the pesto out of bowl and into a mixing bowl. Add the Parmigiano-Reggiano to taste; add the salt and pepper to taste. Keeps for up to one week in an airtight container in the fridge.

Makes about ¾ cup

MADRAS-STYLE CURRY POWDER

As mentioned in the pantry section, curry powder is a highly individualized spice blend typically mixed at home in India. Here's just one way of recreating Madras-style curry; feel free to mix up the amounts and spice combinations as you see fit. You'll need a coffee mill specifically designated for spices to grind the seeds. Curry will keep for a few months in a sealed jar stored in a cool, dark place.

INGREDIENTS

2 tablespoons coriander seeds
1 tablespoon fenugreek seeds
1 tablespoon cumin seeds
1 tablespoon red pepper flakes
2 teaspoons ground turmeric
2 teaspoons ground ginger
2 teaspoons ground cinnamon
2 teaspoons black peppercorns
1 teaspoon ground cardamom

HERE'S WHAT TO DO:

Combine all the ingredients and grind as needed.

Makes about ⅔ cup

APPLESAUCE

INGREDIENTS

A mix of 4 medium-size apples
(Granny Smith, Jonathan,
Empire, to name a few) for a
variety of flavor and texture

Juice of ½ lemon

1 cup water

Pinch of ground cinnamon

Up to ¼ cup sugar (optional)

HERE'S WHAT YOU DO:

Peel and core the apples, then slice into fourths. Place in a medium-size saucepan. Add the lemon juice and water; the apples should be barely covered. Bring to a lively simmer over medium-high heat, then lower the heat and cook at a gentle simmer, allowing the apples to soften, reduce, and thicken into a sauce. This should take no more than 15 minutes.

Stir in the cinnamon, then taste the apples for sweetness and add sugar as you see fit.

The sauce is done when the apples are completely soft and broken. For a more pureed consistency, use a potato masher or wooden spoon.

Serve warm or let cool and store in the fridge. Will keep in an airtight container for up to three days.

Makes 4 servings

A QUART OF ALL-PURPOSE VEG STOCK

I call for veg stock in several places throughout the book, using variations of the template below. The beauty of homemade stock is that you can improvise, depending on what you have on hand or what you're in the mood for. The amounts below will yield one quart of stock, which you can use in myriad ways, from a pot of beans to potpie (page 165). I like the mild flavor that leeks impart in a stock, but don't fret if they're unavailable where you live. Use a larger yellow storage onion instead.

INGREDIENTS

1 leek, thoroughly cleaned, trimmed of its root and cut into fourths (dark green part can be used)

1 medium-size onion, cut into quarters, with skin (clean if need be)

1 stalk celery, cleaned and cut into thirds

3 cloves garlic, peeled but left whole

10 black peppercorns

5 stripped parsley stems

4½ cups cold water

Optional add-ons: 1 medium-size carrot, peeled and quartered (optional, for a sweeter result); 1 (2 x 1-inch) hunk fresh ginger (optional, for Asian-inspired kapow); 1 dried cayenne pepper (optional, for a spicier result)

HERE'S WHAT YOU DO:

Place all the ingredients (including your choice of optional add-ins) in a large saucepan. Bring to a lively simmer, then cook over medium-low heat for 30 minutes. Strain and use as needed.

Makes 1 quart (4 cups). Amounts may be doubled or halved, and when cooled, can be frozen for future use.

METRIC CONVERSIONS

- The recipes in this book have not been tested with metric measurements, so some variations might occur.
- Remember that the weight of dry ingredients varies according to the volume or density factor: 1 cup of flour weighs far less than 1 cup of sugar, and 1 tablespoon doesn't necessarily hold 3 teaspoons.

General Formulas for Metric Conversion

Ounces to grams $\longrightarrow$ ounces $\times$ 28.35 = grams
Grams to ounces $\longrightarrow$ grams $\times$ 0.035 = ounces
Pounds to grams $\longrightarrow$ pounds $\times$ 453.5 = grams
Pounds to kilograms $\longrightarrow$ pounds $\times$ 0.45 = kilograms
Cups to liters $\longrightarrow$ cups $\times$ 0.24 = liters
Fahrenheit to Celsius $\longrightarrow$ (°F − 32) $\times$ 5 ÷ 9 = °C
Celsius to Fahrenheit $\longrightarrow$ (°C $\times$ 9) ÷ 5 + 32 = °F

Linear Measurements

1/2 inch	=	1 1/2 cm
1 inch	=	2 1/2 cm
6 inches	=	15 cm
8 inches	=	20 cm
10 inches	=	25 cm
12 inches	=	30 cm
20 inches	=	50 cm

Volume (Dry) Measurements

1/4 teaspoon = 1 milliliter
1/2 teaspoon = 2 milliliters
3/4 teaspoon = 4 milliliters
1 teaspoon = 5 milliliters
1 tablespoon = 15 milliliters
1/4 cup = 59 milliliters
1/3 cup = 79 milliliters
1/2 cup = 118 milliliters
2/3 cup = 158 milliliters
3/4 cup = 177 milliliters
1 cup = 225 milliliters
4 cups or 1 quart = 1 liter
1/2 gallon = 2 liters
1 gallon = 4 liters

Volume (Liquid) Measurements

1 teaspoon = 1/6 fluid ounce = 5 milliliters
1 tablespoon = 1/2 fluid ounce = 15 milliliters
2 tablespoons = 1 fluid ounce = 30 milliliters
1/4 cup = 2 fluid ounces = 60 milliliters
1/3 cup = 2 2/3 fluid ounces = 79 milliliters
1/2 cup = 4 fluid ounces = 118 milliliters
1 cup or 1/2 pint = 8 fluid ounces = 250 milliliters
2 cups or 1 pint = 16 fluid ounces = 500 milliliters
4 cups or 1 quart = 32 fluid ounces = 1,000 milliliters
1 gallon = 4 liters

Oven Temperature Equivalents, Fahrenheit (F) and Celsius (C)

100°F = 38°C
200°F = 95°C
250°F = 120°C
300°F = 150°C
350°F = 180°C
400°F = 205°C
450°F = 230°C

Weight (Mass) Measurements

1 ounce = 30 grams
2 ounces = 55 grams
3 ounces = 85 grams
4 ounces = 1/4 pound = 125 grams
8 ounces = 1/2 pound = 240 grams
12 ounces = 3/4 pound = 375 grams
16 ounces = 1 pound = 454 grams

# RESOURCES

STOCKING THE PANTRY AND FEEDING YOUR BRAIN

Meatless Monday
www.meatlessmonday.com/

Johns Hopkins Center for a Livable Future
www.jhsph.edu/clf/

World Spice, Seattle
www.worldspice.com/

Penzey's (spices)
www.penzeys.com/

Rancho Gordo Beans
www.ranchogordo.com

Online Latino groceries
www.mexgrocer.com/

Thai groceries, both perishable and non-
www.importfood.com

Map of Asian grocery stores in the U.S.
www.newasiancuisine.com/new_asian/map_grocery_stores.asp

Farmers' markets list from the USDA
www.ams.usda.gov/AMSv1.0/FarmersMarkets

Interactive Farmers' Market Map
   Discovery Health
   http://health.discovery.com/convergence/truth/map/map.html

Seasonal Produce Map by Month
Epicurious
   http://www.epicurious.com/articlesguides/seasonalcooking/farmtotable/seasonalingre dientmap
   Dr. Preston Maring/Kaiser Permanente, the doctor who brought farmers' markets to hospitals around the country
   kp.org/farmersmarketrecipes

Whole Grains A to Z Explainer by Whole Grains Council
   http://www.wholegrainscouncil.org/whole-grains-101/whole-grains-a-to-z

Finding KOD
   www.kimodonnel.com
   trueslant.com/kimodonnel

LEARNING ABOUT FRUITS AND VEGETABLES:

Vegetables from Amaranth to Zucchini by Elizabeth Schneider

LEARNING ABOUT HERBS AND SPICES:

The Spice Lover's Guide to Herbs & Spices by Tony Hill

OLD-SCHOOL RELIABLE PRIMER ON GRAINS:

The Grains Cookbook by Bert Greene

POCKET GUIDES:

The Visual Food Lover's Guide by QA International
   Pictorial for getting more acquainted with fruit, veg, spices, grains, legumes
The Organic Food Shopper's Guide by Jeff Cox
The New Food Lover's Companion by Sharon Tyler Herbst
Notes on Cooking by Lauren Braun Costello and Russell Reich

ACKNOWLEDGMENTS

Giving Thanks

A dream come true. That's what this project has been for me. Without the tireless encouragement and hands-on assistance from the following individuals, it would remain just an idea cloud.

Hats off to my merry band of recipe testers, who volunteered their time, palates, and pantries to share invaluable insight and kitchen smarts:

Julia Beizer, Dan Berko, Phil Berko, Paula Champa and Euan Sey, Dennis Coyle, Rebekah Denn, Janet and Jerry Eber, Karl Eisenhower, Sally Ekus, Dean Ericksen, Stefanie Gans, Jen Sieve-Hicks, Nicole Ladas Fitzgerald and Tim Fitzgerald, Erin Hare, Heather Jones, Leslie Kelly, Liz Kelly Nelson and Dot Kelly, Barbara Kennedy, Eddie Gehman Kohan, Brian Krebs, Susan Mack, Stephanie Marquis, Matthew Greenberg and Maura McCarthy, Dan Murano, Howard Parnell, Steven Shapiro, Nicole Spiridakis, Elizabeth Terry. And to Tara Austen Weaver and Devra Gartenstein for contributing recipes.

Three fingers of bourbon to Jim Eber, who was there when this idea was just a seedling and who has lent a hand, an ear, an eye, and amusement every step of the way. Obi, you da man.

To Stephanie Gailing, who's got a third eye when it comes to line editing, amazing celestial insight, and a heart of gold.

To Jeanne Sauvage, who went beyond the call of recipe-testing duty and magically morphed into a kitchen assistant extraordinaire and a good friend who scraped me off the floor more than once.

To Eddie G., for her eternally bent ear, second set of eyes, and passion for the passion that binds food and politics.

For the sundry love, kindness, assists, and cheerleading from:

Bill Addison, Colin Baugh, Stephanie Bittner, Keren Brown, Kim Carlson, Alex Carrillo, Jacqueline Church, Carrie Ferrán, Rocci Fisch, Leslie Hatfield, Luuvu Hoang, Eleanor Hong, Jules James, Leslie Kelly, Liz Kelly, Shannon Kelly, Destin Joy Layne, Nancy Loggins-Gonzalez, Susan Mack, Jennifer Maiser, Karla McDuffie, Dan Murano, Chris Nelson, Chris Nishiwaki, Jill Nussinow, Lennox Raphael, Kim Ricketts, Jeff Seligman, Leslie Silverman, Frances and John Smersh, Naomi Starkman, Kerry Trueman, Tai Tsang, Hughes Walker.

To the women chefs and authors who have crossed my path, inspired, and paved the way: Diana Abu-Jaber, Nicole Aloni, Monica Bhide, Ann Cashion, Gillian Clark, Fran Costigan, Erin Doland, Nathalie Dupree, Lisa Hamilton, Kate Jansen, Anna Lappé, Mollie Katzen, Pascale LeDraoulec, Susan McCreight-Lindeborg, Isa Chandra Moskowitz, Cynthia Nims, Rosemary Parkinson, Sara Roahen, Jules Shepard, Julia Watson, Virginia Willis, Grace Young.

To my "family" in Eureka Springs: Vicki Kell-Schneider and Cindy Duncan at the Writer's Colony at Dairy Hollow and fellow scribe Kelly Hayes-Raitt; Catherina Bernstein for chakra work and keeping me aligned; David "Fuzzy" White (and his canine friend Jeff), Karen Lindblad, and Barbara Kennedy.

To Chris Elam at Meatless Monday and Ralph Loglisci and Dr. Robert Lawrence at the Center for a Livable Future at Johns Hopkins University, for their continued support and solidarity.

Un beso por Myra Kohn, whose photographic talent is not only evident in these pages but whose capacity for greatness is immense.

To my editor Renee Sedliar, for her human touch and superhuman wizardry, and to the crackerjack team at Perseus for taking good care of me and my "baby."

To Lisa Ekus-Saffer and Sally Ekus, who had faith, shepherded the deal, and who always have my back, even when I least expect it.

To my readers, who have stuck by me for more than a decade, as we learned to cook together and live more mindfully in a digital world.

To Susan and Jim (aka Mister Sausage), Tim and Dorothea, and to John, my immediate family and meat lovers to the core, who have all been good sports, opening their minds, crumb by crumb, to the notion of a little less meat in their lives.

To my dad, whose beloved spirit has been cheering me along the way.

And to Russ, who has washed dishes, wiped away tears, endured many cranky pants episodes, edited like a banshee, and gone on way too many shopping runs. He's all mine.

Photographer Myra Kohn would like to thank the sales and rental department staff at Glazer's Camera for their assistance, infinite knowledge, and encouragement; *un millón de gracias* to my friends Valentina Vitols, Carrie Ferrán, Jeanne Sauvage, and Luuvu Hoang for their generosity of spirit, time, skills, and equipment; to my father for instilling in me the love of photography; to my sister Giselle for a lifetime of adventures together both in front and behind the lens, to my mother for being an everlasting source of inspiration in and out of the kitchen; and to Mr. C, a thousand thanks for being in my life and for your unconditional love and unwavering support.

INDEX

All-Purpose Veg Stock,
  A Quart of, 211
Almonds
  Basil Pesto, 206
  Corn Cakes, 119
  Roasted Green Bean,
    Mushroom, & Shallot
    Medley, 86
  Romesco Sauce, 100
  Susan's Eggplant Stack,
    101–103
Apple, Blue Cheese, &
    Caramelized Onion
    Pizza Topping, 183
Applesauce, 210
Aromatics, about, 13
Arugula
  Arugula Pesto, 205
  Arugula & Seasonal
    Fruit, 37
  Good Ole Marinara
    and Mozzarella (and
    Arugula and Lemon,
    If You're Smart) Pizza
    Topping, 182
  Pear-Arugula Salad, 114
  Rocket Lasagna,
    26–29
Asparagus, in Spring
    Meadow Risotto, 32

Baked Beans, True-Blue, 94
Barbecue, Tofu, 92–93
Barley
  Barley Pilaf, 40
  pearl, about, 18
  Stuffed Bell Peppers,
    98–99
Basic recipes
  Applesauce, 210
  Caramelized Onions, 198
  Lemon-Garlic
    Vinaigrette, 199
  Lime-Cilantro
    Compound Butter, 200
  Madras-Style Curry
    Powder, 209
  Pesto for All Seasons,
    205–208
  Pico de Gallo, 202
  A Quart of All-Purpose
    Veg Stock, 211
  Reliable Stovetop Rice
    that Even My Husband
    Can Make (and
    coconut variation), 203
  Roasted Broccoli Pick-Up
    Sticks (and cauliflower
    variation), 204
  Simple Marinara Sauce,
    197

  Simple Pot of Dried
    Beans, 196
  Tahini Sauce, 201
Basic techniques
  bell pepper, to roast, 194
  bread crumbs, to make,
    195
  corn, to slice kernels from
    cob, 195
  herbs, to chiffonade, 195
  pineapple, to cut up, 194
Basil
  Basil Pesto, 206
  Corn Kernel Salad, 72
  Goat Cheesy Roasted
    Peppers, 107
  to chiffonade, 195
  Zucchini &
    Corn-Studded Orzo,
    105–106
Beans (see also specific type).
    See also lentils
  about, 13
  Black Bean–Sweet Potato
    Chili, 144–145
  Canned Beans & Rice: A
    Template Meant to Be
    Tweaked, 190–191
  Chickpea "Crab Cakes,"
    69–70

Chickpea-Turnip Chili, 38–39
Huevo y Frijoles, 58
Hummus, 87
Hummus-Stuffed Tomatoes, 74
Jamaican-Style Peas & Rice, 62
Jig-Inducing Falafel Burgers, 48–50
Minty Chickpeas, 104
Nonna Caterina's Pasta e Fagioli, 159–160
Quickie Couscous-Chickpea Salad, 78–79
Roasted Beans, Greens, & Squash Rings, 115–116
Roasted Green Bean, Mushroom, & Shallot Medley, 86
Simple Pot of Dried Beans, 196
Smokin' Hoppin' John, 146–147
Spring Cassoulet, 44–46
Stuffed Bell Peppers, 98–99
True-Blue Baked Beans, 94
West Indian–Style Channa Wrap, 52–53
Beet greens
Beets and Greens Quesadillas, 139–40
Gumbo z'Herbes (Green Gumbo), 156–158
Beets and Greens Quesadillas, 139–140

Bell peppers
Goat Cheesy Roasted Peppers, 107
Ratatouille, 110–111
Roasted Red Pepper Sauce, 118
Roasted Red Pepper Soup, 141
Romesco Sauce, 100
Stuffed Bell Peppers, 98–99
to roast, 194
Black beans
Black Bean–Sweet Potato Chili, 144–145
Canned Beans & Rice: A Template Meant to Be Tweaked, 190–191
Huevo y Frijoles, 58
Simple Pot of Dried Beans, 196
Black Bean Sauce & Bok Choy, Braised Winter Squash with, 122–123
Black-eyed peas, in Smokin' Hoppin' John, 146–147
Blue cheese
Apple, Blue Cheese, & Caramelized Onion Pizza Topping, 183
Pear-Arugula Salad, 114
Blue Corn Cakes, 117–119
Blue cornmeal, about, 15
Bok choy
about, 16
Braised Winter Squash with Black Bean Sauce & Bok Choy, 122–123
Go-with-the-Flow Potpie with Cheddar-Biscuity Crust, 165–168

Slurpy Pan-Asian Noodles, 175–176
Veggie Fried Rice Bowl, 185
Braised Winter Squash with Black Bean Sauce & Bok Choy, 122–123
Bread crumbs, to make, 195
Breads
Individual Flatbreads, 135–136
Pizza Dough, 180–181
Skillet Corn Bread, 148
Broccoli
Broccoli Soup, 188
Brocco Mac & Cheese, 150–151
Roasted Broccoli Pick-Up Sticks, 204
Broccoli raab, about, 16
Broccoli Raab, Polenta Squares with Puttanesca Sauce &, 162–164
Bulgur wheat
about, 16
Tabbouleh, 88–89
Burgers, Jig-Inducing Falafel, 48–50
Butter, about, 14
Butter, Lime-Cilantro Compound, 200

Cabbage
Stir-Fried Cabbage and Cumin (or Caraway), 170
Vinegar Slaw, 95
Canned Beans & Rice: A Template Meant to Be Tweaked, 190–191

Cannellini beans
  Canned Beans & Rice:
    A Template Meant to
    Be Tweaked, 190–191
  Roasted Beans, Greens,
    & Squash Rings,
    115–116
  Simple Pot of Dried
    Beans, 196
  Spring Cassoulet, 44–46
Cantaloupe, in Sesame Rice
  Noodles & Melon-
  Herb Salad, 96–97
Caramelized Onion, Pear,
  and Goat Cheese
  Crostata Filling, 36
Caramelized Onion Pizza
  Topping, Apple,
  Blue Cheese &, 183
Caramelized Onions, 198
Caramelized Shallots,
  Tempeh, & Goat
  Cheese, Penne
  with, 155
Carrot tops, in Gumbo
  z'Herbes (Green
  Gumbo), 156–158
Cassoulet, Spring,
  44–46
Cauliflower
  Go-with-the-Flow Potpie
    with Cheddar-Biscuity
    Crust, 165–168
  Roasted Cauliflower
    Pick-Up Sticks
    (variation), 204
  Roasted Cauliflower with
    Tahini Sauce, 89
  Sicilian-Style Roasted
    Cauliflower with
    Pasta, 169
  Thai-Style Red Curry
    Tempeh, 131–132

Winter Veg & Cilantro
  "Curry" with
  Dumplings, 153–154
Channa Wrap, West
  Indian-Style, 52–53
Chard
  about, 14
  Beets and Greens
    Quesadillas, 139–140
  Chard & Feta Crostata
    (variation), 34
  Chard Frittata, 81
  Egg-in-the-Hole,
    41–42
  Gumbo z'Herbes (Green
    Gumbo), 156–158
  Mushroom-Chard
    Scramble (variation),
    120
  Shepherd's Pie with
    Chard-Lentil Filling,
    171–174
  Stuffed Bell Peppers,
    98–99
  to chiffonade, 195
  Wilted Greens in a
    Skillet Vinaigrette, 161
Cheddar
  Beets and Greens
    Quesadillas, 139–140
  Brocco Mac & Cheese,
    150–151
  Egg-in-the-Hole,
    41–42
  Go-with-the-Flow
    Potpie with Cheddar-
    Biscuit Crust,
    165–168
  Grilled Cheese Template,
    186
  Huevo y Frijoles, 58
  Susan's Eggplant Stack,
    101–103

Cheese (see also specific type)
  Apple, Blue Cheese, &
    Caramelized Onion
    Pizza Topping, 183
  Basil Pesto, 206
  Beets and Greens
    Quesadillas, 139–140
  Brocco Mac & Cheese,
    150–151
  Caramelized Onion, Pear,
    and Goat Cheese
    Crostata Filling, 36
  Egg-in-the-Hole,
    41–42
  Garlic Scape Pesto Pasta,
    66–67, 208
  Goat Cheesy Roasted
    Peppers, 107
  Good Ole Marinara and
    Mozzarella (and
    Arugula and Lemon,
    If You're Smart) Pizza
    Topping, 182
  Go-with-the-Flow
    Potpie with Cheddar-
    Biscuity Crust,
    165–168
  Grilled Cheese Template,
    186
  Huevo y Frijoles, 58
  Kale Pesto, 207
  Kopanisti, 90
  Mushroom-Rosemary
    Pizza Topping, 184
  Mushroom-Spinach
    Scramble, 120
  Parmigiano-Reggiano,
    about, 18
  Pear-Arugula Salad,
    114
  Penne with Tempeh,
    Caramelized Shallots,
    & Goat Cheese, 155

Cheese (continued)
  Polenta Squares with
    Puttanesca Sauce &
    Broccoli Raab,
    162–164
  Risotto, Two Ways,
    30–33
  Rocket Lasagna, 26–29
  Seared Halloumi, 75
  Spinach & Feta Crostata,
    34
  Spring Cassoulet, 44–46
  Stuffed Bell Peppers,
    98–99
  Susan's Eggplant Stack,
    101–103
  Whipped Feta, 118
  Zucchini Boats, 76–77
Chickpeas
  Chickpea "Crab Cakes,"
    69–70
  Chickpea-Turnip Chili,
    38–39
  Hummus, 87
  Hummus-Stuffed
    Tomatoes, 74
  Jig-Inducing Falafel
    Burgers, 48–50
  Minty Chickpeas, 104
  Quickie Couscous-
    Chickpea Salad, 78–79
  Stuffed Bell Peppers,
    98–99
  West Indian–Style
    Channa Wrap, 52–53
Chicory, in Gumbo z'Herbes
  (Green Gumbo),
  156–158
Chiffonade, how to, 195
Chili, Black Bean–Sweet
  Potato, 144–145
Chili, Chickpea-Turnip,
  38–39

Chipotle chiles in adobo
  sauce, about, 16
Chips, Kale, 57
Cilantro
  Chickpea "Crab Cakes,"
    69–70
  Corn Kernel Salad, 72
  Huevo y Frijoles, 58
  Jig-Inducing Falafel
    Burgers, 48–50
  Lime-Cilantro
    Compound Butter, 200
  Pepita-Crusted Tofu,
    128–129
  Winter Veg & Cilantro
    "Curry" with
    Dumplings, 153–154
Clementines, in Arugula &
  Seasonal Fruit, 37
Cocktail Sauce, 71
Coconut milk
  Coconut Rice, 124
  Jamaican-Style Peas &
    Rice, 62
  Thai-Style Red Curry
    Tempeh, 131–132
Collard greens
  Gumbo z'Herbes (Green
    Gumbo), 156–158
  KOD's Quickie Collards,
    149
Compound Butter, Lime-
  Cilantro, 200
Cooking oils, about, 14
Coriander, about, 16
Corn
  Corn Kernel Salad, 72
  Stuffed Bell Peppers,
    98–99
  to remove kernels from
    cob, 195
  Zucchini & Corn-
    Studded Orzo, 105–106

Corn Bread, Skillet, 148
Corn Cakes, 119
Cotija cheese, in Huevo y
  Frijoles, 58
Couscous
  Quickie Couscous-
    Chickpea Salad, 78–79
  Stuffed Bell Peppers,
    98–99
"Crab Cakes," Chickpea,
  69–70
Creamy Tomato Soup, 189
Crostata, Caramelized
  Onion, Pear, and Goat
  Cheese, 36
Crostata, Spinach & Feta,
  34–36
Crostini, Roasted
  Eggplant–Lentil Caviar
  on Oversized, 125–126
Cumin
  about, 16
  Red Lentil Dal with
    Cumin-Fried Onions
    & Wilted Spinach,
    133–134
  Stir-Fried Cabbage and
    Cumin (or Caraway),
    170
Curries
  Thai-Style Red Curry
    Tempeh, 131–132
  West Indian–Style
    Channa Wrap, 52–53
  Winter Veg & Cilantro
    "Curry" with
    Dumplings, 153–154
Curry paste, Thai red,
  about, 19
Curry powder, Madras,
  about, 17
Curry Powder,
  Madras-Style, 209

Dairy-optional recipes
Black Bean-Sweet Potato
Chili, 144–145
Frittata, Three Ways,
80–82
Gumbo z'Herbes
(Green Gumbo),
156–158
Mushroom-Spinach
Scramble, 120
Nonna Caterina's Pasta e
Fagioli, 159–160
Sicilian-Style Roasted
Cauliflower with
Pasta, 169
Smokin' Hoppin' John,
146–147
Stuffed Bell Peppers,
98–99
Stuffed Shells with
Lentil Ragout &
Spinach, 137–138
Tempeh Hoagie-letta,
55–56
Dal, Red Lentil, with
Cumin-Fried Onions
& Wilted Spinach,
133–134
Dandelion greens, in
Gumbo z'Herbes
(Green Gumbo),
156–158
Dino-Mash, 130
Dressings. See sauces and
dressings
Dumplings, Winter Veg &
Cilantro "Curry" with,
153–154

Eggplant
Eggplant Rounds,
Roasted or Grilled, 91
Ratatouille, 110–111

Roasted Eggplant–Lentil
Caviar on Oversized
Crostini, 125–126
Susan's Eggplant Stack,
101–103
Thai-Style Red Curry
Tempeh, 131–132
Eggs
about, 14
Egg-in-the-Hole, 41–42
Frittata, Three Ways,
80–82
Huevo y Frijoles, 58
Mushroom-Spinach
Scramble, 120

Falafel Burgers, Jig-
Inducing, 48–50
Family-Style Latke, 43
FAQs, 10–11
Fennel, in Go-with-the-
Flow Potpie with
Cheddar-Biscuity
Crust, 165–168
Feta
Kopanisti, 90
Spinach & Feta Crostata,
34
Stuffed Bell Peppers,
98–99
Whipped Feta, 118
Flatbreads, Individual,
135–136
Fontina, in Mushroom-
Rosemary Pizza
Topping, 184
Fried Rice Bowl, Veggie, 185
Frisée, in Wilted Greens
in a Skillet Vinaigrette,
161
Frittata
Basic Frittata Template,
80

Chard Frittata, 81
Potato Frittata, 82
Zucchini Frittata, 81
Fruit, Seasonal, Arugula &,
37

Garlic
Garlic Scape Pesto Pasta,
66–67
garlic scapes, about, 16
Lemon-Garlic
Vinaigrette, 199
Rosemary-Garlic Roasted
Potatoes, 121
to roast, 194
Gazpacho, 83
Gluten-free recipes
Blue Corn Cakes,
117–119
Caramelized Onions, 198
Dino-Mash, 130
Family-Style Latke, 43
Goat Cheesy Roasted
Peppers, 107
Huevo y Frijoles, 58
Hummus-Stuffed
Tomatoes, 74
Jamaican-Style Peas &
Rice, 62
Kale Chips, 57
Kopanisti, 90
Lemon-Garlic
Vinaigrette, 199
Lime-Cilantro
Compound Butter, 200
Minty Chickpeas, 104
Mushroom-Spinach
Scramble, 120
Oven Sweet Potato Fries,
51
Pear-Arugula Salad, 114
Pepita-Crusted Tofu,
128–129

Gluten-free recipes
(*continued*)
Pesto for All Seasons,
205–208
Pico de Gallo, 202
Pistachio-Raisin Rice
Pilaf, 127
Polenta Squares with
Puttanesca Sauce &
Broccoli Raab,
162–164
A Quart of All-Purpose
Veg Stock, 211
Risotto, Two Ways,
30–33
Roasted Beans, Greens,
& Squash Rings,
115–116
Roasted Broccoli Pick-Up
Sticks (and cauliflower
variation), 204
Roasted Cauliflower with
Tahini Sauce, 89
Roasted Red Pepper
Sauce, 118
Romaine & Balsamic-
Gingery Strawberries,
68
Rosemary-Garlic Roasted
Potatoes, 121
Sesame Rice Noodles &
Melon-Herb Salad,
96–97
Shepherd's Pie with
Chard-Lentil Filling,
171–174
Simple Marinara Sauce,
197
Simple Pot of Dried
Beans, 196
Skillet Corn Bread, 148
Southern Red Rice,
84–85

Stewed Tomatoes, 152
Stir-Fried Cabbage and
Cumin (or Caraway),
170
Stuffed Bell Peppers,
98–99
Susan's Eggplant Stack,
101–103
Tahini Sauce, 50, 201
Tofu Barbecue, 92–93
Top-Shelf Potato Salad,
54
Twice-Baked Sweet
Potatoes, 112–113
Whipped Feta, 118
Wilted Greens in a
Skillet Vinaigrette,
161
Goat cheese
Caramelized Onion,
Pear, and Goat Cheese
Crostata Filling, 36
Goat Cheesy Roasted
Peppers, 107
Penne with Tempeh,
Caramelized Shallots,
& Goat Cheese, 155
Stuffed Bell Peppers,
98–99
Gomasio
about, 16
Slurpy Pan-Asian
Noodles, 175–176
Good Ole Marinara and
Mozzarella (and
Arugula and Lemon,
If You're Smart) Pizza
Topping, 182
Gorgonzola, in Grilled
Cheese Template, 186
Gouda
Brocco Mac & Cheese,
150–151

Grilled Cheese Template,
186
Susan's Eggplant Stack,
101–103
Go-with-the-Flow
Potpie with
Cheddar-Biscuity
Crust, 165–168
Grapefruit, in Arugula &
Seasonal Fruit, 37
Great northern beans
Roasted Beans, Greens,
& Squash Rings,
115–116
Spring Cassoulet, 44–46
Green beans
Roasted Green Bean,
Mushroom, & Shallot
Medley, 86
Veggie Fried Rice Bowl,
185
Green Gumbo (Gumbo
z'Herbes), 156–158
Greens. *See also* chard; kale;
spinach; *specific types
of greens*
Beets and Greens
Quesadillas, 139–140
Greens-Ricotta Lasagna
Filling, 27
Gumbo z'Herbes (Green
Gumbo), 156–158
to chiffonade, 195
Wilted Greens in a
Skillet Vinaigrette, 161
Grilled Cheese Template,
186
Gruyère
Brocco Mac & Cheese,
150–151
Egg-in-the-Hole, 41–42
Grilled Cheese Template,
186

Gumbo z'Herbes (Green Gumbo), 156–158

Halloumi, about, 17
Halloumi, Seared, 75
Havarti, in Grilled Cheese Template, 186
Hazelnuts, in Romesco Sauce, 100
Herbs. *See also* basil; cilantro; mint; parsley
about, 15
to chiffonade, 195
Hoisin sauce, about, 17
Huevo y Frijoles, 58
Hummus, 87
Hummus-Stuffed Tomatoes, 74

Individual Flatbreads, 135–136
Ingredient notes, 13–19

Jamaican-Style Peas & Rice, 62
Jerk sauce, about, 17
Jerk Tempeh, 60
Jicama, in Romaine with Toasted Pepitas and Lemon Vinaigrette, 59
Jig-Inducing Falafel Burgers, 48–50

Kale
about, 17
Dino-Mash, 130
Gumbo z'Herbes (Green Gumbo), 156–158
Kale Chips, 57
Kale Pesto, 207
Roasted Beans, Greens, & Squash Rings, 115–116

Stuffed Bell Peppers, 98–99
to chiffonade, 195
Kid-friendly recipes
Beets and Greens Quesadillas, 139–140
Brocco Mac & Cheese, 150–151
Chickpea "Crab Cakes," 69–70
Egg-in-the-Hole, 41–42
Go-with-the-Flow Potpie with Cheddar-Biscuity Crust, 165–168
Grilled Cheese & Soup for All Seasons, 186–189
Huevo y Frijoles, 58
Jig-Inducing Falafel Burgers, 48–50
Pepita-Crusted Tofu, 128–129
Pizza Night with DIY Dough and Seasonal Toppings, 180–184
Red Lentil Dal with Cumin-Fried Onions & Wilted Spinach, 133–134
RW's Snack Plate, 87–90
Slurpy Pan-Asian Noodles, 175–176
Stuffed Shells with Lentil Ragout & Spinach, 137–138
Veggie Fried Rice Bowl, 185
Kidney beans
Canned Beans & Rice: A Template Meant to Be Tweaked, 190–191
Jamaican-Style Peas & Rice, 62

Simple Pot of Dried Beans, 196
True-Blue Baked Beans, 94
Kitchen tricks. *See* basic recipes; basic techniques
KOD's Quickie Collards, 149
Kohlrabi, in Gumbo z'Herbes (Green Gumbo), 156–158
Kopanisti, 90

Lamb's quarters, in Wilted Greens in a Skillet Vinaigrette, 161
Lasagna, Rocket, 26–29
Latke, Family-Style, 43
Leek-Potato-Parsley Puree, 187
Leftover-bonus recipes
Beets & Greens Quesadillas, 139–140
Black Bean–Sweet Potato Chili, 144
Canned Beans & Rice: A Template Meant to Be Tweaked, 190–191
Chickpea-Turnip Chili, 38–39
Gazpacho, 83
Go-with-the-Flow Potpie with Cheddar-Biscuity Crust, 165–168
Gumbo z'Herbes (Green Gumbo), 156–158
Jerk Tempeh, 60
Jig-Inducing Falafel Burgers, 48–49
Nonna Caterina's Pasta e Fagioli, 159–160

Leftover-bonus recipes
(*continued*)
Penne with Tempeh,
Caramelized Shallots,
& Goat Cheese, 155
Polenta Squares with
Puttanesca Sauce &
Broccoli Raab,
162–164
Ratatouille, 110–111
Red Lentil Dal with
Cumin-Fried Onions
& Wilted Spinach,
133–134
Roasted Eggplant–Lentil
Caviar on Oversized
Crostini, 125–126
Roasted Green Bean,
Mushroom, & Shallot
Medley, 86
Rocket Lasagna, 26–29
RW's Snack Plate, 87–90
Sicilian-Style Roasted
Cauliflower with
Pasta, 169
Smokin' Hoppin' John,
146–147
Spinach & Feta Crostata,
34–36
Spring Cassoulet, 44–46
Stuffed Bell Peppers,
98–99
Stuffed Shells with Lentil
Ragout & Spinach,
137–138
Tofu Barbecue, 92–93
Veggie Fried Rice Bowl,
185
West Indian–Style
Channa Wrap, 52–53
Winter Veg & Cilantro
"Curry" with
Dumplings, 153–154

Lemon-Garlic Vinaigrette,
199
Lentils
about, 17
Nonna Caterina's Pasta e
Fagioli, 159–160
Red Lentil Dal with
Cumin-Fried Onions
& Wilted Spinach,
133–134
Roasted Eggplant–Lentil
Caviar on Oversized
Crostini, 125–126
Shepherd's Pie with
Chard-Lentil Filling,
171–174
Stuffed Shells with Lentil
Ragout & Spinach,
137–138
Lime-Cilantro Compound
Butter, 200

Madras curry powder,
about, 17
Madras-Style Curry Powder,
209
Make It a Meal suggestions,
26
Marinara Sauce, 28
Marinara Sauce, Simple,
197
Matzoh, in Rocket Lasagna,
26–29
Meatless meals FAQs,
10–11
Melon-Herb Salad, Sesame
Rice Noodles &, 96–97
Mint
Fattoush Salad, 73
Minty Chickpeas, 104
Sesame Rice Noodles &
Melon-Herb Salad,
96–97

Tabbouleh, 88–89
to chiffonade, 195
Zucchini & Corn-
Studded Orzo, 105–106
Monterey Jack
Beets and Greens
Quesadillas, 139–140
Grilled Cheese Template,
186
Huevo y Frijoles, 58
Mozzarella
Good Ole Marinara and
Mozzarella (and
Arugula and Lemon,
If You're Smart) Pizza
Topping, 182
Mushroom-Rosemary
Pizza Topping, 184
Rocket Lasagna, 26–29
Susan's Eggplant Stack,
101–103
Mushrooms
Go-with-the-Flow Potpie
with Cheddar-Biscuity
Crust, 165–168
Mushroom Risotto, 31
Mushroom-Rosemary
Pizza Topping, 184
Mushroom-Spinach
Scramble, 120
Roasted Green Bean,
Mushroom, & Shallot
Medley, 86
Tara's Mushroom Ragout,
24
Mustard greens, in Gumbo
z'Herbes (Green
Gumbo), 156–158

Nonna Caterina's Pasta e
Fagioli, 159–160
Noodles. *See* pasta and
noodles

Nuts (see also specific type)
  Arugula Pesto, 205
  Arugula & Seasonal
    Fruit, 37
  Basil Pesto, 206
  Corn Cakes, 119
  Garlic Scape Pesto Pasta,
    66–67
  Goat Cheesy Roasted
    Peppers, 107
  Kale Pesto, 207
  Pear-Arugula Salad,
    114
  Roasted Green Bean,
    Mushroom, & Shallot
    Medley, 86
  Rocket Lasagna, 26–29
  Romesco Sauce, 100
  Sicilian-Style Roasted
    Cauliflower with
    Pasta, 169
  Susan's Eggplant Stack,
    101–103

Oils, about, 14
Okra, Mushroom, & Shallot
  Medley, Roasted
  (variation), 86
Onions
  about, 15
  Apple, Blue Cheese, &
    Caramelized Onion
    Pizza Topping, 183
  Caramelized Onion,
    Pear, and Goat Cheese
    Crostata Filling, 36
  Caramelized Onions,
    198
  Caramelized Shallots,
    Tempeh, & Goat
    Cheese, Penne with,
    155
  Onion Gravy, 174

Red Lentil Dal with
  Cumin-Fried Onions
  & Wilted Spinach,
  133–134
Oranges, in Arugula &
  Seasonal Fruit, 37
Orzo, Zucchini & Corn-
  Studded, 105–106
Oven Sweet Potato Fries, 51

Pan-Asian Noodles, Slurpy,
  175–176
Pantry ingredients, 13–19
Parmigiano-Reggiano
  about, 18
  Basil Pesto, 206
  Garlic Scape Pesto Pasta,
    66–67, 208
  Good Ole Marinara and
    Mozzarella (and
    Arugula and Lemon,
    If You're Smart) Pizza
    Topping, 182
  Kale Pesto, 207
  Mushroom-Rosemary
    Pizza Topping, 184
  Mushroom-Spinach
    Scramble, 120
  Polenta Squares with
    Puttanesca Sauce &
    Broccoli Raab, 162–164
  Risotto, Two Ways,
    30–33
  Rocket Lasagna, 26–29
  Spring Cassoulet, 44–46
  Susan's Eggplant Stack,
    101–103
  Zucchini Boats, 76–77
Parsley
  about, 14
  Chickpea "Crab Cakes,"
    69–70
  Corn Kernel Salad, 72

Hummus-Stuffed
  Tomatoes, 74
Jig-Inducing Falafel
  Burgers, 48–50
Potato-Leek-Parsley
  Puree, 187
Tabbouleh, 88–89
Parsnips, in Go-with-the-
  Flow Potpie with
  Cheddar-Biscuity
  Crust, 165–168
Passover Rocket Lasagna
  (option), 26–28
Pasta and noodles
  Brocco Mac & Cheese,
    150–151
  Garlic Scape Pesto Pasta,
    66–67
  Nonna Caterina's Pasta e
    Fagioli, 159–160
  Penne with Tempeh,
    Caramelized Shallots,
    & Goat Cheese, 155
  rice noodles, about, 18
  Rocket Lasagna, 26–29
  Sesame Rice Noodles &
    Melon-Herb Salad,
    96–97
  Sicilian-Style Roasted
    Cauliflower with Pasta,
    169
  Slurpy Pan-Asian
    Noodles, 175–176
  Stuffed Shells with Lentil
    Ragout & Spinach,
    137–138
  udon noodles, about, 19
  Zucchini & Corn-
    Studded Orzo,
    105–106
Pear, Caramelized Onion,
  and Goat Cheese
  Crostata Filling, 36

Pear-Arugula Salad, 114
Pearl barley
    about, 18
    Barley Pilaf, 40
    Stuffed Bell Peppers,
        98–99
Peas, in Spring Meadow
    Risotto, 32
Peas & Rice, Jamaican-
    Style, 62
Pecans
    Arugula & Seasonal
        Fruit, 37
    Pear-Arugula Salad, 114
Penne with Tempeh,
    Caramelized Shallots,
    & Goat Cheese, 155
Pepitas
    about, 18
    Pepita-Crusted Tofu,
        128–129
    Romaine with Toasted
        Pepitas and Lemon
        Vinaigrette, 59
Peppers. See bell peppers
Pesto
    Arugula Pesto, 205
    Basil Pesto, 206
    Garlic Scape Pesto, 208
    Kale Pesto, 206
Pick-Up Sticks, Roasted
    Broccoli (and
    cauliflower variation),
    204
Pico de Gallo, 202
Pies, savory
    Caramelized Onion, Pear,
        and Goat Cheese
        Crostata, 36
    Go-with-the-Flow
        Potpie with Cheddar-
        Biscuity Crust,
        165–168

Shepherd's Pie with
    Chard-Lentil Filling,
    171–174
Spinach & Feta Crostata,
    34–36
Pineapple, to cut, 194
Pineapple Salad, Zesty, 61
Pine nuts
    Basil Pesto, 206
    Sicilian-Style Roasted
        Cauliflower with
        Pasta, 169
    Susan's Eggplant Stack,
        101–103
Pinto beans
    Canned Beans & Rice:
        A Template Meant
        to Be Tweaked,
        190–191
    Nonna Caterina's Pasta e
        Fagioli, 159–160
    Simple Pot of Dried
        Beans, 196
    True-Blue Baked Beans,
        94
Pistachio-Raisin Rice
    Pilaf, 127
Pizza
    Apple, Blue Cheese, &
        Caramelized Onion
        Topping, 183
    Good Ole Marinara and
        Mozzarella (and
        Arugula and Lemon,
        If You're Smart)
        Topping, 182
    Mushroom-Rosemary
        Topping, 184
    Pizza Dough, 180–181
Polenta Squares with
    Puttanesca Sauce &
    Broccoli Raab,
    162–164

Pomegranate seeds, in
    Arugula & Seasonal
    Fruit, 37
Potatoes
    Broccoli Soup, 188
    Dino-Mash, 130
    Family-Style Latke, 43
    Go-with-the-Flow Potpie
        with Cheddar-Biscuity
        Crust, 165–168
    Potato Frittata, 82
    Potato-Leek-Parsley
        Puree, 187
    Roasted Red Pepper
        Soup, 141
    Rosemary-Garlic Roasted
        Potatoes, 121
    Shepherd's Pie with
        Chard-Lentil Filling,
        171–174
    Top-Shelf Potato Salad,
        54
Pot of Dried Beans, Simple,
    196
Potpie with Cheddar-
    Biscuity Crust,
    Go-with-the-Flow,
    165–168
Provolone, in Susan's
    Eggplant Stack,
    101–103
Puttanesca Sauce &
    Broccoli Raab, Polenta
    Squares with, 162–164

A Quart of All-Purpose
    Veg Stock, 211
Queso fresco, in Stuffed Bell
    Peppers, 98–99
Quickie Couscous-
    Chickpea Salad, 78–79
Quinoa
    about, 18

Quickie Quinoa-
Chickpea Salad
(variation), 78–79
Stuffed Bell Peppers,
98–99

Raisins
Pistachio-Raisin Rice
Pilaf, 127
Sicilian-Style Roasted
Cauliflower with
Pasta, 169
Ratatouille, 110–111
Red beans
Canned Beans & Rice:
A Template Meant to
Be Tweaked, 190–191
Jamaican-Style Peas &
Rice, 62
Simple Pot of Dried
Beans, 196
Red Curry Tempeh,
Thai-Style, 131–132
Red Lentil Dal with
Cumin-Fried Onions
& Wilted Spinach,
133–134
Red Rice, Southern, 84–85
Reliable Stovetop Rice that
Even My Husband Can
Make, 203
Rice
arborio, about, 15
Canned Beans & Rice:
A Template Meant to
Be Tweaked, 190–191
Coconut Rice, 124
Gumbo z'Herbes (Green
Gumbo), 156–158
Jamaican-Style Peas &
Rice, 62
Pistachio-Raisin Rice
Pilaf, 127

Reliable Stovetop Rice
that Even My Husband
Can Make, 203
Risotto, Two Ways,
30–33
Smokin' Hoppin' John,
146–147
Southern Red Rice,
84–85
Stuffed Bell Peppers,
98–99
Thai-Style Red Curry
Tempeh, 131–132
Veggie Fried Rice Bowl,
185
Rice noodles, about, 18
Rice Noodles, Sesame, &
Melon-Herb Salad,
96–97
Rice wine
about, 18
Braised Winter Squash
with Black Bean
Sauce & Bok Choy,
122–123
Sesame Rice Noodles &
Melon-Herb Salad,
96–97
Slurpy Pan-Asian
Noodles, 175–176
Ricotta
Ricotta-Greens Lasagna
Filling, 27
Stuffed Bell Peppers,
98–99
Risotto
Basic Risotto, 30
Mushroom Risotto, 31
Spring Meadow Risotto,
32
Risotto Stock, 33
Roasted Beans, Greens, &
Squash Rings, 115–116

Roasted Broccoli Pick-Up
Sticks (and cauliflower
variation), 204
Roasted Cauliflower with
Tahini Sauce, 89
Roasted Eggplant–Lentil
Caviar on Oversized
Crostini, 125–126
Roasted Potatoes,
Rosemary-Garlic, 121
Roasted Red Pepper Sauce,
118
Roasted Red Pepper Soup,
141
Rocket Lasagna, 26–29
Romaine & Balsamic-
Gingery Strawberries,
68
Romaine Wedges,
Seared, 47
Romaine with Toasted
Pepitas and Lemon
Vinaigrette, 59
Romesco Sauce, 100
Rosemary-Garlic Roasted
Potatoes, 121
Rosemary-Mushroom Pizza
Topping, 184
Rutabaga, in Go-with-the-
Flow Potpie with
Cheddar-Biscuity
Crust, 165–168
RW's Snack Plate, 87–90

Salads
Corn Kernel Salad, 72
Fattoush Salad, 73
Pear-Arugula Salad, 114
Quickie Couscous-
Chickpea Salad, 78–79
Romaine & Balsamic-
Gingery Strawberries,
68

Salads (continued)
  Romaine with Toasted
    Pepitas and Lemon
    Vinaigrette, 59
  Sesame Rice Noodles &
    Melon-Herb Salad,
    96–97
  Tabbouleh, 88–89
  Top-Shelf Potato Salad,
    54
  Vinegar Slaw, 95
  Zesty Pineapple Salad,
    61
Sandwiches
  Chickpea "Crab Cakes,"
    69–70
  Grilled Cheese Template,
    186
  Jig-Inducing Falafel
    Burgers, 48–50
  Tempeh Hoagie-letta,
    55–56
  West Indian–Style
    Channa Wrap, 52–53
Sauces and dressings
  Cocktail Sauce, 71
  hoisin sauce, about, 17
  jerk sauce, about, 17
  Lemon-Garlic
    Vinaigrette, 199
  Marinara Sauce, 28
  Marinara Sauce, Simple,
    197
  Onion Gravy, 174
  Pico de Gallo, 202
  Puttanesca Sauce,
    162–164
  Roasted Red Pepper
    Sauce, 118
  Romesco Sauce, 100
  Tahini Sauce, 201
  Yogurt Rémoulade, 71
Seared Halloumi, 75

Seared Romaine Wedges, 47
Sesame Rice Noodles &
  Melon-Herb Salad,
  96–97
Shallot Medley, Roasted
  Green Bean,
  Mushroom &, 86
Shallots, about, 18
Shaoxing rice wine
  about, 18
  Braised Winter Squash
    with Black Bean Sauce
    & Bok Choy, 122–123
  Sesame Rice Noodles &
    Melon-Herb Salad,
    96–97
  Slurpy Pan-Asian
    Noodles, 175–176
Shepherd's Pie with
  Chard-Lentil Filling,
  171–174
Sicilian-Style Roasted
  Cauliflower with
  Pasta, 169
Side dish suggestions, 26
Simple Marinara Sauce, 197
Simple Pot of Dried Beans,
  196
Skillet Corn Bread, 148
Slaw, Vinegar, 95
Slurpy Pan-Asian Noodles,
  175–176
Smoked paprika, about, 19
Smokin' Hoppin' John,
  146–147
Snacks
  Kale Chips, 57
  RW's Snack Plate, 87–90
Sorrel, in Gumbo z'Herbes
  (Green Gumbo),
  156–158
Soups and stocks
  Broccoli Soup, 188

Creamy Tomato Soup,
  189
Gazpacho, 83
Gumbo Stock, 156
Potato-Leek-Parsley
  Puree, 187
Potpie Stock, 168
A Quart of All-Purpose
  Veg Stock, 211
Risotto Stock, 33
Roasted Red Pepper
  Soup, 141
veg stock, about, 15
Southern Red Rice, 84–85
Spinach
  Egg-in-the-Hole,
    41–42
  Greens-Ricotta Filling, 27
  Mushroom-Spinach
    Scramble, 120
  Red Lentil Dal with
    Cumin-Fried Onions
    & Wilted Spinach,
    133–134
  Spinach & Feta Crostata,
    34
  Stuffed Bell Peppers,
    98–99
  Stuffed Shells with
    Lentil Ragout &
    Spinach, 137–138
  Wilted Greens in a
    Skillet Vinaigrette, 161
Split peas, in Nonna
  Caterina's Pasta e
  Fagioli, 159–160
Spring Cassoulet, 44–46
Spring Meadow Risotto, 32
Squash, summer. See
  zucchini
Squash, winter. See winter
  squash
Stewed Tomatoes, 152

Stir-Fried Cabbage and
    Cumin (or Caraway),
    170
Stocks
    Gumbo Stock, 156
    Potpie Stock, 168
    A Quart of All-Purpose
        Veg Stock, 211
    Risotto Stock, 33
    veg stock, about, 15
Stovetop Rice, Reliable,
    that Even My Husband
    Can Make, 203
Strawberries
    Arugula & Seasonal
        Fruit, 37
    Romaine & Balsamic-
        Gingery Strawberries,
        68
Stuffed Bell Peppers,
    98–99
Stuffed Shells with Lentil
    Ragout & Spinach,
    137–138
Susan's Eggplant Stack,
    101–103
Sweet potatoes
    Black Bean–Sweet Potato
        Chili, 144–145
    Go-with-the-Flow Potpie
        with Cheddar-Biscuity
        Crust, 165–168
    Oven Sweet Potato
        Fries, 51
    Twice-Baked Sweet
        Potatoes, 112–113
    Winter Veg & Cilantro
        "Curry" with
        Dumplings, 153–154
Sweet potato greens, in
    Gumbo z'Herbes
    (Green Gumbo),
    156–158

Tabbouleh, 88–89
Tahini
    about, 19
    Hummus, 87
    Hummus-Stuffed
        Tomatoes, 74
    Roasted Cauliflower with
        Tahini Sauce, 89
    Tahini Sauce, 201
    Twice-Baked Sweet
        Potatoes, 112–113
Tara's Mushroom Ragout, 24
Tatsoi, in Wilted Greens in a
    Skillet Vinaigrette, 161
Tempeh
    about, 19
    Jerk Tempeh, 60
    Penne with Tempeh,
        Caramelized Shallots,
        & Goat Cheese, 155
    Tempeh Hoagie-letta,
        55–56
    Thai-Style Red Curry
        Tempeh, 131–132
Thai red curry paste,
    about, 19
Thai-Style Red Curry
    Tempeh, 131–132
Tofu
    about, 19
    Pepita-Crusted Tofu,
        128–129
    Tofu Barbecue, 92–93
Tomatoes
    Creamy Tomato Soup, 189
    Gazpacho, 83
    Good Ole Marinara and
        Mozzarella (and
        Arugula and Lemon,
        If You're Smart) Pizza
        Topping, 182
    Hummus-Stuffed
        Tomatoes, 74

Marinara Sauce, 28
    Pico de Gallo, 202
    puree, about, 15
    Puttanesca Sauce,
        162–164
    Ratatouille, 110–11
    Simple Marinara Sauce,
        197
    Southern Red Rice,
        84–85
    Stewed Tomatoes, 152
    Susan's Eggplant Stack,
        101–103
Top-Shelf Potato Salad, 54
True-Blue Baked Beans, 94
Turnip greens, in Gumbo
    z'Herbes (Green
    Gumbo), 156–158
Turnips
    Chickpea-Turnip Chili,
        38–39
    Go-with-the-Flow Potpie
        with Cheddar-Biscuity
        Crust, 165–168
    Winter Veg & Cilantro
        "Curry" with
        Dumplings, 153–154
Twice-Baked Sweet
    Potatoes, 112–113

Udon noodles
    about, 19
    Slurpy Pan-Asian
        Noodles, 175–176

Vegan recipes
    Arugula & Seasonal
        Fruit, 37
    Arugula Pesto, 205
    Barley Pilaf, 40
    Braised Winter Squash
        with Black Bean Sauce
        & Bok Choy, 122–123

Vegan recipes (*continued*)
Broccoli Pick-Up Sticks, 25
Broccoli Soup, 188
Canned Beans & Rice: A Template Meant to Be Tweaked, 190–191
Chickpea-Turnip Chili, 38–39
Corn Kernel Salad, 72
Dino-Mash, 130
Family-Style Latke, 43
Fattoush Salad, 73
Gazpacho, 83
Hummus-Stuffed Tomatoes, 74
Jamaican-Style Peas & Rice, 62
Jerk Tempeh, 60
Jig-Inducing Falafel Burgers, 48–49
Kale Chips, 57
KOD's Quickie Collards, 149
Lemon-Garlic Vinaigrette, 199
Minty Chickpeas, 104
Oven Sweet Potato Fries, 51
Pepita-Crusted Tofu, 128–129
Pico de Gallo, 202
Pistachio-Raisin Rice Pilaf, 127
Potato-Leek-Parsley Puree, 187
A Quart of All-Purpose Veg Stock, 211
Quickie Couscous-Chickpea Salad, 78
Quickie Couscous-Chickpea Salad, Quinoa Variation, 79

Ratatouille, 110–111
Red Lentil Dal with Cumin-Fried Onions & Wilted Spinach, 133–134
Roasted Beans, Greens, & Squash Rings, 115–116
Roasted Broccoli Pick-Up Sticks (and cauliflower variation), 204
Roasted Cauliflower with Tahini Sauce, 89
Roasted Eggplant–Lentil Caviar on Oversized Crostini, 125–126
Roasted Green Bean, Mushroom, & Shallot Medley, 86
Roasted Red Pepper Sauce, 118
Roasted Red Pepper Soup, 141
Romaine & Balsamic-Gingery Strawberries, 68
Romaine with Toasted Pepitas & Lemon Vinaigrette, 59
Romesco Sauce, 100
Rosemary-Garlic Roasted Potatoes, 121
Seared Romaine Wedges, 47
Sesame Rice Noodles & Melon-Herb Salad, 96–97
Simple Marinara Sauce, 197
Simple Pot of Dried Beans, 196
Slurpy Pan-Asian Noodles, 175–176

Stewed Tomatoes, 152
Southern Red Rice, 84–85
Tabbouleh, 88–89
Tahini Sauce, 50, 201
Thai-Style Red Curry Tempeh, 131–132
Tofu Barbecue, 92–93
Top-Shelf Potato Salad, 54
True-Blue Baked Beans, 94
Twice-Baked Sweet Potatoes, 112–113
Veggie Fried Rice Bowl, 185
Vinegar Slaw, 95
West Indian–Style Channa Wrap, 52–53
Wilted Greens in a Skillet Vinaigrette, 161
Zesty Pineapple Salad, 61
Veggie Fried Rice Bowl, 185
Veg stock, about, 15
Veg Stock, A Quart of All-Purpose, 211
Vinaigrette, Lemon-Garlic, 199
Vinegar Slaw, 95

Walnuts
Arugula Pesto, 205
Arugula & Seasonal Fruit, 37
Basil Pesto, 206
Garlic Scape Pesto Pasta, 66–67
Goat Cheesy Roasted Peppers, 107
Kale Pesto, 207
Pear-Arugula Salad, 114
Roasted Green Bean, Mushroom, & Shallot Medley, 86
Rocket Lasagna, 26–29

Sicilian-Style Roasted Cauliflower with Pasta, 169
Susan's Eggplant Stack, 101–103
Watermelon, in Sesame Rice Noodles & Melon-Herb Salad, 96–97
West Indian–Style Channa Wrap, 52–53
Whipped Feta, 118
White beans
Canned Beans & Rice: A Template Meant to Be Tweaked, 190–191

Simple Pot of Dried Beans, 196
Spring Cassoulet, 44–46
Wilted Greens in a Skillet Vinaigrette, 161
Wine-Braised Lentils, 173
Winter squash
about, 19
Braised Winter Squash with Black Bean Sauce & Bok Choy, 122–123
Go-with-the-Flow Potpie with Cheddar-Biscuity Crust, 165–168
Roasted Beans, Greens, & Squash Rings, 115–116

Winter Veg & Cilantro "Curry" with Dumplings, 153–154
Wrap, West Indian–Style Channa, 52–53

Yogurt Rémoulade, 71

Zesty Pineapple Salad, 61
Zucchini
Ratatouille, 110–11
Zucchini Boats, 76–77
Zucchini & Corn-Studded Orzo, 105–106
Zucchini Frittata, 81

ABOUT THE AUTHOR

Kim O'Donnel is a trained chef, nationally recognized online food personality, and longtime journalist. She is a graduate of the Institute of Culinary Education and the University of Pennsylvania. Formerly of the *Washington Post*, she has also written for *Real Simple*, the Huffington Post, True/Slant.com, and Smithsonian .com. She is a regular contributor to Culinate.com. She is the founder of Canning Across America, a collective dedicated to the revival of preserving food. Born and raised in Philadelphia, she lives in Seattle with her husband, Russ Walker.

Visit Kim at www.kimodonnel.com

Follow her on Twitter at twitter.com/kimodonnel